THE VIETNAM WAR AND POSTMODERNITY

UNIVERSITY OF MASSACHUSETTS PRESS *Amherst*

Edited by Michael Bibby

THE
VIETNAM
WAR

AND POSTMODERNITY

ISBN 1-55849-237-2 (cloth); 238-0 (paper)

Designed by Milenda Nan Ok Lee

Set in Trump Mediaeval and Futura Book by Graphic Composition, Inc.

Printed and Bound by Sheridan Books, Inc.

Library of Congress Cataloging-in-Publication Data

The Vietnam war and postmodernity / edited by Michael Bibby.
    p.   cm.
    Includes index.
    ISBN 1-55849-237-2 (cloth : alk. paper). — ISBN 1-55849-238-0
(pbk. : alk. paper)
     1. Vietnamese Conflict 1961–1975. 2. Postmodernism. 3. United
States—Civilization—1970– I. Bibby, Michael, 1957– .
DS557.7.V56659   2000
959.704'3—dc21   99-36757
                                        CIP

British Library Cataloguing in Publication Data are available

This book is published with the support and cooperation of the
University of Massachusetts Boston

CONTENTS

THE VIETNAM WAR AND POSTMODERNITY

INTRODUCTION

Michael Bibby

Since the mid-seventies, "postmodernism" has become one of the keywords of cultural criticism and theory. Perhaps not coincidentally, the blossoming of postmodern studies occurred in the shadow of that moment when the last Huey lifted off from the U.S. embassy in Saigon, bringing to an ignominious close one of the most heinous chapters in twentieth-century history. And since the founding of the Wall in Washington, D.C., there has been an increased production of critical work concerning the literature, film, and cultural representation inspired by the Vietnam War. To date, however, there has been no book devoted to situating these two congruent and, perhaps, mutually constitutive historical phenomena in relation to each other in any extended and meaningful way. The present collection seeks to address this gap, both by investigating the postmodernity of American cultural representations inspired by the war and also by questioning the historical and theoretical relationships of postmodernity and the war. Previous studies of Vietnam War representation have made use of the critical vocabulary associated with postmodernism, yet none has focused specifically on how the war might problematize and/or make possible postmodernity, or how what we know now about the war, how we express and represent it, may be postmodernist. The essays collected here offer varying, sometimes conflicting positions on these issues. This book, then, does not hope to provide definitive answers on the questions of the war's relationship to post-modernity; rather, it has been my hope that these essays might encourage further engagement with the enduring traces of the war in contemporary experience.

Although postmodernity's periodization remains in contention, varying widely across the century, perhaps few events better capture the sense of an epochal rupture and the dawning of postmodernity than the frantic withdrawal of U.S. forces from Vietnam, its last helicopters uneasily lifting off from the roof of the U.S. embassy in Saigon. Philip Beidler's "The Last Huey" evocatively explores this image and the Bell UH-1 Iroquois Helicopter, otherwise known as the Huey in the popular vernacular, as the meta-sign of the Vietnam War's postmodernity. Beidler argues that as a machine, the Huey represents the reification of performativity Lyotard and others point to as indicative of postmodernity. It is the "locomotion" in Michael Herr's "La Vida Loca," "chopping" up space, geography, and time for the soldiers who rode it and the people it invaded. The Huey also exaggerates the failings of the U.S. military's "technowar" strategies in Vietnam, its hyperbolic entrance into any territory always signaling well in advance to the Vietcong and NVA the presence of U.S. troops. Beidler sees the image of the last Huey lifting off from the U.S. embassy in Saigon in 1975 as a primal scene for U.S. cultural history, the Fall that would usher in a new era and become the Repressed returning repeatedly to haunt post-Vietnam literature and films. For Beidler suggests that the last Huey must finally be taken as iconic, a spectral meta-sign of the tragedies of the U.S. intervention.

In important ways the first "TV War," as it has so often been called, necessarily calls into question the nature of representation, image, iconography, and simulacra, central obsessions of postmodernity. Although all war can be said to be generally about representation and spectacle, the Vietnam War experience for many Americans has always been profoundly specular in ways seemingly unique to contemporary history. Michael Clark's "The Work of War in the Age of Mechanical Reproduction" takes up Walter Benjamin's notions about representational technologies and reconsiders them in light of the experience of the Vietnam War. Clark argues that Vietnam War narratives demonstrate an absence of the historical agency idealized in modernity. In place of this agency, he argues, we find instead spectatorship. It is this subject position and the hegemony of specularity in late capitalism that Clark considers paradigmatic of postmodernity and, consequently, symptomatic of the postmodern aesthetics of Vietnam War narratives and post-Vietnam War cinema. Pointing to the saturation of U.S. culture by cinematography, Clark considers the ways in which cinematic technologies construct a spectator-subject analogous to the subject of Vietnam War narratives. Discussing *Apocalypse Now, The Stunt Man, 84 Charlie Mopic, Universal Soldier,* and *Jacob's Ladder,* Clark draws crucial and disturbing parallels between war in postmodernity and the experience of filmic spectatorship. The Vietnam War, according to Clark, manifests the emergence of war as specular experience, which would later culminate in the videomatics of the Gulf War. It is in the post-World War II U.S. military's increased reliance on and development of representational technologies that Clark sees a collapse of the differences between "watching" and "doing" in war. In the Gulf War, this collapse would become practically total, so that the subject position of soldier and TV viewer merge; watching the "smart bombs" hit their targets through the very same video lens of the soldier firing the bombs erases boundaries between viewer and actor, citizen and soldier.

Although on one level the Vietnam War could be said—following Guy Debord—to have moved away into representation, foreclosing on authenticity, memory, and historicity, becoming the locus of dis(re)-membering, and thus, obsessively rearticulating the tropes of "fragging" central to its narratives, it has also become a rich site for anxious, even hysterical attempts to rearticulate national memory and identity. Cynthia Fuch's "'What do we say happened here?': Memory, Identity, and the Vietnam War" examines these obsessions by reading several post-Vietnam films that deploy the war and its tropes as sites for staging memory and identity. Fuchs interrogates the use of hyperviolence and white masculinity in *Universal Soldier* and *Jacob's Ladder* to rework and restage an identity always already disremembered such that it both ironically underscores its generic conventions and concomitantly elides them. By way of contrast, she investigates *Boyz N the Hood* and *Dead Presidents* as films that invoke the war's tropes in order to bring it home to the hood, refusing to idealize identity and memory in relation to a pre-Vietnam experience, underscoring rather than eliding the structural racist oppression that organizes the national narrative.

Brady Harrison's essay, "'This movie is a thing of mine': Homeopathic Postmodernism in Michael Herr's *Dispatches*," also takes up notions of filmic representation to identify the postmodernism of Vietnam War narratives. Harrison deploys Baudrillard's theories of simulation in order to understand Herr's text as a filmic projection. Departing from Baudrillard and Jameson, however, Harrison argues that Herr's simulacra reproduce the "secret history" of a war thoroughly constituted as simulacrum, a war made hyperreal through a meaningless dissemination of information and movie imagery, what Herr's text called "informational freak-o-rama." Harrison argues that Herr renders the "real" of the war into the "filmic," into simulacra traced in fragmentation on a screen, a "hyper-space" of depthlessness. Harrison points to the book's character of Sean Flynn, a figure overdetermined by Hollywood encodements, as Herr's paradigm of postmodern subjectivity. In Sean Flynn, Herr seeks to recuperate subjectivity and historicity through a valorization of the simulacrum. Harrison sees the character of Flynn as both simulation of the Hollywood male hero subject and also as a resistance to the commodification of subjectivity. In his reading, Harrison follows Jamesonian dialectics rather than Baudrillardan apocalyptics, seeing in Herr's deployment of simulacra both its positivity and negativity at once. For Harrison, then, Herr's text instantiates a Jamesonian "homeopathic" engagement with postmodernism, a strategy that deploys the methods of postmodernism to dismantle postmodernism.

Although many critics discussing the postmodernism of Vietnam War representations emphasize them as resistant to hegemony, it is also important to discern how they confirm and legitimize the very ideology that could be said to have underwritten American imperialism. Tony Williams's essay, "Rites of Incorporation in *In Country* and *Indian Country*," considers how these two novels, central to the canon of Vietnam War literature, manifest the characteristics of, what Hal Foster has called, a "reactionary postmodernism." While Bobbie Ann Mason's *In Country* and Philip Caputo's *Indian Country* ostensibly pose as critiques of the war, Williams demonstrates that their narratives construct what he calls "rites of incorporation," which undercut their critiques. Drawing on the work of Arnold van Gennep, Williams posits "rites of incorporation" as inherently conservative narrative conventions that ameliorate the historicity of the U.S. intervention in Vietnam. Williams argues that by reincorporating their protagonists into the U.S. social community unproblematically these novels validate masculinist bonds and erase the complicity in war-making that such masculinism bears. According to Williams, by suppressing the historical complexities of the Vietnam War, these novels also reinvest in the narrative conventions the historical experience of the war specifically called into question. Consequently, rather than offering any engagement with the war as deconstructive of the grand narratives of U.S. mythmaking, these novels reify such narratives. It is through these ahistorical and reaffirming rituals of incorporation that Williams sees the postmodernity of these novels as inherently reactionary.

Literary and cultural images of the war have played a significant role in postmodernity's attempts to rethink and rearticulate key problems of subjectivity, memory, and history. Although a number of critics have discussed such problems in prose narratives of the Vietnam War, few have engaged them in poetic representations of the war. Eric Gadzinski's "Bruised Azaleas: Bruce Weigl and the Postwar Aesthetic" argues for a reading of the veteran poet Bruce Weigl's poetry as exemplary of a post-Vietnam War, postmodern aesthetic of melancholy, grief, and borderline subjectivity. Gadzinski's analysis draws on Julia Kristeva's notions of abjection and melancholia and the growing work in the psychology of survivor trauma and survivor testimony. According to Kristeva, the post-World War II era manifests a "rhetoric of apocalypse" that is the historical expression of the incomprehensibility of the Holocaust and the liminal position of the survivor's subjectivity. Kristeva notes that this rhetoric can be characterized by an image-laden, yet nondemonstrative language. Gadzinski shows how Weigl's poetry exemplifies this rhetoric and, thus, demonstrates the abject, borderline conditions of survivor subjectivity for Vietnam veterans. For the U.S., then, Weigl's work is emblematic of a postmodern "rhetoric of apocalypse."

Ultimately, the etymology of postmodernity calls upon temporality and the historical, inviting periodization. Although Fredric Jameson once called it "the first terrible postmodern war," the extent and duration of the Vietnam War, the fact that Vietnam's colonial subjection and anti-imperialist response involved most of the metropolitan states from the turn of the century to the mid-seventies and that the consequences of the U.S. intervention continue to be felt not only in society and politics, but in the global market, all demand that a more assiduous account of the historical relationships between the war and the postmodern be attempted. In "The Post-Vietnam Condition," I challenge historicizations of postmodernity that fail to account adequately for the epochal nature of the Vietnam War and its impact on the structure of contemporary experience. Interrogating Jameson's famous comment on the war I demonstrate slippages in his narratives of postmodernity that place its epochal rupture variously in the 1940s, 1950s, and 1960s. Jameson never considers the Vietnam War as constitutive of postmodernity, but rather as an expression of it, suggesting that a cultural, historical period might transcend the longest foreign war ever fought by the U.S. I argue that given the Vietnam War's well-documented impact on the structure of contemporary history, especially economically, politically, and socially, and given that an organized discourse on postmodernism was not widely available until after the war, it seems more historically accurate to read postmodernity as an expression of a post-Vietnam condition rather than the other way around. Further, I interrogate the failure of postmodern studies and theory to enunciate the name of the war, arguing that its very rhetoric has been inflected by the war experience.

Chris Hables Gray argues in "Postmodernism with a Vengeance: The Vietnam War" that the Vietnam War marks a significant break from previous forms of warfare, a rupture distinct enough to qualify the war as "postmodern." For Gray, the categories *modern* and *postmodern* are considered less as aesthetic and more as military-historical categories. Marking the introduction of nuclear weaponry as the last stage of modern warfare's drive to produce new technologies for total war, Gray's analysis suggests that the structure of warfare in Vietnam can be considered the effect of the limitations to warmaking brought about by the threat of nuclear war and symptomatic of the consolidation of economic, political, and social practices significantly constituted under the shadow of nuclear war. In this, Gray sees the explosive proliferation of technologies, especially information technologies, after World War II as key to the emergence of postmodernity. This proliferation not only correlates to the multiplication of the various narratives available, which necessarily results in the devaluation of the "grand narratives," it also results in a proliferation of the versions of war and war production. This in turn has led to a proliferation of "little wars" throughout the globe, so that the notion of war itself has become fragmented. The technologies that make available an almost infinite array of information make it also possible for numerous micropolitical groups to stage wars. In an era when "total war"—the "grand narrative" of all historical disasters—must always be prepared for yet never enacted, "war" must be waged in a fragmentary network of "limited" conflicts in order to maintain a sustainable level of production and expenditure in the military economy. At the heart of this, Gray pinpoints key paradoxes in the structure of post-nuclear war's discursive construction, which suggest the ultimate dissolution of postmodern war.

On the other hand Douglas Kellner's "From Vietnam to the Gulf: Postmodern Wars?" raises troubling questions about any attempt to call the Vietnam War postmodern; these questions lay bare undertheorized concepts of postmodernity and problematize the notion of "postmodern war." Based on his readings of the text most often deemed a "postmodernist" account of the war, Herr's *Dispatches*, Kellner shows how this work is fundamentally *modernist* in its aesthetic practices. Further, Kellner argues that the account of the war in *Dispatches* is modernist precisely because the war should be considered modern. Kellner draws on James William Gibson's historical analysis of the war's operation to reveal that the U.S. military's Cold War mentality and the national liberation motivations of the Vietnamese correspond to historical conventions of modernity. Turning to an analysis of the U.S.-Iraq War, Kellner argues that with its substitution of video-game imagery for any "signified" and its evacuation of any semblance of truth, this war, rather than the Vietnam War, might be considered the first postmodern war. Yet, Kellner ultimately expresses doubts about the legitimacy of qualifying the historical brutalities of any war with terms derived from cultural-aesthetic practices. His analysis reveals significant continuities between the two wars that challenge any notion of a historical rupture necessary to designate a "postmodernity" in the contexts of these wars. Kellner concludes that the U.S.-Iraq War signals an important shift toward postmodernity, but that it fails to render a complete break from the practices of the Vietnam War.

Although these essays take varying perspectives on the relationships between the Vietnam War and postmodernity, they all raise significant questions about those relations and invite further interrogation of the terms by which we have framed an understanding of recent history and culture. What all these essays demand is the recuperation of the war's significance in any account of the postmodern. Perhaps through further interrogation and critical discussion, we can ensure that a war that has made such a lasting impact on the shape of U.S. and global history not fade away—and with it the lessons we have to learn from this war—into the "jargon stream."

This book's long journey has been guided by a number of people who deserve acknowledgment here. Kali Tal, managing editor of the vital forum for Vietnam War cultural studies, *Viet Nam Generation* and its various offshoots, first sponsored and promoted this project and to her we all owe a great debt. Paul Wright's support and encouragement gave this book new hope. I also thank the anonymous readers whose comments helped me rethink the structure of the book and gave us all a better sense of direction. Barbara L. Tischler's support and enthusiasm have also been inspirational throughout.

Personally I want to thank the contributors for not only their interest and support but also their perseverance through the process. I thank as well Shari Horner for patience and endurance above and beyond the call of duty. And thanks to Nicholas for giving this work new meaning.

ONE

ILLUMINATION ROUNDS

1

THE LAST HUEY

Philip D. Beidler

April 29, 1975. In the familiar photograph, a last helicopter, barely perched on its skids, waits to lift off from an apartment rooftop in downtown Saigon. Evacuees jam the ladder reaching upward from the next level as if on some forlorn stairway to nowhere. The aircraft markings are hard to determine. Mainly silver rather than olive drab green or camouflage brown, it is not army or marine. It might be air force. Actually—as the photo ID tells us with a providential irony—the helicopter in question belongs to Air America, by now known to the world, in this vast, ungovernable, loose-cannon business, as the aviation arm of the United States Central Intelligence Agency.

Meanwhile, over on the nearby roof of the embassy, where it had begun for the Americans so long ago, with Lansdale and Lodge, Bao Dai, Diem, Big Minh, and the rest, another prepares to go. Aboard will be one last U.S. vice regent, his wife, some Vietnamese retainers, and the station flag.

The unmistakable vignettes, the first real, the second essentially "true," but reconstructed from imagination, configure a freeze-frame vision of the end. As to American assumptions of national innocence and historical infallibility, it is the geopolitical equivalent of the Fall conflated back into the Freudian primal scene—a return of the repressed resulting in the emergence into a new historical subjectivity;

and, as revealed in our subsequent literature and history, we cannot let it go.[1] Was either of these the last helicopter? Probably not. Most of the evacuation flotilla, in fact, consisted of larger and, to the un-schooled observer, less familiar aircraft—cargo helicopters such as the CH-46, -53, and -54. Most of them, in fact, were naval and marine helicopters, a relative rarity anywhere south of the DMZ or I Corps during the conflict itself, here deployed from offshore aircraft carriers as evacuation shuttles. Whatever few "escape" Hueys made it out to sea, often commandeered by Vietnamese, themselves became the subject of other indelible images, pushed overboard from the pitching decks to make room for the American craft. We will never really know what the last helicopter was. Still, one just somehow has to make it into a Huey. That would be the final shot and fade-out, the signature of a fatal iconography.

One speaks here, obviously, of images of the end in Vietnam in a sense identified through postmodern theories of representation and meaning as comprising a dominant "textual" medium of cultural discourse: images in the sense articulated by Jean Baudrillard as the iconography of a world in which signs persistently outrun refer-ents, where they create a media reality that does not so much medi-ate between ourselves and the world as it simply self-reifies and self-proliferates into patterns of its own endlessly devised self-referentiality. Given this identification, however, one may also begin to speak here of postmodernism's discovery of the image in a certain iconic configuration—such as that of the Huey dominating the ico-nography of the American experience of Vietnam—as a critical open-ing out of the seamless welter of nagging presence it seems to create. If certain iconic images truly make history, then they also supply us with a certain archaeology of vision—at once semiotic and episte-mic—whereby we may inquire into the means through which it has been made. Similarly, they may perhaps point us toward the future technologies of vision whereby it can be newly made.

The Huey. The Bell UH-1 Iroquois Helicopter.[2] It was beyond anything else the showpiece, in attitudinal expectation *and* in opera-tional fact, of what James William Gibson, in his study of the failure of American technological-managerial arrogance in Vietnam, has entitled *The Perfect War*. It became the corporate embodiment of our assumptions of historical innocence and politico-military invincibil-ity, positive thinking become the ultimate positivism, a mentality of the operational totally identifying the thing with the function. "Performance," to use Susan Jeffords's acute phrasing from Jean Lyotard, became literally the thing. The Huey, in all our dreams of Vietnam and beyond, was the thing, "the ability to enact display . . . the capacity for staging spectacle." ('Think here," she reflects in brilliant parenthesis, "of American helicopters invading Grenada playing Wagner, 'imitating' *Apocalypse Now.*")[3] And appropriately, the Saigon the last Huey lifted off from in 1975 became for Americans the capital of a new domain of consciousness, the place where those assumptions had finally come face-to-face with a vision of their utter, unprecedented historical defeat.[4]

It is well for history that such lasting images of the American fall into history should be so configured. And it is well, for the sake of interpretation, that new codes of reading across a vast range of genre and mode continue to be devised that refuse to let us separate cultural history from cultural critique. To put this another way, there are images and there are images: the images that quite literally "make" history, before, during, and after the fact; and the images that help us to make sense of it, if not to unmake it, at least to re-make it or perhaps newly make it. The Huey focuses these dynamics for the American experience of Vietnam. It is surely the "image" of American "performance" in the war that got us there, energized us there, eventually hypnotized us there, kept making us believe we could not lose there, kept us from knowing that it was no longer, had in fact never been our place to be there. It is also, however, an "image" of such "performance" in the larger sense of historical hermeneutic, a way of constructing a history out of the twinned resources of memory and imagination that might have helped us not "go there" in the same fashion anywhere else in the world again.[5]

In the first sense of the word image, the Huey most surely in many ways *was* the American project of Vietnam, from start to finish and everywhere in between, in our actualized experiencings and also in our mentalized imagings of what was happening there, the ultimate wedding of conventional close combat with the perfection of twentieth-century nonnuclear, counterinsurgency, rapid-reaction technowar. It came in innumerable configurations and nicknames: slicks, gunships, hogs, dustoffs, log birds, command and controls. It also came, one will be surprised to remember, among a dizzying panoply of helicopters: Hooks, Skycranes, Sea Stallions, Cobras, Loaches. As Alasdair Spark has asserted in "Flight Controls," a brilliant and richly documented "social history," as he calls it, "of the helicopter as a symbol of Vietnam," no other icon of memory from the war save perhaps the Vietnam Veterans Memorial can claim status as "the archetypal symbol of Vietnam."[6] But the one we see, hear, remember, imagine: that one is the Huey. It is the master vehicle, emblem, image of the war.

It is the cavalry to the rescue. It is commuting to a firefight. It is overhead management of the battlefield. It is instant medical evacuation. It created an entire argot of speed, power, aggression, decision: air assets, lift company, preparation, insertion, extraction, Lima Zulu, Papa Zulu, Hot, Cold. The Bell UH-1 series Iroquois helicopter. It is for Vietnam, the ultimate American power trip, the ride to the end of the twentieth-century technomilitary production line.

Indeed, even today, one continues to write the book basically on Vietnam by detailing an American Huey obsession in which disastrous day-to-day consequences kept up some dreadful footrace with new mythic symbologies. Spark, for instance, cites P. Starr's *Discarded Army* on the recollections of a pilot who described flying, in Spark's phrasing, as "the mental equivalent of a cinematic 'jump-cut': 'One morning you're flying medevac and you'll see guys who haven't had a meal in four days. And [next] you're going to fly the general around [and he] brings you in to eat in an air-conditioned room with a tablecloth and sterling silver. . . . '"[7] Similarly, in *Self-Destruction*, detailing the U.S. Army's overall failure of performance during the war, a career officer writing under the name of "Cincinnatus" reveals how helicopter tactics served to telegraph any major tactical move. Such air operations, he writes, "regularly gave away to the enemy the information that a search-and-destroy mission was beginning. Aerial-reconnaissance flights, sweeping back and forth across a particular grid of terrain in ever narrowing arcs, were a dead giveaway to hidden observers in the jungle below that an operation was about to be launched in the vicinity. They could often pinpoint the LZ selected by the Americans and, if they wished, be there waiting to ambush the G.I.s as they offloaded from their choppers."[8]

Thus the Huey inscribed the whole mindset of American energy, know-how, decisiveness, and determination regnant, of measurable progress, of inevitable triumph; and exactly in that measure it reigned as the ultimate emblem of misplaced faith, of a geopolitical ignorance and a technological arrogance literally wrecking itself against the great, ancient, impassive face of Asia.[9] It was, in sum, the prime conveyance to "apocalypse now," to encounter with a small Asian country—even as we attempted to "waste" it in nearly every sense of the term—electing itself as the first one ever not to succumb to us in armed conflict, and thus for Americans a trip to the end of history in its traditional western sense—history as the inevitability of progress, the perfectibility of man, the victory of technology, the utopian fulfillment of reason, science, objective knowledge.

The transportation to, from, and amid all of that was provided by the Huey; or perhaps, rather, all the Hueys that came to comprise, as Michael Herr called it at the time, one incredible

> collective meta-chopper . . . the sexiest thing going; saver-destroyer, provider-waster, right hand-left hand, nimble, fluent, canny and human; hot steel, grease, jungle-saturated canvas webbing, sweat cooling and warming up again, cassette rock and roll in one ear and door-gun fire in the other, fuel, heat vitality and death, death itself, hardly an intruder.

He goes on:

> Helicopters and people jumping out of helicopters, people so in love they'd run to get on even when there wasn't any pressure. Choppers rising straight out of small cleared jungle spaces, wobbling down onto city roof-tops, cartons of rations and ammunition thrown off, dead and wounded loaded on. Sometimes they were so plentiful and loose that you could touch down at five or six places in a day, look around, hear the talk, catch the next one out. There were installations as big as cities with 30,000 citizens, once we dropped in to feed supply to one man. God knows what kind of Lord Jim phoenix numbers he was doing in there, all he said to me was, "You didn't see a thing, right Chief?"

"Choppers like taxis," he rhapsodizes, the locomotive and the loco-motion in "La Vida Loca."[10]

Choppers everywhere, while it was happening and long after it has gone. And always, somehow, the chopper is a Huey. Hear, for instance, the narrator of Ward Just's *The American Blues* on a late winter's afternoon in New England, 1975, standing on the deck out-side his house, looking for literary-cultural closure, the end of a his-tory of the war he is attempting to write, while, on the television inside, the actual end crowds upon him. Suddenly, having watched all the lift ships on all the Saigon rooftops, he somehow knows that he is about to see one here as well, somewhere just out beyond the horizon. Then it comes, the Huey, somewhere on the landscape of America; and once again it becomes the image of the history for which no ending perhaps can be written:

> It could have been a wilderness anywhere, these deserted and silent highlands. . . . No one who has ever heard the sound in wartime will ever forget, slap*slap*slap*slap*. I watched him approach over my empty quarter, dipping a little, then rising, flying contour only a few feet above my firs and bare maples. Very close now, the nose suddenly dipped and the Huey turned like a runner reversing field, skidding, its engine screaming and banked dizzyingly away, rising higher in circles and flying off to the south. I watched it go, seeing the pink excited face in the passenger seat, a quick grin and a too-casual salute—my banker friend, Eurodollar Ed, scouting the valley for a developer.[11]

For Americans scouting the valleys in Vietnam, sitting in base camp offices or motor pools, running across tarmacs to trundle wounded into operating rooms, the real Hueys were every bit as ubiquitous and hypnotic as those imaged here. Likewise, for Americans at home, they came regularly as TV nightly news Hueys. Then, shortly they would begin to come as movie Hueys. At some point, as H. Palmer Hall notes in a perceptive essay situating the helicopter and the pungi stick as comparative technologies, they would all just start to blend in. And he is right. The one John Wayne uses in *The Green Berets* to ferry himself, David Janssen, and Aldo Ray into a beleaguered Special Forces camp in the Highlands merges with the one in *Platoon* carrying Charlie Sheen out, on the last day of his tour, to the heartbreaking whispers of Samuel Barber's *Adagio*. That one merges into the one rattling the windows of the hotel room in Saigon where Charlie Sheen's father Martin Sheen awaits his upriver heart-of-darkness odyssey in *Apocalypse Now*. That one has already emerged from the one flittering back in the burning treeline while Jim Morrison, voice-over, does "The End." Eventually it will lead the air assault conducted by the mad surfing colonel in the cavalry hat to the tune of "Ride of the Valkyries" (and, as noted earlier, replicated in grim parodic fact during the invasion of Grenada). Meanwhile, out at the end of the pipeline, where no one is in charge of the war, that one will merge into the one supplying The Ride of the Playboy Bunnies. And that one in turn will get commandeered by Rambo, pretty much the way John Wayne used to pick up a dismounted machine gun, for the hell-bent revenge mission of *First Blood, Part II*.[12]

These become the endlessly proliferated imagings of our energy, our prodigality, our violence, our haste, our waste. And, as in the movies, so in the books, they haunt our representations. Indeed, as themselves the pre-texts often of a visual sine qua non—in promotional posters, advertising copy, design features of record sleeves and book jackets—they preside over our very ideas of those representations. They become our first visualizations of texts with names like *Writing Under Fire, America Rediscovered, The Fire Dream, Message from Nam, To Bear Any Burden, The Fall of Saigon*. They make our breathless descent into titles such as *Landing Zones* and *Search and Destroy*. And that, of course, is not to mention the spate of texts quite literally about the chopper war: *Chickenhawk, CW-2, Let a Soldier Die, Weary Falcon*.

Then there are the imagings that proliferate within the texts themselves. In one of the earliest, for instance, and, as Alfred Kazin called it, most "astringent"[13] metafictions of the war, William Eastlake's *The Bamboo Bed*, the titular aircraft is pure sex, a flying platform above the battlefield where medevac pilots spend their time between dustoffs on autopilot, copulating with compliant nurses. Another, Norman Mailer's *Why Are We in Vietnam?*, depicts its Texas-rich, gun-nut protagonists on heliborne hunting assault in the Brooks Range of Alaska, laying waste to anything that moves on the last American frontier. (On the last page, the young buckaroos, we discover, are "off to see the Wizard in Vietnam. . . . Vietnam. Hot Damn."[14] Robert Stone's *Dog Soldiers*, the chronicle of a doomed, idiotic heroin scam bringing the war back home, basically encapsulates the madness in the theory of The Great Elephant Zap, where, one of the protagonists recalls, "the Military Advisory Command, Vietnam, had decided that elephants were enemy agents because the NVA used them to carry things, and there had ensued a scene worthy of the *Ramayana*." He goes on:

> Many-armed, hundred-headed MACV had sent forth steel-bodied flying insects to destroy his enemies, the elephants. All over the country, whooping sweating gunners descended from the cloud cover to stampede the herds and mow them down with 7.62-millimeter machine guns.
>
> The Great Elephant Zap had been too much and had disgusted

everyone. Even the chopper crews who remembered the day as one of insane exhilaration had been somewhat appalled. There was a feeling that there were limits.

And as for dope, Converse thought, and addicts—if the world is going to contain elephants pursued by flying men, people are just naturally going to want to get high.[15]

And, lest fiction suggest that such imaging begins to outrun itself, one may also be directed to an inclusion in Tom Wolfe's classic anthology, *The New Journalism*. About a helicopter ride with General James F. Hollingsworth, assistant division of commander of the First Infantry, it is entitled "The General Goes Zapping Charlie Cong." Or, one may review the case of the only U.S. general officer court-martialled during the war, "prosecuted for shooting civilians from his command helicopter," as Spark phrases it, "'gook hunting.'"[16] As with fiction, one here may also leave the rest, as the saying goes, to the reader's imagination.

In a host of other narrative texts, the inscription becomes richly and deeply codified. The last machine in *Machine Dreams*, Jayne Anne Phillips's chronicle about a family weathering this nation's midcentury of wars, is the helicopter carrying the last male to death in Vietnam. In *Meditations in Green*, the record of a drug-addled veteran's attempts to imagine the green of old war into the green of new hope, the woman who becomes his confidante and soul mate is named Huette Mirandella. In one of the farthest imaginative flights back into memory, in Tim O'Brien's recent *The Things They Carried*, a GI's choppered-in hometown girlfriend becomes the eternal war, out there waiting, "The Sweetheart of the Song Tra Bong." In James Park Sloan's ambitious metafiction, *War Games*, a Huey on a "leaflet flight" becomes the platform for one of the great antiwar orations and pissing contests in a war that deeply needed to be pissed on from the start. "We stood in the open doors," the narrator recalls, "and shouted challenges a thousand feet down."

"Come on you bastards, mix it up. I paid good money for this goddamn seat. Let's see some punches. Candy asses!"

"Come on, nick me so I can get a Purple Heart."

Our machine guns useless in the dark, we poured barrage of mucus and urine upon the countryside.

As K. C. unbuttoned his fly, I recalled my childhood wish to see the heavens open and an airliner empty its toilets on the head of the corner cop.

"You mothers that can't swim better head for the sampans."[17]

The Huey likewise pervades our poems. One of the earliest soldier-poets of the war, for instance, Basil T. Paquet, in a kind of "Death of the Ball Turret Gunner," Vietnam version, recreates the medical evacuation scene of "Night Dust-off":

> A sound like hundreds of barbers
> stropping furiously, increases;
> suddenly the night lights,
> flashing blades thin bodies
> into red strips
> hunched against the wind.
> of a settling slickship.
>
> Litters clatter open,
> hands reaching
> into the dark belly of the ship
> touch toward moans,
> they are thrust into a privy,
> feeling into wounds,
> the dark belly all wound,
> all wet screams riven limbs
> moving in the beaten night.[18]

Similarly, in "Wichita Vortex Sutra," the foremost of the antiwar poets, Allen Ginsberg, finds the same vehicle, at once literal and metaphoric, for the imaging of the manic anguish:

> American Eagle beating its wings over Asia
> million dollar helicopters
> a billion dollars worth of Marines
>   who loved Aunt Betty
>   Drawn from the shores and farms shaking
> from the high schools to the landing barge
> blowing the air through their cheeks with fear
>   in *Life* on Television

> Put it this way on the radio
> Put it this way in television language
> > Use the words
> > > language, language,
> > > > "A bad guess"[19]

Finally, in one of the most enduring poems of the war, Bruce Weigl's "Him, On the Bicycle," "the worst old dream of aerial murder," as I have described it elsewhere becomes "a new ecstasy of flight."[20] The "Him" who was the enemy again rides the bicycle on the Ho Chi Minh Trail. The "I" who is the poet again rides the "liftship." But now something miraculous happens. "He pulls me out of the ship," the poet writes,

> there's firing far away.
> I'm on the back of the bike
> holding his hips.
> It's hard pumping for two,
> I hop off and push the bike.
>
> I'm brushing past trees,
> the man on the bike stops pumping,
> lifts his feet,
> we don't waste a stroke.
> His hat flies off,
> I catch it behind my back,
> put it on, I want to live forever!
>
> Like a blaze
> streaming down the trail.[21]

In the recent evolution of popular drama, however, may be found perhaps a most singular current imaging of the last Huey, and that is the one presiding over the set of the Broadway hit musical, a Madame Butterfly after the Fall entitled *Miss Saigon*. In a trenchant observation on the possible significance of such an attempted vision of closure, Robert Stone wishes for the best. In such coming to terms, he suggests, "there's reason to hope that being just another country in the world may turn out to be less demeaning than we feared." Yet he also speculates on the more likely message it sends us. "With the

New York opening of 'Miss Saigon,' the Vietnam experience begins its final slide into the past, into history, make-believe, and melodrama."[22]

To put these matters into a broader historical context, contrast all this with the iconography of World War II, the jeep, the Sherman tank, or, even out at the far end of Heller-Vonnegut-Pynchon techno-paranoia, the bomber or the rocket. Compare now the totally sanitized iconography of Desert Storm, a war that was actually contrived to look like a video game: live fireworks from an air attack on the center of Baghdad; film of a smart bomb going down the air shaft of a huge building; videotape during a briefing of a truck driver speeding across a bridge, caught for a moment in radar lock, and then watching Armageddon in the rear-view mirror as the real target disintegrates behind him, with the general and the press chuckling communally over the scaredest man in Iraq.

In the wake of all this, we need to ask an important question about the power of images in the world that a particular image of Vietnam described here continues to make imperative. What will the world look like when the last Huey we see really turns out to be the last Huey? And it is already happening. In Panama, the main troop carrier was the Blackhawk. In the Persian Gulf, the main weapons platform was the Apache.

Before that happens, I would suggest, one should continue to listen to someone who still carries the image of a UH-1 helicopter on the inside of his or her head; someone, that is, still around who knows how a Huey war looked, smelled, sounded; someone who remembers, for instance, like this GI in Mark Baker's *Nam*, what it was always like after the latest rocket attack:

> I would put my helmet on and sometimes my flak jacket and I would sit on the sandbags outside my hooch and watch the war. Flare light everywhere, the smoke trails making patterns all over the place and strange shadows in the sky. Tracer bullets coming down. All the catalogue of noises. Picking out an RPG sound. Our mortars or their mortars. AKs as opposed to our M-16s. All those noises that I know that at ninety I would be able to recognize and differentiate. I still look up every time I hear a Huey.[23]

So, always, as noted earlier, does the fictional journalist-historian in Ward Just's *The American Blues*. So, always, does the actual veteran critic writing to you on this page. It is true. You can always tell a vet, I am convinced, by how he acts around a helicopter, how he stops, gets quiet, looks up, listens. He will easily tell if it's a Huey or something else, and, if it's something else, he'll likely stop looking. If it is a Huey, he will follow it all, the series of patterns, reverberations, pitches. Whether it's out-of-small-arms-range high or treetop low, inbound or outbound, low speed or high speed, about to land or heading off somewhere else, point-to-point. Moreover, I hope the scene enacted, whether in a life or in a literary moment, will stay true. Images may be what we have, and in them dizzying significations may endlessly proliferate. Even if so, I would assert, images must serve. As long as we have people who think it might be important to remember Vietnam, what happened to us and the Vietnamese there, and what we can do to keep it from happening again, I suggest that we never junk the last Huey, that we ought to keep at least one around, that we never allow the last Huey in the world to become the last Huey in our minds. And we should do so, I propose, not just to remember, the way they do with B-25s and Zeros and Messerschmitts. Rather, through new representations and new attempts at sense making, we should do so exactly for the sake of the power of images to help us both remember and imagine, as they say, for future reference.

NOTES

1. To give just one measure of the obsessive power of the scene, the well-known Vietnam writer Philip Caputo returned literally once and has literarily returned three times since to the moment of the fall. A first account comprises a kind of coda and reprise in his autobiographical narrative, *A Rumor of War*. A fictionalized version figures heavily in his novel, *Del Corso's Gallery*. A third, configured, as he suggests, somewhere in between, appears in his recent memoir, *Ways of Escape*. Readers familiar with the literature of the war will also note a number of book-length accounts of the fall of Saigon, the most dramatic and engaging being David Butler's book of that title. The scene has also played heavily in postwar fiction ranging from the prizewinning work of Ward Just to the mass-market productions of Danielle Steel. A major retrospective volume of the Vietnam poet Walter McDonald is similarly entitled *After the Fall of Saigon*.

2. Why Huey? There is the obvious, and deeply American practicality of a functional onomatopoeia. GP equals jeep, etc. Beyond that, one also suspects, for a generation of GIs brought up on Saturday morning TV, a strong cartoon logic. Maybe it is Baby Huey, duckling in a diaper, fat, ungainly, not too bright, but lovable and somehow impervious to all manner of possible

harm. Maybe it is Huey as in Huey, Dewey, and Louie, nephews of Donald, grandsons of Scrooge. This would be of a piece with the same cartoon logic that often seemed to make Vietnam, as Bernard Fall wrote just before his death, a "Batman war." Certainly, it was the logic projecting from countless Huey nose bubbles through the familiar face of the feckless, Roadrunner-chasing, disaster-bound Wile E. Coyote and his plaintive "Why me?"

As to the "Iroquois" part, the American military seemed to see helicopter development as somehow a natural extension of Indian Wars. On this point, Spark offers a catalog of names so used: "Sioux, Choctaw, Shawnee, Chickasaw, Mohave, Iroquois, Cayuse, Kiowa, Chinook, Tarke, Cheyenne." Alasdair Spark, "Flight Controls," *Vietnam Images: War and Representation,* ed. Geoffrey Walsh and James Aulich (New York: St. Martins, 1989), 89.

3. Susan Jeffords, *The Remasculinization of America: Gender and the Vietnam War* (Bloomington: University of Indiana Press, 1989), 14.

4. A further, definitive vignette of the whole airmobile "scene" at the last is provided by David Butler, in the opening pages of *The Fall of Saigon,* where he describes an embassy official, detailed to cut down an ancient tamarind tree to provide a ground-level landing zone, self-consciously hesitating to give the order because he knows it will constitute his admission to himself that defeat is final. David Butler, *The Fall of Saigon* (New York: Simon & Schuster, 1985), 26–27.

Meanwhile, out on the ships, as Spark notes, a corresponding debacle was being enacted through some familiar old metaphors. Citing William Gibson, he observes of the "dumping overboard of helicopters," it was "'as if an imaginary Western had turned into a horror show—the Cavalry was shooting its horses after being chased by the Indians back to the fort,'" Qtd. Spark, "Flight Controls," 87; James William Gibson, *The Perfect War: Technowar in Vietnam* (New York: Atlantic Monthly Press, 1986), 4.

5. One might have been emboldened in the years just after the war to use the more hopeful expression, "may yet help us not to 'go there' any more." One is forced to the past conditional on the basis that if one counts Grenada, Panama, and Saudi Arabia, we have by now "gone there" again thrice already.

6. Spark, "Flight Controls," 86.

7. Ibid., 99.

8. Cincinnatus (pseud.), *Self-Destruction: The Disintegration and Decay of the United States Army during the Vietnam Era* (New York: Norton, 1987), 79. Speaking as a former combat platoon leader, I can also testify to the reality of the "squad leader in the sky" syndrome that often quite literally put an unbridgeable distance between field-grade commanders and tactical unit commanders on the ground. One former compatriot, cited by both Cincinnatus and Gibson, crystalizes it dramatically:

> We always had a horror that one day things would come to a standstill. Overhead would be circling our battalion commander. Above him would be his brigade commander. Higher than both would be the division commander and hovering over him would be his corps commander. All circling in their "charlie-charlie" [command and control] choppers,

all demanding to know what was going on down on the ground. So much command and control would be present that those with their "ass in the grass" would no longer be able to function at all. It never happened, but it came close. (Cincinnatus, 82)

It was suggested by some analysts that the helicopter would eliminate the dugout, bunker, rear command-post generalship of earlier wars. In fact, the Huey often replicated the communications mess described above as a matter of command perspective as well. One of the problems of a commander away from the actual terrain is that things appearing feasible on a map prove for various reasons utterly impracticable on the battlefield. So, for a commander in orbit above that battlefield, the terrain often seemed to become simply a living version of the same topographical map. Measures that seemed workable from the air often translated themselves into futility on the ground. See discussions of the problem in Cincinnatus, *Self-Destruction*, 81.

9. Both Cincinnatus and Gibson again record acutely, in this regard, the observation of Sir Robert Thompson, architect of British response to the Malaysian insurgency of the 1950s, that the helicopter exactly "exaggerated the two great weaknesses of the American character—impatience and aggressiveness." See Cincinnatus, 81; and Gibson, 105. Gibson then adds, "note how in this formulation an entire world-view and system of warfare became reduced to one technological artifact, the helicopter" (105).

10. Michael Herr, *Dispatches* (New York: Knopf, 1977), 8–9.

11. Ward Just, *The American Blues* (New York: Viking, 1984), 16.

12. Indeed, as Susan Jeffords notes, in terms of writing the male body into the machine, the Rambo series uses the helicopter here to up the ante on itself, given the viewer's likely remembrance of such literal machine-gun slinging by the hero with an M-60 (unlike John Wayne's dismounted weapons, actually designed, among other uses, to be fired from the hip) in the original film. Jeffords, *Remasculinization*, 11–14.

13. Alfred Kazin, B*right Book of Life* (New York: Delta, 1974), 91.

14. Norman Mailer, *Why Are We In Vietnam?* (New York: Putnam's, 1967), 208.

15. Robert Stone, *Dog Soldiers* (Boston: Houghton Mifflin, 1974), 41–42.

16. Spark, "Flight Controls," 100.

17. James Park Sloan, *War Games* (Boston: Houghton Mifflin, 1971), 126.

18. In *Carrying the Darkness: American Indochina — The Poetry of the Vietnam War,* ed. W. D. Ehrhart (New York: Avon, 1985), 217.

19. Allen Ginsberg, *Planet News* (San Francisco: City Lights, 1968), 116–17.

20. Bruce Weigl, *A Romance* (Pittsburgh: University of Pittsburgh Press, 1979), 196.

21. Ibid., 9–10.

22. "*Miss Saigon* Flirts with Art and Reality," *New York Times* 2 (7 April 1991): 1, 30.

23. Mark Baker, ed., *Nam: The Vietnam War in the Words of the Men and Women Who Fought There* (New York: Morrow, 1981), 143.

THE WORK OF WAR AFTER THE AGE OF MECHANICAL REPRODUCTION

Michael P. Clark

Airmobility, dig it, you weren't going anywhere. It made you feel safe, it made you feel Omni, but it was only a stunt, technology.

> Michael Herr, *Dispatches*

Today men's nerves surround us; they have gone outside as electrical environment. The human nervous system itself can be reprogrammed biologically as readily as any radio network can alter its fare.

> Marshall McLuhan, "Notes on Burroughs"

Many of the novels, oral histories, and films about the Vietnam War express what critics identify as a "Modernist sensibility" that seems to belie their date of composition and the naturalistic genre of war stories.[1] The sensibility emerges most often as a sense of alienation and as an inchoate, intuitive awareness of the power of symbolic forms to shape the perception of reality. This anomic disengagement is summarized by a remark in Mark Baker's oral history *Nam:* "You want to hear a gen-u-ine war story? I only understand Vietnam as though it were a story. It's not like it happened to me."[2] To be sure, such untutored aestheticism bears little resemblance to what T. S. Eliot might recognize as "tradition" or a "consciousness of the past." Nor do we find much evidence of the exquisitely tuned sensitivity of the poet in Ezra Pound's "Mauberly," who is plunged into despair when "The tea-rose tea-gown, etc. / Supplants the mousseline of Cos" and "The pianola 'replaces' / Sappho's barbitos." Yet, if the canonical jetsam of Pound's poem seems dated and comically distant from most of the work on Vietnam, his poet's bitter denunciation of empty patriotism and political hypocrisy in the great fourth and fifth sections of "Mauberly" still resonates in the resentment and bitterness that dominate much writing about Vietnam. And more surprisingly, even the oral histories taken from combat veterans often express a fundamentally Modernist self-consciousness about the mediated character of their experience that foregrounds narrative convention at the expense of personal feeling or existential immediacy. "What the fuck do you *think* happened?" a soldier responds when asked to describe an ambush that killed the rest of his patrol, "We got shot to pieces." But when the reporter starts to write down that answer, the soldier adds, "make that 'little pieces.' We were still shaking the trees for dog tags when we pulled back out of there."[3]

Philip Beidler has pointed to this persistent motif of narrative self-consciousness as one of the most distinctive characteristics of popular writing about Vietnam. Soldiers have always told war stories, and they have always taken comfort in projecting familiar images onto strange and threatening scenes. But writing about Vietnam usually lacks the counterbalance of what might be called epiphany or moments of illumination in which a heightened sense of the real war supplants romantic fantasies. Conventions and stereotypes are not so much measured against the "truth" of eyewitness accounts as they are confounded by broader uncertainties and by a nagging sense of failure to distinguish between fiction and reality. Surveying the early oral histories of the war, Beidler notes that the "truth-burdened" immediacy of these firsthand accounts is usually accompanied by a sense of their own narrative formation that emerges in the "recurrent, almost startlingly routine demonstration of clearly 'aesthetic' attributes of focus and design, point, coherence, and closure.... There it is," Beidler concludes. In the accounts of the war by men who fought it, "as if through bizarre mirror image, fact likewise seems to make its most visible meanings by recurrently calling attention . . . to its inherent and essential fictiveness."[4]

This narrative self-consciousness is uncommon in war stories such as the ones reported in these oral histories, but the form it takes in most writing about Vietnam remains equally distant from the highly articulated theological systems, mythological narratives, and elaborate metaphorical traditions of High Modernist art. There are, of course, some examples of pretentious allusion and empty culture-mongering in works that seem determined to lift the war into art on the backs of Wallace Stevens and e. e. cummings. The idealizing tendency of Modernist aestheticism is echoed more frequently in Vietnam literature, however, by comments scattered through oral histories that suggest a casual, if sometimes calculated, awareness on the speaker's part that authenticity depends on narrative persona and point of view as much as on lived experience. The aesthetic traditions of high culture were largely inaccessible and irrelevant to the lower classes from which most Vietnam combat units were composed—and to the mass culture from which most of the imagery about the Vietnam war has come.[5] Even the elementary irony characteristic of so many novels and films about World War II is missing from much of this later work. Traditional symbols and themes have been replaced by less complex motifs borrowed from commercial logos, rock music, and the simplistic stereotypes that populate television series and animated cartoons. So instead of a holy war or a defense of the free world, the Vietnam War was fought according to a script from the Saturday matinees and prime-time sit-coms that had rehearsed their scenes for such a long time in living rooms back home. It is no accident, Philip Beidler says, that the generation fighting and dying in this war was the same one whose "sense-making faculties" had been informed by

> Golden-age TV: cartoons, commercials, cowboys, comedians and caped crusaders, all coming across together at quantum-level intensity . . . child-world dreams of aggression and escape mixed up with moralistic fantasies of heroism beleaguered yet ultimately regnant in a world of lurking, omnipresent dangers and deceits—in sum, a composite high-melodrama and low-comedy videotape of the American soul.[6]

The curious migration of images from television commercials to the battlefield of war might therefore be explained by the semantic weightlessness of those images as they function in the popular media. Given the commercial basis of this symbolic repertoire, the feelings of alienation and confusion so often associated with the use of these reductive figures by veterans trying to make sense out of their experience may be read simply as extrapolations of contradictions inherent in our media-saturated lives but obscured by the acquiescent silence of the masses in everyday life. James Wilson suggests as much when he traces the connection between the conduct of the Vietnam War and the typical practices of late capitalism. Motivated by the single need to stimulate increasingly higher levels of consumption, our culture strives to destroy "All vestiges of tradition, all orthodox ideologies, all continuous forms of reality," Wilson says. "The same holds true of Vietnam, where history and culture had to be negated in order to mass market the consumer entity known as South Vietnam." Those who write about Vietnam and make films about the war merely "take to an extreme the unreality, the discontinuity, and the loss of values that may characterize much of our experience in America today," an experience made up of "isolated individuals, victims of a culturally conditioned alienation, estranged from external reality, from history, and from binding values."[7]

Perhaps it is the inane, empty commercialism of mass culture in late capitalism that explains why the self-consciousness of symbolic mediation in oral histories of the Vietnam War so seldom translates into the active historical agency imagined by many Modernist artists. Rather than inspiring a creative freedom to remake the world in the image of their own fictions, the disengagement from immediate experience described by many of the veterans leads to a sense of their being passive observers, similar to their positions vis-à-vis the popular media back home. As one of the veterans says in *Nam*,

> I was a grunt radioman, so I used to hang back with the CO and keep squad together. I got to watch the whole war with my eyes. I loved to just sit in the ditch and watch people die. As bad as that sounds, I just liked to *watch* no matter what happened, sitting back with my homemade cup of hot chocolate. It was like a big movie. (93)[8]

The radioman's perspective is unique, given his special duties. But the scenario of "watching" the war as a spectator in a movie theater is a common motif in much writing about Vietnam. Another veteran told Baker that he began to feel that he possessed an inner faculty he called "The Watcher" and observed that in Vietnam, "[e]verybody watched. There was a kind of implied voyeurism without the nasty connotations" (142). However awful such an attitude sounds in retrospect, watching constituted a distinct source of pleasure that at times even drew the spectator into the scene in macabre ways. "I loved to just sit in the ditch and watch people die," the radioman says of his big movie. He remembers looking at disemboweled corpses and thinking only "'Oh, wow. So that's what they look like.' . . . You do things that seem not right now, but which seemed right at the time." After confessing that he used to play with the intestines of the dead men, he says "I can actually say I never felt bad about anything I did in Nam, except for doing something like that once in a while. Or getting the pleasure out of it" (93–94).

The specular structure of cinematic experience is such a familiar part of popular culture in the United States that it is not surprising to see veterans associate it with extraordinary circumstances for which no ordinary discourse is readily available. In addition, as Christian Metz has shown, the "filmic pleasure" of watching a movie has important structural parallels with more general forms of scopophilia (the "passion for perceiving") that psychoanalysis has likened to voyeurism. Unlike voyeurism, though, filmic pleasure lacks the "nasty consequences" of perversion because its carnivalesque respite from the constraints of everyday life takes place within the broader symbolic order of social relations as figured by the narrative coherence of the film and, more concretely, by the technology of production that makes the cinematic image possible in the first place.[9]

The paradoxical character that Metz attributes to filmic pleasure suggests why the experience of movie-going works so well to represent war. Like a film, war is a moral "reserve" in which actions normally restricted by society are permitted and even encouraged, though only with certain boundaries. In war, soldiers do what civilians only watch on the movie screen back home. For the soldier, translating the action into terms of watching limits the horrific consequences of that action and domesticates the violence. This translation of scenes from the war into civilian fantasy is exemplified by Tim O'Brien in his autobiographical journal of his experience in Vietnam, *If I Die in a Combat Zone*, where he reports overhearing the following conversation among four soldiers in a foxhole. They have found a starlight scope and one is looking through it.

"What's out there?"
"A peep show," Chip murmured. "Sweet, sweet stuff. Dancing soul sisters." He giggled and stared through the scope.
"Starlight, star bright."
"Don't *hog* it, man."

"Dreamland!"

"Come on, what do you *see*?"

"All the secrets. I see 'em all out there."

"Hey—"

"Fairy-tale land," Chip whispered. . . ."I *see*. Yeah, now I *see*."

"Evil."

"No, it's sweet, real nice." Chip giggled. "I see a circus.
No shit, there's a circus out there. Charlie's all dressed up in clown suits.
Oh, yeah, a real circus."[10]

The loss of agency inherent in assuming the position of a spectator is apparent in such accounts. Yet, it would be a mistake to dis-
count the watching described by these examples merely as lower-
class *ressentiment* or a degenerate passivity bred by the degraded
mass culture Pound scorned in "Mauberly" as the "prose-kinema."
These viewers express a degree of enjoyment that suggests a more
active engagement in what is unfolding before their eyes than mere
"watching" would allow. A Modernist rhetoric of estrangement and
alienation, with its nostalgic reference to a real, substantial world
against which passive disengagement might be measured, ignores the
pleasure derived from the production and circulation of these images
by the people who see, imagine, and report them. Many of these allusions to the specular structure of the cinematic scene do characterize
the position of the subject as a passive viewer, but at other times that
specular position suggests a new kind of agency for the subject that
confounds traditional distinctions between watching and doing by
emphasizing the act of receiving and communicating those images
to others. While neither the radioman nor the soldier with the starlight scope are immediately engaged in the scenes they watch, they
are nevertheless crucial participants in the circulation of information about those scenes.

Neither active participant nor passive spectator, the position of
the subject described in these scenes is more that of a symbolic relay
determined entirely by the technological apparatus used to represent
the war and direct its violence: the radio and the night-scope and the
huge network of information technology that produced them. Many
of the combat veterans who have written or spoken about their experiences describe the extent to which their interaction with representational technologies in Vietnam overwhelmed any direct personal contact with the enemy, their own units, or even themselves; as scout

sniper James Hebron described sighting his target down the barrel of his rifle, "it is pure symbolism at that point. Everything is symbolism that you're living on."[11] This engagement with symbolic apparatus is dramatized even more concretely by another account reported in *Nam* about a firefight that began one night while a film was being shown. While the story strains credulity by its very appropriateness to this point, the scene is worth considering in its full length because it so explicitly traces the connections suggested by the preceding examples among the prefabricated images of mass culture, actual combat, and the representational apparatus that joins them.

> "This is a story of long, long ago, when the world was just beginning . . ." a resonant voice booms out of the darkness. The makeshift movie screen explodes in a vortex of lava fire like rolling napalm. The following quiet is filled with the rattle of the old projector and the very real night sounds of Southeast Asia. "One Million Years B.C." Dadumm.
>
> Gar hadn't seen a movie in a long time. In fact, he'd been in the field almost four months straight. But Da Nang was a big base. They had an outdoor theater with a wooden wall painted white and rows of benches for the men to sit on. Gar couldn't complain about the choice of films either—cavemen clad in animal skins, grunting, fighting, hunting with their hands, chased by giant iguanas that smacked their scaled lips. It seemed particularly relevant to his life these days. When Raquel Welch appeared, a lynx bikini slung low on her hips, cascades of red hair billowing over bare shoulders, a whoop went up from the crowd. "Oh, yeah! Shit, she look good," Gar yelled.
>
> In the distance, someone else yelled, "Incoming! Incoming!" Raquel faded and vanished as the projector clacked to a stop. Most of the men ran for their bunkers, including the projectionist in spite of a voice in the audience that threatened, "Turn that thing back on or I'll blow you away."
>
> Only Gar and a few other grunts from the field were left. In the red glare of the rockets, with mortar shells bursting all around them, they flipped the projector back on and settled in for the rest of the movie. Beyond the flickering light somebody called, "They're infiltrating!"
>
> "We shot our rifles off all around us," Gar told me. "Everybody knew not to come in there while we were watching the film, because we would shoot them. Everybody was enemy at that point." (217–18)

This scene begins with the simplest conflation between the reality of the war and the fantasy of the movie. The images of the cavemen are read as imaginary projections of the grunt's own experience, and the beginning of the world as a battlefield; but the violence of that world quickly yields to desire when Raquel Welch suddenly appears on the screen, a shift facilitated by the moral ambiguity Metz described as inherent in cinematic pleasure. The delicious perversity of that fantasy then quickly dissolves under the very real threat of the incoming shells, and most of the audience suspend their imaginary places beside Raquel to seek shelter and assume their defensive positions. But Gar and his friends refuse this orderly transition from the imaginary realm to their military role as soldiers. They seize control over the production of the fantasy, violating their positions as spectators while at the same time defying their role in the hierarchy of command and the obligation to defend their position against the enemy. Reversing their cinematic roles from viewer to projectionist disrupts the regulations by which the military authority has organized their relation to the people around them as friend or foe, just as it violates the conventional protocols of "watching." The violence that inhabited their fantasy spills over the frame of the imaginary scene in the film, canceling symbolic distinctions between ally and enemy and spreading at random across the field: "Everybody was an enemy at that point."

In this case, the cinematic scene does not domesticate the forbidden pleasure of violence and desire, nor does that scene contain the perversity of that pleasure within a broader symbolic stability, as Metz would predict. Rather, these men use cinematic terms to indicate an abrupt dislocation in their position as subjects within the symbolic structure of the war that had codified the enemy as "other" and so channeled the violence of war along ideological lines, just as the film directed desire toward the figure of a conventional sex object. Standing beside the projector, firing at anyone who would threaten his control over the machine that supports his fantasy, Gar disrupts, at least momentarily, the symbolic apparatus that would otherwise govern his behavior and determine his relation to imaginary objects of desire and even to the very real threat of death. From that perspective, distinctions between watching and doing, between the screen and the battlefield, collapse into an ecstatic reverie that projects the untamed violence of the fantasy outward onto the world. In this scenario, the creative "stylist" of Pound's Modernist aestheticism has yielded to a postmodern projectionist whose power derives not from artistic creativity so much as technical mastery of the representational machinery that sustains the life of his desire even as it threatens to destroy his body.

II

This emphasis on the mechanical apparatus of representation and its effect on the subject complicates the themes of alienation and "self"-consciousness that a more conventionally Modernist reading of these texts would suggest. Those complications point toward a postmodern sense of the powerful influence of representational technologies over all aspects of individual identity, an influence so pervasive that it determines not only forms of consciousness but also one's sense of the body and its place in the world. As we shall see, this postmodern sensibility relies on electronic and biochemical technologies—and their metaphors—rather than on the machinery of cinematic production that dominates the speech of the veterans discussed above. It is this disjunction between the veterans' postmodern experience and the modernist metaphors they often use to describe it that has led critics occasionally to impose on the veterans' remarks a rhetoric of alienation or distortion that does not quite fit the obvious expressions of pleasure and satisfaction in the mediating apparatus that determined the veterans' vision of the war and their place in it.

Rather than treating allusions to films and movie-going simply as updated metaphors for the mediating symbols of High Modernism, Walter Benjamin offered an early analysis of the ideological impact of emerging representational technologies in "The Work of Art in the Age of Mechanical Reproduction" that comes closer to addressing the way those allusions function in the examples we have just seen.[12] While his analysis of the "decay of aura" brought about by the mechanical reproduction of images in photography smacks of the existential rhetoric of authenticity and a nostalgic fondness for what he calls the "unarmed eye" (223), Benjamin is acutely aware of the powerful appeal of photography and cinema in the modern world. "The shooting of a film . . . affords a spectacle unimaginable anywhere at any time before this," he says (232). Through editing, special camera angles, lighting machinery, and other devices, film can construct a position for the subject—not just a point of view but a place to be—that is impossible outside the studio and yet that constitutes what we see as our place in the world:

> [I]n the studio the mechanical equipment has penetrated so deeply into reality that its pure aspect freed from the foreign substance of equipment is the result of a special procedure, namely, the shooting by the specially adjusted camera and the mounting of the shot together with other similar ones. The equipment-free aspect of reality here has become the height of artifice; the sight of immediate reality has become an orchid in the land of technology. (233)

Commenting on the technological innovations that made photographic reproduction possible, Benjamin notes that photography transferred to the eye the productive artistic functions formerly reserved for the hand of the craftsman, sculptor, and painter. Images can now be composed with a look through the lens rather than with a brush stroke or a hammer and chisel, and that capability has reduced the physical immediacy between the representational artifact and the presence of the body. Consequently, in addition to blurring the distinction between looking and doing, the mechanical reproduction of images has also altered our relation to spatial distinctions. Benjamin claims that this newfound omniscience, which can put a distant mountain range in the palm of our hand, quickly led to a sense of omnipotence over reality itself, the reward for our disengagement from the world we reproduce.

It takes little imagination to read Benjamin's remarks about the evolution from an art of the hand to an art of the eye as a commentary on the development of modern weaponry, which has largely substituted the eye for the hand as the anatomical source of violence. In the epilogue to his essay, Benjamin himself makes explicit the association between film and war in his discussion of the appalling success of fascism and its enthusiastic incorporation of film into its ideological program.

The principal problem facing fascism, Benjamin says, is organizing the newly created masses without disturbing the property structure that those masses threaten. Most important, he says, fascism gives the masses a chance to "express" themselves:

> It is inherent in the technique of the film as well as of sports that everybody who witnesses its accomplishments is somewhat of an expert. . . .

Similarly, the newsreel offers everyone the opportunity to rise from passer-by to movie extra. In this way any man might even find himself part of a work of art. . . . At any moment the reader is ready to turn into a writer. (231–32)

Channeling such "self-expression" into the technology controlled by the state, fascism is able to construct a place for the subject without according to individuals any political rights. The only way to effect that solution, however, is to introduce aesthetics into political life: "The violation of the masses has its counterpart in the violation of an [aesthetic] apparatus which is pressed into the production of ritual values" (241). And the only possible outcome of this conjunction between politics and aesthetics is war. Hence, fascism "expects war to supply the artistic gratification of a sense perception that has been changed by technology" (242). Benjamin concludes his argument by sketching an aesthetics of imperialistic war that provides an apt commentary on the radioman's confession in *Nam* that he liked playing with the intestines of dead bodies:

[T]he aesthetics of today's war appears as follows. . . . The horrible features of imperialistic warfare are attributable to the discrepancy between the tremendous means of production and their inadequate utilization in the process of production. . . . Imperialistic war is a rebellion of technology which collects, in the form of "human material," the claims to which society has denied its natural material. Instead of draining rivers, society directs a human stream into a bed of trenches; instead of dropping seeds from airplanes, it drops incendiary bombs over cities. . . . [Our] self-alienation has reached such a degree that it can experience its own destruction as an aesthetic pleasure of the first order. (242)

Benjamin's characterization of imperialistic war as a rebellion of technology against nature has taken on an appalling prescience after the defoliation of Vietnam's countryside and the ecological disasters unleashed in the Gulf War. Similarly, the continuing market for commercial videotapes of dogfights over the Arabian desert, tank combat, and smart bombs seeking their targets in Baghdad testifies to the aesthetic pleasure that the Gulf War continues to yield despite subsequent revelations of a body count that belies the sanitary blips on the video screen and a fail rate for the Patriot missile that may have actually gone over 50 percent. This persistent discrepancy between the experience of war and the images in which that experience is reproduced and circulated is obviously crucial to the ideological justification of this devastation, and it could only exist in what Debord has described as a world where "everything that was directly lived has moved away into representation" and reality has reached "its absolute fulfillment in the spectacle, where the tangible world is replaced by a selection of images, which exist above it and which simultaneously impose themselves as the tangible."[13]

The strategic censorship of information and images from combat during wartime is not peculiar to modern times, but in the Gulf War it took on an unusually productive and celebratory tone. More traditional forms of censorship that simply suppressed disturbing images of the battlefield have been rendered obsolete by the military use of video images of targets that convert the object into information as a condition of the violence directed toward it. Sighting the target and censoring its reality become one with the technology that transmits its image, and it is that same technology that makes the image so easily portable between the cockpit and living room. This technology, used so extensively by the U.S. during the Gulf War (and now in the bombing of Yugoslavia), allows the viewer at home to participate in the sighting and elimination of the enemy target without conveying even the mediated sense of presence and context experienced by the soldiers viewing the same image in their cockpits and tanks. Along with the usual footage of troops marching, planes taking off and landing, and tanks rolling out on maneuvers, the Gulf War also came home in exactly the same form that it appeared to many of the people fighting it, as an image on the video screen. Watching a blurry shape being framed by the electronic sight on a tank, the Iraqi landscape slide past the sighting screen on a fighter-bomber, or a bridge grow larger and larger as a smart bomb plunged toward its target, the viewer quite literally saw the same image of the war as the soldier and in fact *did* what the soldier did: looked. As Mark Poster puts it in his discussion of the role of television in the Gulf War, "the sense of being there was figured through powerful framing devices that subverted realism as they enacted it. . . . The more television images attempt to convince the viewer of the reference to reality, the more the image itself becomes the reality."[14]

Poster's remarks suggest a world in which Benjamin's concern about a mechanized triumph over space seems antique and naïve. As electronic transmission begins to replace not only the "mechanical reproduction" of images but also the actual presence of targeted objects on the battlefield in the eyes of a gunner, the difference between being "there" in combat and "here" at home seems even more ambiguous than Benjamin feared. As the reality of objects and their situation in a real world apart from the viewer's gaze begins to fade into the electronic image, feelings of alienation and disengagement yield to what Jean Baudrillard has called an "ecstasy of communication":

> Private "telematics": each person sees himself at the controls of a hypothetical machine, isolated in a position of perfect and remote sovereignty, at an infinite distance from his universe of origin.
>
> . . .The era of hyperreality now begins. What I mean is this: what was projected psychologically and mentally, what used to be lived out on earth as metaphor, as mental metaphorical scene, is henceforth projected into reality, without any metaphor at all, into an absolute space which is also that of simulation.[15]

This "hyperreality" differs most significantly from the cinematic scene described by Benjamin in the lack of any reference to the real that characterizes more traditional forms of mediation or representation. Without that reference to the real, the conventional affective weight of the image also tends to disappear, along with the "subject" or self associated with it. "Distance" connotes a clear sense of self and other, Baudrillard says, and it correlates with an intense sense of the private self as the scene of identity. In hyperreality, such distinctions no longer hold, and all space is literally "*ob*scene":

> [T]his private universe was alienating to the extent that it separated you from others—or from the world, where it was invested as a protective enclosure, an imaginary protector, a defense system. But it also reaped the symbolic benefits of alienation, which is that the Other exists, and that otherness can fool you for the better or the worse. Thus consumer society lived also under the sign of alienation, as a society of the spectacle. But just so: as long as there is alienation, there is spectacle, action, scene. It is not obscenity—the spectacle is never obscene. Obscenity begins precisely where there is no more spectacle, no more scene, when all becomes transparence and immediate visibility, where everything is exposed to the harsh and inexorable light of information and communication.
>
> We are no longer a part of the drama of alienation; we live in the ecstasy of communication. (130)

Whether the battlefield appears in the eerie glow of a starlight scope, the computerized grid projected before a pilot's eyes, or the video image broadcast into a tank or living rooms back home, these images have realized Baudrillard's vision of an obscene hyperreality that translates bodies into information and violence into communication, "without any metaphor at all." We have seen how many of the oral histories testify to an intuitive grasp of this new kind of experience, either through the rapture of projected vision—*I see! I see!*—or through a more unsettling sense that ethical distinctions between watching and doing are uncertain in a transparent world of instant communication between the safety of home and the danger of war. But as Gar's story shows, this "telematic" eye is no longer alienated in Benjamin's sense. Postmodern subjects worry less about their difference from the projected vision than about their dependence on the projector itself, the source of the image and the position from which both the viewer and the vision are constituted. In that position, the anxiety of alienation gives way to the compound euphoria of omniscience and omnipotence: "Airmobility, dig it, you weren't going anywhere," Michael Herr says in *Dispatches.* "It made you feel safe, it made you feel Omni, but it was only a stunt, technology" (13).

III

Given the prevalence of cinematic allusions and technological motifs in the discourse of many Vietnam veterans, it is surprising that it took so long for filmmakers to begin incorporating those allusions in their work about Vietnam. Constrained in part, no doubt, by the naturalistic conventions of most war movies,[16] and perhaps unprepared to attribute any aesthetic self-consciousness to their unschooled characters, most early films about Vietnam aspired either to a transparent realism or overt ideological critique. Testaments to the influence of film and other media in our perspective on the war were often inadvertent, the product of obtrusively wooden writing, stiffer acting, or comically egregious faux pas such as the ending of *The Green Berets* (1968), where the sun sets meaningfully over the eastern horizon of the South China Sea. Several years after the end of the Vietnam War, however, the role of cinematic production in that war and in our memory of it began appearing as an explicit motif in popular films about Vietnam, and with the appearance of this motif came a more subtle understanding of the relation between representational technologies and the people subject to their control in war and at home.

The most famous film to incorporate filmmaking into its diegesis is undoubtedly Francis Ford Coppola's *Apocalypse Now* (1979). Early in the film, as Captain Willard lands on shore during a chaotic firefight, he walks directly into a battle scene being shot by a documentary filmmaker played by Coppola himself. The filmmaker is ordering the soldiers around in the scene we see, just as Coppola directs the actors in the film that we are watching. For the few seconds in which Coppola's character is on screen, the world of the war represented by the film becomes a mirror for the cinematic apparatus that produced that world and our relation to it as spectators. This detour in the usual passage from the narrative signifier to its diegetic signified is repeated as *Apocalypse Now* moves from one scene to another that blurs the distinction between staged spectacles and real violence. Moreover, Coppola repeatedly draws our attention to the techniques used to produce those spectacles as we see the base setting up the stage for the USO show, and as we listen to the photographer played by Dennis Hopper explaining at great length to Captain Willard how they both have roles to play in the creation of Kurtz's legend.

Less predictably, Coppola also reminds us of the constructed nature of mythological significance as well when the camera pans slowly over a copy of *The Golden Bough* and a cheap paperback of *From Ritual to Romance* among the clutter of mementos in Kurtz's room. This attention to the purely textual origins of Modernist primitivism as represented in the notes to *The Waste Land*—not to mention its commodification in the form of mass-marketed texts—undermines the high seriousness of Modernism's effort to discover a natural or spiritual link between "civilized" and "savage" cultures. The absurdity of that appropriative effort is emphasized even further in the second half of *Apocalypse Now* through the debilitating, nearly parodic self-consciousness of the film and particularly of Kurtz's rambling, mumbled monologue. The self-consciousness of such mythologizing also compromises the mystical parallel between Kurtz's murder and the sacrificial killing of the animal that is suggested by intercutting scenes from both events, a hackneyed technique that fails by dissolving the significance of Kurtz's murder into a spectacle of sheer cinematic technique. By the end of the film, when the closing credits are rolling over the apocalyptic flames that consume the jungle with colors that exist nowhere outside of a movie theater, Coppola has reduced both the war and Modernism to by-products of a representational technology that equates victory and meaning with the aesthetic pleasure of cinematic reproduction and the disembodied perspective of a mechanical gaze.

Apocalypse Now is audacious in its equation of war, realism, and ritual as products of a representational technology, but Richard Rush's dark comedy *The Stunt Man* (1980) overtly thematizes the technological basis for that equation in the process of moviemaking. In doing so, Rush raises Coppola's stylistic associations to an explicit critique of the connections among ideology, illusion, and war. Based on a novel published in 1970 by Vietnam veteran Paul Brodeur, *The Stunt Man* casts Peter O'Toole as the megalomaniacal film director, Eli Cross, who is making an antiwar film about World War I. Steve Railsback plays a Vietnam veteran named Cameron, who is running from the police and who stumbles into a scene Cross is filming on a deserted bridge. When the film's stuntman is killed during the scene, Cross coerces Cameron into filling in for him, and the rest of the film deals with Cameron's peculiar fascination with Cross as the director who dominates and manipulates everyone around him.

After being repeatedly tricked into performing several dangerous stunts, Cameron eventually decides to run off with the leading lady during the final stunt of the film, which is to be a retake of the scene on the bridge. Rather than driving the car off the side of the bridge as he is supposed to do, Cameron plans to keep on driving right out of the film and, presumably, off into the sunset with his new love, who will be hiding in the trunk of the car. Unfortunately, as they are crossing the bridge in the car, an explosive charge blows out a tire and the car careens off the bridge, just as it did in the earlier scene. Cameron is rescued, and it turns out that Cross and the heroine of the film had planned the whole escape just to get Cameron to do the scene. The film then concludes with Cameron and Cross dickering over a walkie-talkie about Cameron's fee for the next picture as Cross soars out of sight in his helicopter.

The Stunt Man is usually read as a self-reflexive satire on moviemaking and the affable credulity of audiences eager to be tricked by the technology of cinematic realism. This point is made clearly by a scene early in the film, before Cameron and Cross meet. Cameron is walking along a bluff above a beach where Cross is filming another scene. Along with Cameron and the rest of the onlookers, we see that scene being set up: actors are positioned, lines are re-hearsed, and the cameras are moved into place. But when the ancient biplane comes swooping down, Rush shoots the scene from the per-spective of the cameras that we have just seen being positioned on the beach, and the result is an absolutely realistic battle. Our eye is replaced by the camera, the editing establishes a credible vision of decapitated bodies and mangled flesh, and we are "there," as we have been in so many war movies. The effect is impressive, for although we have literally watched the scene being constructed, the conven-tions are so familiar, and our reading of them so habitual, that it is impossible not to react with horror and revulsion at the bodies strewn about on the sand and at the moans of the victims as the camera lingers over their open wounds. Suddenly, a jump cut shows us the crowd on the bluff. They, too, have become alarmed at the vision that emerges from the smoke of the explosions, and Cameron begins screaming "Medic! Medic!" The film then cuts back to the beach where, under Cross's watchful eye, the dead rise, the maimed walk, and grips begin collecting the artificial limbs for the next day's shooting. "Assholes," Cameron mutters as he realizes what has hap-pened, but there is a smile on his face.

Deliberate confusion between the "reality" of characters in a film and the illusions they create within their world has been a com-monplace since Buster Keaton dove into the screen in *The Camera-man* (1928). What makes *The Stunt Man* unusual is the extent to which it represents that confusion between the characters' fantasies and the diegetic "reality" of *The Stunt Man* as governed by the self-conscious strategies of domination associated with the director, Cross. Rather than emphasizing the power of film to blend fact and fantasy in the illusion of realism, Rush shows how that power is the product of specific technological mechanisms in the hands of totali-tarian authority. Cross's direction of the film, his crew, and the people around him is a marvel of machinery and cinematic industry. The first time we see him, Cross swoops down out of the air in a helicop-ter like a chopper pilot from Herr's *Dispatches*, reveling in the illu-sion of "omni" power over the world as he shoots it through the cam-era lens.

Until he flies off in the helicopter at the end of the film, disap-pearing into a cloud of colored smoke while his disembodied voice continues to harangue Cameron, Cross inhabits the screen like a de-mented director *ex machina*, soaring through space on the elaborate chairlifts and tracking cars that he commands. Despite his painfully thin, etiolated body and apparent sexual impotence (or at least indifference), Cross exercises a formidable power over those around him, fusing the reality of the machine with the reach of his vision to a degree that suggests he is not compensating for the weakness of the flesh so much as celebrating the triumph of its technological extension. "If God could do the tricks that we can do," Cross tells Cameron at one point, "he would be a happy man."

Cross's fascination with Cameron stems from the threat of danger and madness he associates with the young man. Cross suspects that Cameron is fleeing a murder charge, and he is drawn to the violence behind this strange person who "reeks of blood" and who constantly invokes his years in combat during the Vietnam War as a point of reference for his current situation. (This association between Cameron and violence was reinforced for the film's original audience by a fortunate bit of casting: just before *The Stunt Man* was released, Railsback had appeared as Charles Manson in a popular television movie *Helter Skelter.*) Cameron's connection to Vietnam holds a more personal attraction for Cross as well, for we later find out that Cross had wanted to produce an antiwar film during the Vietnam War and could not get the backing for the project. Now he has the backing, his scriptwriter remarks, but no war. Similarly lacking a context for his war stories, Cameron finds that most of his attempts to impress people with his stay in Vietnam elicit no more than idle curiosity or bored disinterest. "Nam? Ancient history," the stunt director tells Cameron when he refers to his combat experience to prove his survival skills, and in another scene Cross casually deflates the dinner-table bravado of Cameron's war stories with a wave of the hand and the casual remark "Vietnam, long gone." Cross's solution to this problem is to produce his own war. Cameron's role in that production solves his problem, too, since doing the dangerous stunts establishes him as a hero on the set, and the film crew and cast give him the appreciation and honor that he says he missed when he got back from Vietnam. So the disturbing tension between past and present that Vietnam represents for both Cameron and Cross is alleviated as the precise machinery of the film reproduces the chaos of the battlefield, and the elaborate choreography of the stunts controls the threats posed to Cameron's body by the very real heights and terrifying falls called for by Cross's script.

Like any successful comedy, *The Stunt Man* lets us in on the joke early by systematically removing any trepidation in our enjoyment of the dilemmas faced by the characters as they move toward the happy ending. Once we have been tricked by the scene on the beach, we tend to be wary of all scenes that occur before our eyes. Despite the undeniable power of continuity editing and line-of-sight camera angles that draw us into the illusion of Cross's war, we nevertheless suspect long before Cameron does that the danger he faces is only one more illusion, and we are always right. The threat of death is replaced by the pleasure of spectacle, and we come to trust the omnipotent omniscience of Cross's eye. We continue to identify with the director's vision even when the images we see situate us entirely within the simulated world on the screen and when those scenes are played for all of the suspense and fear they can generate in the viewer.

The Stunt Man teaches us that our relation to the world we see around us has its origin in the mechanical apparatus of cinematic illusion rather than anything we see through our own eyes. By the end of the film, we have come to identify with that apparatus itself rather than the perspective it constructs for our eye through the techniques of realism. Cameron's dickering with Cross at the end of the film may suggest at least the remnants of some subjective autonomy from technological control and from the ideological order that control suggests. Nevertheless, the willingness of the veteran to put his life in danger again for the sake of a realistic scene in the film indicates the extent to which the very real dangers encountered in Vietnam have been displaced in Cameron's mind by the apparent safety of Cross's power. Cameron's complicity in Cross's authority reflects the loss of innocence inherent in the eye of the viewer, which has been educated by the film to distrust what it sees yet which yields repeatedly to the power of the image before it. Rush's film does conceal the machinery of its own production—we never see Rush filming his fictional director, for example—and in doing so seems to impose a limit to this self-reflexivity by implying an end to the proliferation of illusion at the edge of the screen. Yet, since the technique of concealment is portrayed in the film as the foundation of cinematic realism, the very *absence* of explicitly fictional markers comes to testify to the constructed character of the "reality" we would normally infer from such a reference point. Consequently, the film contaminates *all* reality, on-screen and off, with the suspicion of illusion and, more important, with the pleasure inherent in the power over reality that illusion inspires. *The Stunt Man* thus goes beyond distinctions between the "reality" and "illusion" of images to dramatize the process by which our sense of self, our relationship with the past, and our place in the world around us are constituted by and communicated within the technological network of cinematic production.

In the years since these early manifestations of a postmodern skepticism about easy distinctions between reality and illusion in the "absolute space" of simulation, films about Vietnam have pushed the connection between human individuals and technological representation far past concerns about alienation and mediation between autonomous subjects and the reality external to them. The figure of a dominant, authoritarian director has been replaced by the influence of an anonymous, omnipresent technology, and the resistant force of individual identity has been reduced to little more than an efficient relay through which flows a continuous stream of information. One of the most striking and original examples of this changing attitude toward the role of representational technology is *84 Charlie Mopic* (1989), which is shot entirely through the perspective of a camera held by a documentary filmmaker who is following a patrol on a reconnaissance mission in the field.

84 Charlie Mopic is thoroughly conservative in terms of character and theme, and there is no suggestion in the film that the eye of the documentary camera controls or dominates the people it frames the way Cross controls the characters in *The Stunt Man*. In fact, the film clearly privileges the expertise and capability of the soldiers on patrol, whose experience will be used to teach new recruits how to survive in the bush and who dictate to the cameraman where that camera will go and what it will see. Nevertheless, the unusual first-person technique used throughout the film literally subordinates the person of the cameraman to the camera he holds. The film ironically "humanizes" the cinematic perspective by associating it with a body in the story: the soldiers talk to the cameraman by speaking directly into the camera, and the frame jiggles and tilts as the cameraman runs and takes cover. But the film also mechanizes that body by subordinating it to the act of transmitting and recording the scene it frames: the cameraman is referred to only by the slang for documentary motion picture, "mopic," and we see only those parts of the cameraman's body that accidently get into the frame while he is shooting the film. It is not until the cameraman himself is shot during a firefight at the end of the movie that we see the body behind the camera, and then the screen quickly goes blank because the life of the image is so nearly coterminous with the life of the body.[17]

84 Charlie Mopic thus identifies the first-"person" perspective with the technological production of the cinematic image rather than with the imaginary figure of a human character. This technique suggests an ironic inversion of priority between the machine and the imaginary body that reflects the subjection of human flesh to the rigors of military hardware in modern warfare. Beyond this predictable conclusion, though, lies a more radical identification between ordinary self-consciousness and the technological apparatus that constitutes the position of that self in the world. This latter issue is the central theme of two later films about Vietnam veterans, *Jacob's Ladder* (1990) and the execrable *Universal Soldier* (1992).[18] Both of these films portray Vietnam veterans as victims of an omnipotent bureaucracy that has literally invaded the very cells of their bodies and reconfigured their biochemistry to fit military needs. Though stylistically more conventional than the films discussed above (and vastly less sophisticated conceptually), *Universal Soldier* and *Jacob's Ladder* demonstrate the extent to which the erosion of individual autonomy by the pervasive penetration of microtechnologies into the tiniest and most intimate recesses of the body is no longer seen as a threat but rather as the given condition against which any subjective sense of self or freedom must emerge.

The "Unisols" of *Universal Soldier* are dead soldiers whose bodies were collected from the battlefields of Vietnam and literally kept on ice until they could be regenerated by "hyperaccelerating" their metabolism. Once up to speed and outfitted with various weapons and communication devices, the unisols are intended to be used as an antiterrorist unit. Unfortunately, some of them suffer from flashbacks into their past—"regressive traumatic recall"—that obstruct their efficiency. One of the unisols, GR44 (Jean-Claude Van Damme) finally remembers enough to become disillusioned with his posthumous assignment and escapes to the dilapidated family farm in rural Louisiana where his parents still live. He is pursued by an evil unisol, GR13 (Dolph Lundgren), who has killed the human leader of the project and assumed command. The film ends predictably with a grotesquely violent fight in which GR44 kills GR13, saves Ma and Pa, and wins the heart of the spunky girl reporter he met along the way.

Universal Soldier passed into richly deserved obscurity shortly after its release. Still, its premise deserves some comment because it extends the theme of the "technologized" body to an enlightening if absurd extreme. As in *84 Charlie Mopic*, a large part of the initial action sequence is shot through the Minicam eye patches of the unisols, which convert the objects they survey into digitalized images that resemble the targets photographed by the smart bombs in the Gulf War rather than the naturalistic scenes on the screen as viewed by the human characters. This electronic vision immediately transmits what the unisols see back to the operating center, where the commander can direct their actions by radio. This combination of looking, acting, and transmitting joins roles that were distinct in earlier technologies and presents the veteran as the literal embodiment of the "telematic eye" described by Baudrillard. Here the human body is no longer subjected merely to mechanical control or bionic enhancement; it has been remade from the cells up and the inside out. The veterans have become the perfect soldiers, physically superior organic machines that carry out orders immediately because they have no minds to complicate their obedience—except, of course, for those troublesome memories that finally destroy the project.

This "regressive traumatic recall" obviously echoes the very real psychological disruption caused by posttraumatic stress, and it serves to establish some limit to the biochemical power of modern science in the film. That limiting function is reinforced by the association of memory in GR44 with a nostalgic humanism illustrated by his parents' farm, which has been equipped from a Luddite catalog of antiquated machinery updated only by the power thresher needed for the big fight scene. Yet the suggestion of a limit to the power of biochemical technology is unpersuasive, for the only way GR44 can triumph over GR13 is with an injection of the same high-tech "muscle enhancers" that gave GR13 his invincible strength. So, for all of their sepia tones, homey memorabilia, and comforting score, home and hearth appear in the film more as a childhood fantasy to be protected than as a viable alternative to the technology that would destroy them.

Any attempt to suggest a coherent allegorical reading for *Universal Soldier* runs up against the cheerful stupidity with which the film was made. Nevertheless, against the background of *The Stunt Man* and other films in which the body of the Vietnam veteran is subjected to medical discipline and technological control, the regeneration of dead flesh to create advanced weapons seems less like outlandish science and more like ideological inevitability. Rather than evoking a spiritual afterlife to inspire the troops, *Universal Soldier* offers a technological eternity in which a mediating chaplain is re-placed by the rejuvenating technician, and heavenly glory is sup-planted by the opportunity to wage perpetual war in the service of one's re-maker. There are also further, uncomfortable associations between this fantastic regeneration of frozen corpses and the tor-tured grief of families of MIA's whose anxiety and uncertainty about the fate of their loved ones are shamelessly exploited in the home-coming scenes between GR44, who had been reported missing in action, and his parents. To be sure, *Universal Soldier* is careful to distinguish the paramilitary science of the unisol project from re-spectable military operations: at one point, the commander of the project snarls, "Do you think those wimps at the Pentagon would allow the regeneration of soldiers, *American* soldiers?" Neverthe-less, the biochemical fantasy that enables the film's premise barely disguises a desperate but very real faith in a transformative technol-ogy that can turn the memory of Vietnam, represented by the figure of the veteran, into the perfect war machine, operated by a body that is invulnerable because it is already dead and that is obedient because it lacks any consciousness of its own expropriation.

Jacob's Ladder also stages the drama of reminiscence in the mind of a Vietnam veteran whose body has been chemically altered by the army to create a better weapon. Fortunately, superior writing and acting, not to mention a greater feasibility in the chemistry in-volved, lends *Jacob's Ladder* a poignancy and seriousness lacking in *Universal Soldier.* In *Jacob's Ladder,* Jacob Singer (Tim Robbins) is a Vietnam veteran suffering from what seem to be hallucinations in which faceless, humanoid monsters are trying to kill him. He fears that he is going insane, but when he discovers that several men from his army unit also fear they are being pursued by these creatures, Singer begins to suspect that their problem stems somehow from their experience in Vietnam, where they had been the only survivors of a vicious firefight. Eventually, Jacob meets a man who says he was a chemist who had been forced by the army to administer hallucino-genic drugs to soldiers in Vietnam as an experiment to heighten their aggressive traits. He tells Jacob that the Vietcong had never attacked Jacob's unit at all and that the U.S. soldiers had in fact turned on themselves after receiving the drug.

Plunged even further into despair by the chemist's story, Jacob is finally abducted by some mysterious strangers and seriously injured. After he escapes, he is taken to a hospital where he receives an injection into his brain and is wrapped in bandages and a leg cast. Suddenly, his chiropractor bursts into the room, frees Jacob from the wires and bandages that bind him to the bed, and takes him back to his office, where he begins manipulating Jacob's body while encouraging him to accept the inevitability of his death. The chiropractic treatment quickly heals Jacob's body and allows him to stand. Jacob slowly makes his way home and finds his son waiting for him, although he knows that his son was killed in a traffic accident sometime earlier. The little boy comforts his father and then leads him upstairs toward a bright light. At that moment, the scene suddenly shifts, and we discover that Jacob has in fact been in a field hospital in Vietnam all along and that the entire film has been a deathbed dream. The film ends when the doctors declare him dead and leave the room.

This summary of the story neglects the moving and entirely convincing account of Jacob's psychological evolution from denial to acceptance of death, which is the most impressive achievement of *Jacob's Ladder*. As the title suggests, the film also aspires to a metaphysical seriousness that generalizes Jacob's plight beyond that of a victimized veteran and turns his story into a meditation on human mortality. Unfortunately, the very generality of the film's philosophical ambitions tends to undermine the motif of the body and its violation by the biochemical technology of the military, which is figured in the dream by the grotesque humanoid creatures stalking Jacob. For that reason, *Jacob's Ladder* lacks the powerful antiwar impact of *Johnny Got His Gun* (1971), which continually measures the fantasies of the mutilated veteran from World War II against the reality of the dismembered, mummified body lying on the hospital bed. Nevertheless, in its fantastic projection of the violated human body as a band of threatening monsters, *Jacob's Ladder* suggests the increasingly ambivalent status of death and the body in contemporary societies and the wars they wage. In the firefight where Jacob is wounded, the threat to the body is very real, but the "enemy" is a projection outward based on the internal transformation of the soldier's brain chemistry, which has been manipulated by an outside agency, the army. Biochemical technology has created an "absolute space" in which information about the body's position in relation to what lies outside it circulates in a closed loop that confounds distinctions between self and other, here and there, inside and outside, and even life and death. The paradoxical topography of that space is reflected in

Jacob's dream through images of convoluted passageways (a deserted subway system), narrow alleys (where he is almost run down by a car), his claustrophobic apartment, and the Kafkaesque chaos of a hospital in Jacob's dream, where doors open up onto straight-jacketed bodies vibrating with explosive energy, bloody organs and amputated limbs are scattered on the floor, and hallways are covered with open grids that disclose a swarming mass of humanity ranging from naked nursing mothers to amputees to aging madmen sneering through the wire floor as Jacob passes beneath them: all vivid externalizations of Jacob's obsessions and fears and of the ruptured integrity of his violated body.

The chiropractor's office is the antithesis of the battlefield and hospital. Suffused with warm colors and furnished in wood and leather, this office provides a safe haven in which Jacob's body is re-stored to its proper alignment, physically and metaphysically, by ma-nipulative techniques that depend on human touch and conversation rather than chemicals and steel. Jacob is desperately dependent on the chiropractor throughout the film, and at the end it is the chiro-practor who finally relieves Jacob's pain and persuades him that the monsters pursuing him are really angels taking him to heaven. That belief relieves Jacob's anxiety and allows him to accept his death without fear. The final scene of the film complicates this serene con-clusion, however, for the phantasmatic restoration of the body in Ja-cob's dream corresponds to the death of the actual body in the hospi-tal in Vietnam. Just as Cameron's fears and desires and his dreams of escape are repeatedly discovered to be stage props for Cross's movie in *The Stunt Man*, the vision of wholeness and corporeal autonomy associated with organic life in Jacob's dream finally fades in the harsh light of the hospital tent, where the film ends as a bored clerk slowly types Jacob's name into his files.

The suspicious or overtly hostile portrayal of bioengineering in these later films about Vietnam veterans appears antiquated against the postmodern fashion for constructed realities and the hardwired bio-forms of cyberpunk fiction. Some theorists have even gone so far as to argue that simulated experience is a more direct and unmedi-ated engagement with contemporary technology than is available through the unassisted senses.[19] Still, for all of their revolutionary rhetoric and pseudosophisticated scientism, the heroic fugitives and ingenious cyborgs that populate such speculative fantasies are usu-ally entirely dependent upon and implicated in the repressive social forms that support the technology they embrace, and that complicity is dramatically evident in the world outside these works. For example, the fantasy of an anarchic interzone carved out from the interstices of a technocratic bureaucracy and populated by bionic outlaws pales before the reality of SIMNET, the computer-simulated battlefield constructed through network links that the U.S. Army uses to train soldiers for tank warfare.

SIMNET is a product of the Defense Advanced Research Projects Agency, the same group that developed the civilian computer network Internet and that is closely aligned with the military agencies and private corporations that meet regularly at the Interservice/ Industry Training Systems and Education Conference (I/ITSEC). At a meeting of I/ITSEC in the early 1990s, General Dynamics displayed a new tank simulator; a new proposal to simulate the entire surface of the earth for military training purposes was demonstrated ("Project 2851"); and papers were presented on such topics as "Hypermedia: A Solution for Selected Training and Prototyping Applications." In addition, plans were circulated for the Distributed Simulation Internet, a "Virtual Training Device" that superannuates SIMNET and that was developed by a cartel of military agencies, private industries, research firms, and public universities that make the "military industrial complex" Eisenhower feared look like a high school project for Junior Achievers.[20] The nostalgic humanism inherited from High Modernism and so often associated with popular representations of Vietnam veterans over the past decade may well be incapable of addressing such a world, but revolutionary fantasies of bionic anarchists and cyborg artists are equally remote from the complex relations of power in which that world is mapped, reproduced, transmitted, and governed.

The ambivalent attitude toward the technologies of representation and the body that is represented by Vietnam veterans in recent films may therefore be less a product of ideological slippage or thematic confusion than an expression of ironic disengagement from more traditional oppositions between nature and the machine, the real and the illusory, and even life and death that have been so complicated by the increasingly simulated nature of our social reality. In an article on the statistical representation of social life and the phenomenon of popular opinion polls, Baudrillard has suggested that a similar disengagement has emerged generally among "the masses" toward the media that propose to represent them. He characterizes it as an "ironic and antagonistic" distance from representational forms. Repudiating the "technological optimism" of McLuhan's dream of global community through mass communication, and also rejecting the pessimistic vision of his own earlier work that saw mass media as a repressive "speech without response," Baudrillard claims that the relation of the masses to media today can better be described as a strategic *"refusal of will."* This refusal represents a challenge to everything that was demanded of the subject by philosophy, Baudrillard says; it is a challenge to "all rationality of choice and to all exercise of will, of knowledge, and of liberty." At the heart of this "radical antimetaphysics" lies a deep awareness by the masses "that they do not have to wish; that they do not have to know; that they do not have to desire." Media have thus become the "strategic territory" in which the masses exercise "their concrete power of the refusal of truth, of the denial of reality." Admitting the addictive power of the media, Baudrillard concludes that it is

> a deep result of this phenomenon: it is not a result of a desire for culture, communication, and information, but of this perversion of truth and falsehood, of this destruction of meaning in the operation of the medium. The desire for a show, the desire for simulation, which is at the same time a desire for dissimulation. This is a vital reaction. It is a spontaneous, total resistance to the ultimatum of historical and political reason.[21]

Whether or not we agree with Baudrillard's description of this attitude as "vital," his account of an ironic detachment from the technologies that represent and direct our desire accurately summarizes the ambivalent relations between individuals and media depicted in many of the films and oral histories about Vietnam. Unlike the more familiar attitudes of alienation or naïve identification with imaginary heroes described in earlier works about the war, we find instead an ironic capitulation of desire and judgment in the radioman's remarks, in Gar's willingness to die to keep the projector running, and in Cameron's bantering about the fee for his next stunt after his escape fails. All of these moments express a "joyful *expulsion* of all the encumbering superstructures of being and of will" that Baudrillard says is the only strategy of resistance left ("Masses," 217). This "hyperconformist simulation of the very mechanisms of the system" ("Masses," 219) serves as a protective coloring to save the subject from total assimilation the way a mantis mimics the leaves in which it hides from its predators. Abandoning the illusion of autonomy while at the same time insisting on the autonomy of illusion as a means of resistance if not escape, the figure of the Vietnam veteran has come to represent a strategic refusal of political and historical meaning. This latest manifestation of the veteran in the works discussed above is therefore doubly ironic, because in this role he can neither be repelled from the social system as alien (the psychotic killer) nor fully assimilated within it (as the patriotic hero).[22] Instead, he marks the functional limits of that symbolic order, the point at which the technologies of simulation have so saturated the social space that organic vitality reappears as an illusive dream and death a comic parody of technological efficiency.

NOTES

1. The phrase is from James C. Wilson, *Vietnam in Prose and Film* (Jefferson, N. C.: McFarland and Company, 1982), 101.

2. Mark Baker, *Nam: The Vietnam War in the Words of the Men and Women Who Fought There* (New York: William Morrow, 1981), 17. Further references will be cited parenthetically in the text.

3. Herr, *Dispatches*, (New York: Avon Books, 1978), 24–25.

4. Philip Beidler, *American Literature and the Experience of Vietnam* (Athens: The University of Georgia Press, 1982), 197, 199.

5. A distinction should be made between this analysis of the way images function in the syntactic and narrative context of the texts in which they appear and the interpretation of archetypal patterns evoked by those images when they are read against what John Hellmann calls "American mythic assumptions" (149). For a mythological analysis of historical themes in films and novels about Vietnam, see Hellmann's *American Myth and the Legacy of Vietnam* (New York: Columbia University Press, 1986).

6. *American Literature and the Experience of Vietnam*, 11.

7. *Vietnam in Prose and Film*, 101–02.

8. I discussed some of these cinematic motifs and techniques in an earlier article; see "Vietnam: Representations of Self and War," *Wide Angle* 7, no.4 (1984): 4–11.

9. Christian Metz says that

> The cinema retains something of the prohibited character peculiar to the vision of the primal scene . . . but also, in a kind of inverse movement which is simply the "reprise" of the imaginary by the symbolic, the cinema is based on the legalisation and generalisation of the prohibited

practice. Thus it shares in miniature in the special regime of certain activities . . . that are both official and clandestine, and in which neither of these two characteristics ever quite succeeds in obliterating the other. For the vast majority of the audience, the cinema (rather like the dream in this) represents a kind of enclosure or "reserve" which escapes the fully social aspect of life although it is accepted and prescribed by it: going to the cinema is one lawful activity among others with its place in the admissible pastimes of the day or week, and yet that place is a "hole" in the social cloth, a *loophole* opening on to something slightly more crazy, slightly less approved than what one does the rest of the time.

The Imaginary Signifier: Psychoanalysis and the Cinema, trans. Celia Britton, Annwyl Williams, Ben Brewster, and Alfred Guzzetti (Bloomington: Indiana University Press, 1982), 65–66. See esp. chapter 4, "The Passion for Perceiving."

10. Tim O'Brien, *If I Die in a Combat Zone* (New York: Dell, 1979), 38.

11. Reported in Al Santoli, *Everything We Had: An Oral History of the Vietnam War by Thirty-Three American Soldiers Who Fought It* (New York: Random House, 1981), 99.

12. In Walter Benjamin, *Illuminations,* trans. Harry Zohn (New York: Schocken Books, 1969), 217–51. Further references will be cited parenthetically in the text. Originally published in *Zeitschrift für Sozialforschung,* vol. 1, 1936.

Benjamin complains that the reproduction of images in general "detaches the reproduced object from the domain of tradition." Film is the most powerful agent of that detachment, Benjamin adds, and he claims that the social significance of film "is inconceivable without its destructive, cathartic aspect, that is, the liquidation of the traditional value of the cultural heritage" (221).

13. Guy Debord, *Society of the Spectacle,* trans. anon. (Detroit: Black and Red, 1977), paragraph 36.

Margot Norris has traced the various strategies by which the U.S. government disguised the scale of carnage in the Gulf. Principle among those strategies was the attempt to control the way dead bodies were represented in the press and especially on television. "The strategies of necrological control have created an illusion that a ludic substitute for war has already been discovered, and that technology has ushered in a new Enlightenment in which a set of rational and logical strategies designed to disarm the enemy . . . can be implemented with weapons that greatly minimize, if not totally eliminate, human killing" (231). See "Military Censorship and the Body Count in the Persian Gulf War," *Cultural Critique* 19 (1991): 223–45.

14. "War in the Mode of Information," *Cultural Critique* 19 (1991): 221. Poster claims that the instantaneous transmission during the Gulf War of images from the battlefield to living rooms in the U.S. rendered the "rhetoric of realism" meaningless.

15. Jean Baudrillard, "The Ecstasy of Communication," in *The Anti-Aesthetic: Essays on Postmodern Culture,* ed. Hal Foster (Port Townsend, Wash.: Bay Press, 1983), 128. Further references will be cited parenthetically in the text.

16. A notable exception to the prevailing realism of earlier films about war and the veterans who fought them is Preston Sturges's *Hail the Conquering Hero* (1944), in which the plot turns on the effort by several soldiers returning home from World War II to help a civilian pass himself off as a war hero in his hometown. While there are no explicit references to cinematic representation in the story, the obsessive interest in spectacle, costume, and war stories lays bare the fictional basis of patriotism and heroism, and in doing so Sturges's film provides a powerful ideological critique of the close connection between politics and aesthetics in World War II.

17. In an appreciative review of *84 Charlie Mopic,* Roger Ebert praises the authenticity of the film and says he has "never seen a combat movie that seemed this close to actual experience." The fact that Ebert would say that about a film that *foregrounds* the mediating presence of the camera testifies to the extent to which "actuality" has become the product of technological production, at least for this film critic. (Ebert also notes that Orson Welles had hoped to film *Heart of Darkness* from a first-person point of view, a prescient ambition given the metacinematic dimension of *Apocalypse Now.*) See *Roger Ebert's Movie Home Companion* (New York: Andrews and McMeel, 1991), 84.

For an analysis of the extent to which the authenticity of actual documentaries about the Vietnam War depends on the techniques of cinematic realism, see John Carlos Rowe, "Eyewitness: Documentary Styles in the American Representations of Vietnam," in *The Vietnam War and American Culture,* ed. John Rowe and Rick Berg (New York: Columbia University Press, 1991), 148–74.

18. *Jacob's Ladder* (1990). Written by Bruce Joel Rubin. Produced by Alan Marshall. Directed by Adrian Lyne. Starring Tim Robbins. *Universal Soldier* (1992). Written by Richard Rothstein, Christopher Leitch, and Dean Devlin. Produced by Allen Shapiro, Craig Baumgarten, and Joel B. Michaels. Directed by Roland Emmerich. Starring Jean-Claude Van Damme and Dolph Lundgren.

19. Since William Gibson's *Neuromancer* (New York: Ace Science Fiction, 1984), the term "cyberpunk" has been used to refer to a wide range of writing, most but not all of which falls within the genre of science fiction. More recently, a body of theoretical writing dealing with motifs and issues typical of cyberpunk fiction has begun to develop as well, though much of this writing also draws explicitly on more general themes of poststructuralism. For a good introduction to all of this work, see *Storming the Reality Studio: A Casebook of Cyberpunk and Postmodern Fiction,* ed. Larry McCaffery (Durham, N. C.: Duke University Press, 1991). On the cyborg as a more direct form of engagement with a technological culture, see Donna Haraway, *Primate Visions: Gender, Race, and Nature in the World of Modern Science* (New York: Routledge, 1989).

20. These remarks about SIMNET and I/ITSEC are based on information in Bruce Sterling's article on simulated warfare, "War is Virtual Hell," *Wired* 1.1 (1993).

21. Jean Baudrillard, "The Masses: The Implosion of the Social in the Media," trans. Marie Maclean, in *Jean Baudrillard: Selected Writings,* ed. Mark Poster (Stanford, Calif.: Stanford University Press, 1988), 215–17, passim. Further references will be cited parenthetically in the text.

22. I have discussed the history of these two alternatives in "Remembering Vietnam," in *The Vietnam War and American Culture,* 177–207.

3

"WHAT DO WE SAY HAPPENED HERE?": MEMORY, IDENTITY, AND THE VIETNAM WAR

Cynthia Fuchs

What you remember is determined by what you
see, and what you see depends on what you
remember.

Tim O'Brien, *Going After Cacciato*

We don't need to remake society, we just need to
remember who we are.

George Bush, 1988

This is only a story. From the real.

Wutang Clan

"NOTHING HAPPENED HERE AT ALL!": IMAGINING IDENTITY

Universal Soldier (Roland Emmerich 1992) opens with the death of
its protagonists. The scene is repeated, as the characters' shared
memory, a kind of ritual instant that binds them across time and
place throughout the film. Titled "Vietnam—1969," this scene establishes the film's general over-the-topness while offering a first
rush of "Vietnam" iconography that is all too familiar. That is, for
viewers as well as characters, memory becomes repetition. At the
same time, as it is mediated, reproduced, blurred, and shifting, mem-

ory is made unstable and untrustworthy, the same and different, again and again.

Private Luc Devereaux (Jean-Claude Van Damme) charges through a dark and rainy jungle, a handheld point-of-view camera representing his disorientation. He comes upon another marine who is visibly afraid. "What happened to the others?" asks Luc. "Fucking dead!" comes the answer. "The whole fucking platoon. The sarge totally lost it, went nuts, killed everyone!" Sergeant Scott's (Dolph Lundgren) madness is soon confirmed when Luc finds him about to execute two Vietnamese civilians. Scott wears a necklace of human ears and his eyes are rolled back in his head: the necklace indicates that he's "gone native," his unhinged barbarism the result, apparently, of too much time "in country." When Luc asks him, "What the hell happened here?" the sergeant's answer is framed in a tight, underlit close-up shot from below, so that he looms, half monster and half victim. Trapped in the frame as he is in the war, Scott literally can't tell what happened; he can only say what didn't happen: "They wouldn't listen." And Luc's response indicates his own entrapment, in memory: "I just wanna go home," he says wearily. Scott explodes. "You're just like the others! You just wanna leave. Like none a this shit ever happened. It happened! It doesn't just go away."

Indeed, "it" continues to happen. Scott turns way from Luc to shoot one prisoner in the head (an image composed to repeat and radically refigure the famous photograph and footage of South Vietnamese police chief Nguyen Ngoc Loan executing a "Vietcong suspect").[1] But if Scott's immersion in his immediate past ("It happened. It won't go away") motivates him, Luc's more remote, longed-for past (as simple Louisiana "farm boy") dictates what he does next, which is to kick the gun loose from Scott's hand and attempt to rescue the remaining Vietnamese prisoner, a girl. His attempt is unsuccessful, and the ensuing fight between the two marines leaves all three characters quite "fucking dead." Fade-out. Then, morning dawns, choppers appear, the opening credits roll. A squad of U.S. military types arrives to clean up after the apparently illegal assault on the village. As Scott's and Luc's bodies are zipped up into body bags, a young U.S. clerk asks his superior, "Sir, how do I write this one up? I mean, what do we say happened here?" The officer keeps his gaze steady, his eyes dead to the carnage in front of him. "Nothing happened here at all. MIA."

With the onset of the postcredits, "present-day" plot, the science-fictionish consequence of this official erasure becomes clear. Luc, Scott, and several other multi-culti muscle heads killed in Vietnam are resurrected as "unisols" (short for universal soldiers, the term taken ironically from Buffy Sainte-Marie's anti-Vietnam War song); the unisols are military cyborgs monitored and directed from a mobile, high-tech command center (it resembles a big black RV, complete with one-way windows and self-sustaining life support and power sources). Their first deployment is against a band of foreign terrorists who have taken hostages at a Nevada desert tourist site. That the soldiers' enemies this time are broadly "Arabic" underlines their participation in a New World Order, as the scenario mixes and matches images from the Iran Hostage Crisis, the Gulf War, and the World Trade Center Bombing. These anonymous villains are quickly dispatched (their motives are glossed over: they're Arabs, which is enough to mark them as "bad" in 1990s terrorism-paranoia movies, such as *True Lies* or *Executive Decision*), in order to focus attention on this film's "real" criminals, the profit-minded collaborators on the "off the shelf" unisol project. These bad guys—mostly white and middle-aged, with a couple of black, younger techies along for the ride—have come up with a new design for unquestioning, terminally loyal jarheads. The unisols are regenerated, hormone-enhanced corpses, priced at $250 million each ($6 million men after inflation and after morality is even a vague concern for corporations). Moreover, the unisols are identityless: their memories are "cleared," replaced by programs and directives. In other words, the unisols are perfect weapons systems, unkillable, conscienceless, and unselfconscious. They point and they shoot.

This extraordinary plot continues to unravel, but I want to pause briefly to consider its gloss on what Michael Rogin calls the "postmodern American empire," pervaded and determined by "secrecy and spectacle, demonology and male heroism."[2] To this point in its narrative, *Universal Soldier* provides some straight-ahead Vietnam War movie conventions: a good private, a bad sergeant, a worse military-civilian business collusion. The repetition of these clichés illustrates how media imagery and collective memory work together to produce a sense of national, and vaguely imperial identity. Arguing that secrecy and spectacle are "entangled" in postmodern culture and social practices, interdependent in their apparent opposition,

Rogin writes, "Political spectacle in the postmodern empire is itself a form of power and not simply window dressing that diverts attention from the secret substance of American foreign policy" (500). Reflecting this interrelationship, *Universal Soldier* generates lots of effects (signs of the movie industry's extravagant power and money) and yet, generally ineffective diversion: its "secret substance" is pretty plain to see. But if its conservative ideological framework is obvious, it is also confused (and looks forward to similarly confused imagery in director Emmerich's *Stargate* [1994], *Independence Day* [1996], and *Godzilla* [1998]).

On the one hand a yahoo-macho-proud movie, reveling in standard white-guy action-flick heroics, on the other, it's also an antiestablishment diatribe, ironically positing Luc as the poor boy abused by the humungo-budget military-entertainment formation that allows its existence. It's not news that popular media remix imperialism, sexism, and racism with splashy imagery in order to please "international" audiences (presumed to have low tolerance for thoughtful social or political critiques, complex characters and situations, or even dialogue). And it's not news that such media representations are increasingly self-conscious, clever, and ironic concerning exactly these conventions and expectations. The "postmodern empire," in other words, is sustained by its media's extratextual excesses and preemptive overlays, its media's refractions of imperial inclinations as nonthreatening comedy or action hijinks, repetitions of formula that accentuate as well as obfuscate grand delusions of national or other identities (see, for example, the *Robocop, Jaws, Lethal Weapon, Die Hard,* or even *Alien* franchises, variously self-deceptive and self-conscious regarding the many gender, race, class, sexuality, and age anxieties they expose); the "empire" is thus destabilized by its media's revisions and disarticulations of "what happened," not to mention what will happen or what might have happened. Without the certainty averred by fixed memories or identities, the "empire" can only continue to produce and consume itself.

The rise of popular conservatism since the Vietnam War is often attributed to the public's willfully short memory and to the concomitant dumbing down of mass mediated imagery. In what follows, I want to complicate this cultural paradigm by examining the play of memory and identity in several Vietnam War movies. As well, I will consider in detail four 1990s films that use the war to map processes of national memory and amnesia, specifically through images of death, repetition, and identity. These movies are *Universal Soldier,* *Jacob's Ladder* (Adrian Lyne 1991), *Boyz N the Hood* (John Singleton 1991), and *Dead Presidents* (Albert and Allen Hughes 1995). In each text, memory is the site of incoherence and crisis, individual and collective. My point is not to render subversive readings of mainstream texts, but to extrapolate from their inconsistencies and anxieties—reflected in part in a manifest distrust of their own narrative structures, and dependence on fragmentation and breakdown—in order to trace movements in and out of recognizable categories of identity.

"THE PROPER MOVEMENT OF HISTORY"

Oliver Stone's *Born on the Fourth of July* (1989) boasts what may be the most brilliantly hysterical collapse of Vietnam War memory onto masculine identity ever put to celluloid. Paraplegic and rowdily drunk veterans played by Tom Cruise and Willem Dafoe find themselves abandoned by their Mexican cabdriver on a desert road to nowhere. Engrossed in their increasingly ugly argument with each other, they barely notice their predicament, screaming at one another while the cab drives off in a literal cloud of dust. At stake for each character is the authenticity of his war-induced emotional damage (their corollary physical damage is of course marked by their wheelchairs). Their identificatory ground zero: Who is the "real" Vietnam vet? Who "really" was forced to kill babies? As the debate intensifies, their exchange reduces to linguistic bare bones: "Fuck you!" "No! Fuck you!" Eventually, they can't even speak, but can only spit on each other and throw air punches, until both men throw themselves from their chairs. They stop, stunned. Finally, they're lying at the edge of the road, exhausted and unable to move.[3]

The emotional effectiveness of this scene stems from its interrogation of memory as a measure of identity. The first worst thing either character can imagine is to be a vet who "killed babies." But the other worst thing, *equally* horrible, is to be a vet who didn't "kill babies." And as the baby-killer identity was entrenched in U.S. popular culture—as a cogent distillation of U.S. atrocities and amorality—these two dying-with-guilt veterans feel compelled to remember it, internalize it, be it. The film in general and this scene in particular are rife with such abuses of memory, incoherent bodies, horror-movie flashbacks, and vehement disarticulations ("Fuck you!" again and again, more a litany than a statement or response), the ultimate effects and permutations of an unrealized and unrealizable U.S. national identity after the Vietnam War. And there's no going back. But, then again, there is. Just ask Oliver Stone, who has made a career of revisiting the Vietnam War. In fact, most U.S.-made Vietnam War movies are all about going back in time in order to recuperate a national identity, pride, purpose, and survivable memory. Like the protagonists of *Universal Soldier, Jacob's Ladder,* and *Dead Presidents, Born on the Fourth of July*'s Ron Kovic (Cruise) seeks a narrative to authenticate, legitimate, and secure his lost experiences, some forgotten or repressed, some never had.

Certainly, a trenchant and recurring emblem of this search is the MIA. As long as the body is missing, what happened (to it, around it, because of it) is uncertain, and identity (in the abstract and in practice) is obscured. In the standard MIA plot, especially as it has been popularized in films, novels, and television, à la *Rambo* or *Missing in Action,* the enemy is less the Vietnamese communists (who are, after all, fighting a war with regular weapons and strategies) than the fact-and-body-suppressing U.S. bureaucracy. In this plot, Elizabeth Traube writes, "the proper movement of history" is suspended, precisely because of the MIAs and POWs whose absence is a gap blocking the expected rhythm and progression of "time" (as much as history is a function of time and storytelling). History is restarted only when the hero recovers the bodies, literally (whether these bodies be alive or dead, they denote events now explained or retraceable, say, in DNA identification processes). The recovery in these formula movies prompts what Traube calls a "transformation of knowledge" that is predicated on a set cause and effect, where "what happened" is uncovered, recorded, and violently rectified (leaving behind plenty of dead Vietnamese, for some reason still dedicated to torturing U.S. boys, not to mention occasional abuse-deserving U.S. paper-pushers). Then, history (and the national identity defined and redefined by its incessant narrative processes) can move on toward a collective redemption (this, according to Traube, would be the "proper movement," seeking to salvage, revise, and consolidate any number of specific pasts).[4]

In 1990s movies focusing on the fragmentation of veterans' memories and identities, such as *Universal Soldier, Jacob's Ladder,* and *Dead Presidents,* narrative events seem to conspire against linear story lines and ordered knowledge, privileging instead disjointed memories that disrupt viewer expectations, so that heroic self- and other-recoveries are rendered, if not quite meaningless, then quite antiredemptive. *Born*'s "who's-a-baby-killer" scene is atypically complex in its representation of the interrelations of collective (cultural, public) and individual moral failures. Even the film's triumphant resolution remains painfully knotted: Kovic the character (like Kovic the real person) is invited to give a speech at the 1976 Democratic National Convention, but the speech itself is significantly unseen and unheard, as the screen fades to white just when he wheels himself to the podium, before a cheering and flag-waving crowd. The speech's absence suggests that the moment, and its implication that Ron has recovered and now celebrates his identity, as a man, U.S. citizen, decorated, resolved, and/or grateful veteran, are both beyond representation and inextricable from it.

Universal Soldier, Jacob's Ladder, and *Dead Presidents* all extend this insight, which might be called a "crisis of representation," strenuously resisting the possibility of national recuperation through restaging.[5] As its title implies (referring both to military delusions of grandeur and oppressive anonymity), *Universal Soldier*'s central problematic is the simultaneous diffusion and instability of identity. More precisely, the film is about losing the illusion that identity is fixed over time. The film insinuates, especially in its science-fictional dimensions, that time, cataloged by or as memory and measured by bodies, is a deceptive construction, a function of identity and a means to name it. Generically, *Universal Soldier* is also super-action cinema, pomo to the max, characterized in part by outrageous stories and big-name stars in deranged, ultraviolent, and loud circumstances. This genre loves repetition: sequels, formulas, and stars who play the same character again and again, no matter the specific narrative frames.

Repetition becomes cartoonish in *Universal Soldier* in ways that resituate history as cyclical and unfixed, especially as it is reimagined and consumed by and through media. Like other pomo action flicks, *Universal Soldier* is by turns inventive and formulaic, self-aware and willfully ignorant. Also like many of its generic cousins, the film focuses on hyperreal bodies that can inflict and survive unbelievable violence. John McTiernan's *Last Action Hero* (1993) offers one of the genre's most overtly "meta" critiques of stable and embodied identity in its looping of time and character: Arnold Schwarzenegger plays a sequelized action hero and "himself," the actor who plays the action hero. And the genre is expanding, such that its conventions appear in what might otherwise be considered straight-ahead action plots. Richard Donner's *Lethal Weapon 3* (1992) and *Lethal Weapon 4* (1998), Tony Scott's *The Last Boy Scout* (1992) and *True Romance* (1993), any of Steven Seagal's films (for instance, *Under Siege* in 1992, *Under Siege 2: Dark Territory* in 1996), Brian De-Palma's *Mission: Impossible* (1996), and even Andrew Davis's films with Harrison Ford, *The Fugitive* (1995) and *Air Force One* (1997), put diversely endowed, and often reluctantly heroic protagonists into extreme situations so that they can kick serious ass, while cracking wise and reclaiming some deep, previously estranged, familial bond (with wife, daughter, brother). In each of these films—not to mention one of Van Damme's more elaborate looney-tune pictures, *Double Impact*, directed by Hong Kong action expert Tsui Hark in 1997 and co-starring human cartoon Dennis Rodman—realism and linear sense give way to a hysterical excess that is nevertheless logical.

This logic is conditioned by what viewers know and anticipate concerning the genre, what they anticipate and what they desire to anticipate. The hero's inevitable sufferings are entertainingly overstated so as to allow his exaggerated affect and our mixed response. We're watching (and even wincing at) graphic images of torture and emotional horrors, while knowing (and enjoying this knowing) that Mel Gibson or Bruce Willis is going to eat that smug, cruel villain for breakfast. And as the stakes of these fighting-man displays are escalated (each successive installment, in sequels and even within single films, demanding more realistic effects and more evidence of excruciating pain), these prescriptive indulgences redouble audience identifications. So, the films use a traditional apparatus (by which viewers identify with characters) in order to expose that apparatus as artifice, as well as to demonstrate viewers' collusion in the effect (visceral, emotional, whatever).

Yvonne Tasker notes that action cinema typically occurs in a cultural and political context that is "new" in the eighties and nineties, one that recognizes "both production and consumption, one for which the critical models formulated in relation to classic Hollywood are not appropriate."[6] Or, at least, these models are made contingent and precarious. Tasker's point is an important one: to castigate *Universal Soldier* (as numerous critics have done) for its misogyny, racism, and nationalism is, while not exactly irrelevant, certainly less than revelatory. Its ideological ground is satirized even as it's laid out. Its interrogation of the masculine anxieties that inform action cinema—regular and pomo—is perceptive even if it's crazy and comic. Tasker writes that action movies depend "on a complex articulation of both belonging and exclusion, an articulation which is bound up in the body of the hero and the masculine identity that it embodies" (8).[7] The genre's conservatism is clear enough in this articulation, but so is the anxiety regarding such ideological trappings. The interconnections of "production and consumption" (including the expanding universe of multiple tie-in products, from children's action figures to hamburgers [and bear in mind that it's no longer unusual for movies to be based on toys, as well as vice versa]) comprise processes of identification and projection, such that elaborate fantasies of agency and memory are erected for both characters and viewers.

In the metatextual world of *Universal Soldier*, we and the characters remember and expect what might or does happen: we've seen it before. We can predict Luc's and Scott's identity-reconstruction trajectories, because we know the formula. Both marines recall their joint death scene in Vietnam, and both realize that they are not MIAs, but prisoners of an impacted war between the still pissed-off military lifers and the cowardly civilian government that won't "go all the way" (a reductive opposition alluding to well-rehearsed Vietnam War policy debates from the sixties and seventies).[8] Their jolted memories initiate not a "proper movement of history," but a repetition in the extreme, a literal replay of their deranged primal scene: over the course of the film, they kill each other again. And again. And again.[9] Unlike Robocop—and emphatically unlike Rambo, who does, eventually and twice, in the second and third movies in the series, get to "win"—Luc and Scott endure grueling redemptions that only return them to death, the ultimate climax and sign of failure. This return operates along two narrative tracks.[10] First, linear time is plotted through a radically fixed identity. The unisols suffer "regressive traumatic recall" (RTR), a severe version of posttraumatic stress disorder (PTSD). RTR occurs as the unisol body overheats, which it must, given its perpetual hyperacceleration. RTR, says the doctor who invented it (Jerry Orbach), is "trauma inflicted at the time of death. In Luc's case, he wanted to go home. When he awoke as a unisol, he returned to that single emotion. As for Scott, he thinks he's still in Vietnam, fighting the insurgents. He doesn't realize he's alive."[11]

As Luc points out at this juncture, however, neither he nor Scott is "alive" in any conventional sense. The symptoms of RTR are deemed specific to corpses. Which leads to the film's second narrative track, which effectively undoes the work of the first. Because of his own memory of Scott murdering the Vietnamese kids, Luc is compelled to save and then continue to protect a feisty girl reporter, Ronnie (Ally Walker), from Scott's attempt to murder her. In a set-up that recalls the Vietnam scene, with Ronnie on her knees and his weapon aimed at her head, she replaces the Vietnamese girl Luc couldn't save, and in her comes his chance for redemption (ironically, she has just told her photographer sidekick seconds before he was murdered by Scott, that she has discovered the unisols project, and that the story is her "redemption," for screwing up on her job). To save Ronnie, Luc destroys the unisol bus and, finally, kills Scott sensationally, impaling him on the thresher at his family's farm outside New Orleans (in a moment suggesting nothing less incredible than the return of the rural, where the ideal "American" prodigal son triumphs over the military-industrial goons). But Luc's dead body is consuming itself as we watch: he is, of course, the perfect product and consumer at the same time, a kind of robo-junkie. He beats Scott only when he shoots up, slamming the hormone-potion hypodermic into his chest like a shot of Popeye's spinach. He can only, according to the film's earlier pseudoscientific explanations, exist with his drugs and the technology that he's just blown to smithereens. Luc and Ronnie share a last embrace as the movie ends, but it's far from clear that he will survive or that they will be a couple. Their embrace emulates a happy ending that cannot be.

But we aren't about to remember all that now.

"MEMOREE-AH!": AUTHENTIC AMNESIA[12]

For all its emphasis on remembering "what happened," *Universal Soldier* is really about forgetting.[13] Even when he's apparently triumphant over the repressive repetition embodied by Scott, Luc is consigned to a heroic cliché, a nostalgic, even amnesiac emblem of pre-Vietnam War idealism, back on the farm (owned by his sweet-natured, supportive, but eerily American Gothic-looking parents), and still dead. This means that he's simultaneously a sign of "original" identity (a son, an innocent, an idealist) and its parodic distortion, an action figure stranded in an imaginary the-war-comes-home recuperative nightmare, a veritable poster boy for postmodernity. Lawrence Grossberg writes, "The sensibility of postmodernity defines a logic of 'ironic nihilism' or 'authentic inauthenticity.'"[14] The sensibility is inauthentic in its lack of political or emotional investment, or more to the point, its definitive loss of faith that any such investment might make a difference. In "assuming a distance from the other which allows it to refuse any claim or demand which might be made on it," Grossberg continues, this postmodern sensibility "deconstruct[s] the inherent possibility of investing in any single image" (225). Pyrotechnic, preposterous, and seemingly unconcerned with emotional or historical coherence, *Universal Soldier*'s dead protagonists make "nihilism" ironic: crowded with big biceps and bigger guns, the movie makes violent fun out of viewer affects, asking us to wince, cheer, and laugh along with the patent absurdity of the whole shebang.

For Grossberg, the disturbing underside to postmodernity's lack of investment is its capacity for political and ideological conservatism. Further, he writes, "[i]f every identity is a fake, a pose taken, then authentic inauthenticity celebrates the possibilities of poses without denying that this is all that they are" (Grossberg 226). *Universal Soldier* would seem to act out the political trajectory Grossberg traces as it celebrates the possibilities of unisol "poses" in its explosive excesses, then takes a nostalgic, conservative turn in lamenting Luc's inability to recover fully his identity or life once he's rediscovered them.

However, the film's commercial slipperiness may be less insidious than it looks. It makes contradictory emotional and intellectual appeals, making Luc a moralistic victor and Scott an entertaining villain, and both victims of larger, diabolic forces. And these appeals make for some specific political effects. Dana Polan writes that postmodernist "qualities" like superficiality and pastiche "can still work in support of dominant power by encouraging a serialized sense of the social totality as something one can never understand and that always eludes one's grasp."[15] Even aside from both Polan's and Grossberg's concerns that the pervasiveness of postmodernity enables its subjects' disinvestment (posing) "without guilt," the "serialized sense" works another cultural nerve. This model of postmodernist discourse paradoxically continues to situate itself in time, delineating distinctive intellectual contours and confirming a notion of "proper movement," of history "progressing," of (selective) public memorializing and forgetting. If many mainstream representations of the Vietnam War mark its relation to earlier discourses, with reference to a fixed, heroic, national identity, some, like *Universal Soldier*, also suggest the irrevocable alteration of this identity, and the Vietnam War's difference from previous wars and wars to come (for example, the Gulf War, so tightly contained and cleanly represented in media).

Locked in time and trauma, narratives of the Vietnam War tend to emphasize affect as a means to articulate or understand effects. Linda Dittmar and Gene Michaud argue that "realism" obtains in Vietnam War texts through visceral identifications; viewers are typically invited to feel pain, boredom, anger, and horror in movies as ideologically diverse as *Apocalypse Now* (Francis Ford Coppola 1979), *Platoon* (Oliver Stone 1986), *Full Metal Jacket* (Stanley Kubrick 1987), and *84 Charlie Mopic* (Patrick Duncan 1989). Dittmar and Michaud say that realism secures affective responses to manage "short-term considerations of profit" as well as "a politic of erasure and long-term ideological investment in maintaining existing social structures and practices." Echoing Grossberg and Polan, their reading of such "erasure" suggests that once meaningful signs of political investment are reduced to "authenticating props."[16] That is, "real" elements are turned into "realistic" effects, including period soundtracks, slangy dialogue, blood and guts, and elaborate stunts. When these effects become the dominant social experience of the war, of what importance is "what happened," which continues to resist consensus and definition?

Drawing on their audience's experience in theaters and in front of television sets (viewers know how to watch and evaluate these effects as effects, while also anticipating their emotional or visceral appeals), the 1990s versions of Vietnam War films are cagier. Assuming spectators' cynicism and denial, they're quite ready to restage wartime as a video game. As Vietnam War representations produce inconstancy in what Rick Berg and John Carlos Rowe call the "American memory" of the war, they also cast doubts on the conventional measures of national identity.[17] On one hand, Berg and Rowe write, popular U.S. images reinforce traditional ideologies: the "means of imagining Vietnam as the mirror we hold up to ourselves, as the searching, critical 'self-image' of our collective failure as a democratic people, are themselves the essence of the new brand of imperialism that we continue to sell in the furthest reaches of the world" (2–3). On another hand, these images reveal ongoing uneasiness over national, familial, political, and individual dispositions. It's not that the war in Vietnam (and the various political "movements" of the era) caused a breakdown in modern social institutions like "the nuclear family," Berg and Rowe argue, but rather that it helped to expose the artifice and tenuousness of such institutions from jump (5). As it enables a retrofitting of events, the "Vietnam" of U.S. popular culture deconstructs the "proper movement of history," showing that it is less forward than dynamic, circuitous, and continuous.

"BODY COUNT BODY COUNT BODY COUNT BODY COUNT": MEDIA INVESTMENTS

In this process of revision and resistance, how do bodies count?[18] Of what value are bodies to history, aside from their statistical use? Consider Luc's status as Representative Body. Initially the character, contextualized in this particular fiction, seems a familiar "genidentity," which, as defined by Baastian C. Van Fraasen, is located and reflected in an "enduring subject over time."[19] Luc's identity is ludicrously fixed and unfixed at once, caught up in a cyborg body that restages subjectivity as a series of allusions, fragmentations, inconsistencies, and a slew of self-referential jokes. Luc is a "Van Damme character" in a "Van Damme vehicle," running the actor's expected big dick action-pic routines. It may be possible for this movie's spectators to invest in Luc's quaint desire to "go home," but it's unlikely: they want to see the pecs, the splits, the head-butts. Who cares, really, if he reaches his destination, except as it's the ideal site for his showdown with Scott, complete with farm machinery and a family to protect? This is a postmodern movie in the broadest, most commercial sense, about itself and its genre, about its big silly bodies flying every which way, preferably in yucky pieces. The characters offer a variety of temporary emotional investments, cultural and political implications, as predictable and orchestrated as any of its elaborate stunts or vehicle chases.

Predictable maybe, but still, these effects can be unstable in address, representation, and meaning. Take the film's closing credits, which scroll under Ice T's speed-metal band's self-naming song, "Body Count." Aside from its obvious pitch for the movie soundtrack on CD, the song serves several other functions. Connecting the Vietnam War and inner city violence, the song makes a clearly politicized point concerning the relation between the U.S. underclass and "organized" violence: bodies merely counted are disremembered, relegated to media imagery, blips in TV-news graphics. Van Damme's performative violence and vengeance will never pose the same threat to social order as Ice T (who actually used Arnold Schwarzenegger's killer-cyborg ripping through a cop station in *The Terminator* to counter the charge that Body Count's song, "Cop Killer," narrated excessive violence against police). As Judith Halberstam argues, the public controversy over "Cop Killer" illustrates the threat of "imagined violence" when posed by particular bodies. She writes, "Imagined violences create a potentiality, a utopic state in which consequences are imminent rather than actual, the threat is in the anticipation, not the act."[20] This threat is clearly not possible in a body like Van Damme's, for he represents no "authentic" stake or potentiality.[21] And *Universal Soldier* underlines this marketable lack of authenticity in its mocking references to Schwarzenegger and Stallone stunts, its self-acknowledged limitations (for example, though Luc's parents have no accents, his background is called "Cajun" in a lame attempt to explain his die-hard French-Belgian accent), and its standard, pretty-boy-naked appeals to Van Damme's fans, straight and queer.[22] If Schwarzenegger, as Fred Pfeil argues, is a "specifically postmodern icon" in his mutation of the deadpan, dead-souled lineage of Bronson, Eastwood, and Chuck Norris, what are we to make of the meta-mutations of Schwarzenegger-wanna-be Van Damme?[23]

Transgressive and regressive at once, Van Damme/Luc's media-immersed body incarnates confusions about his identity. The ambiguous relation between masculine and national identity that Tasker sees in the regular action hero is revealed precisely in Luc's strained relation to media as memory, specifically, Richard Nixon on a motel television screen. As he stares dumbfounded at a TV documentary, Luc is dropped into a weird *media res* bewilderment: "And now back to *Nixon: The War Years, Part Seven*," the offscreen narrator intones over Nixon's pasty, beard-shadowed face. Cut to footage of Vietnamese prisoners, accompanied by Nixon's voice-over, "We will keep America the strongest nation in the world. And we will couple that strength with firm diplomacy. No apologies, no regrets." Luc is stricken. "The war is over," he says, believing the TV without question. Pause. Deep breath. His own body mirrored, obliquely, in those of the Vietnamese prisoners, Luc has nowhere to go, feels marched along a trajectory of time that has ignored him. His identity, grounded in his will to "go home," to claim locality and nationality amid the chaos of "the World," is suddenly revoked because the time is not his, the national memories have nothing to do with him.

No regrets. Luc's alarm at Nixon on television is triggered by his sense of temporal displacement. But his loss reflects a national identificatory and representational crisis as well, remembered for us in the play of Nixon as media image. Here he is as recuperated elder statesman, discussing his culpability for Watergate alongside his diplomatic record. If this is hard for an informed audience to grasp, an audience with its memory in order, Luc's instant lack of context is an effective allusion to the 1990s, an era when memory is famously in constant turnaround. Where the eighties, as Susan Jeffords argues, saw the rise of "hard bodies" in U.S. popular culture, the nineties' masculine representations are increasingly unresolved, ambiguous, hysterical. The Reagan Revolution's "normative body," writes Jeffords, "enveloped strength, labor, determination, loyalty, and courage."[24]

If Rambo and Robocop could recover their identities (even Schwarzenegger's Terminator was allowed to "recover" one in *Terminator 2: Judgment Day*, as John Connor's relentless father figure), Luc cannot. He's a media effect. He doesn't count.[25] Luc is surely determined, courageous, and exceptionally well-trained, and his body is nothing if not hard, but his sweet naïf characteristics are repeatedly the occasion for comedy and ridicule. When, for instance, he realizes that he and Ronnie are being tracked by the hardcore unisols (assigned to "search and destroy" the "traitorous" couple), he strips and instructs Ronnie to find the device implanted in his body. "Look for something unusual," he says, "Look for something hard." She's shot from between his naked legs, scanning his body, plainly looking at his penis, which is, after all, the punchline (we don't see it, but she assures us that it's "perfectly normal"). This punchline is redoubled when Ronnie does locate the device in the back of Luc's leg and grimaces while removing it, following his own self-inflicted, bloody gash ("Ewww, this is sooo gross," she whines). Clearly, nothing about this body is "normal."

As Luc is disappointed when he sees Nixon as a liar (Luc's

"America" is no "strongest nation"), so Scott offers a hysterical response to Rambo as hero. Our reluctant hero, Luc, refutes mediated history while our ostensible villain embraces all of that history's inversions and inaccuracies as his own. Scott, who has brought the war home with a vengeance, pointedly recalls Colonel Trautman's (Richard Crenna) warning that the supertrained Rambo has internalized the war ("What you call hell, he calls home"). And then Scott, with a flourish only Lundgren could muster, turns this warning on its head, being the bona fide sociopath that Rambo could never dream of being.[26] Stopping at a local grocery store to "cool down" his overheated unisol buddies in the meat locker (which emphasizes the embodiedness, the meat as opposed to the matrix, of these cyborgs), Scott educates a nonplussed crowd of locals, who stand about wearing cowboy hats and jeans. "What the hell are you staring at?" he accuses them. "Do you have any idea what it's like out there? Do you? Well, I'm fighting this fucking war. These shitheads. These yellow traitoring motherfuckers. They're everywhere." Some uniformed guards show up, waving their weapons at Scott in an effort to take him quietly. Scott shoots them dead in an instant. "See?" he says, smug, as his assessment of the traitorous world is summarily confirmed. "They're everywhere."

Drawing on the memory of Schwarzenegger's police station massacre in *The Terminator*, Scott's assault on anonymous uniforms is less startling than hilarious. While "See? They're everywhere" would seem to erect a rigid barrier between him and them, it also suggests a dissolution of boundaries between "out there" ("everywhere") and a self that is so emphatically defined by its performance and reception, its positioning by them "out there." Scott's/Lundgren's diatribe is highly performative, framed by its injunction ("See?") to spectators, both the diegetic folks gathered round the hamburger patties and chicken thighs, understandably disturbed, and the movie viewers who cheer on his rampage. Rogin writes, "Spectacle is the cultural form for amnesiac representation, for spectacular displays are superficial and sensately intensified, short-lived and repeatable" (507). The relation between amnesia and spectacle lies in their mutual production of "illusory unification and meaning": in postmodern culture, observes Rogin, "[i]nstead of dissolving the subject into structures or discourses, the concept of amnesia points to an identity that persists over time and that preserves a false center by burying the actual past" (508). The image of Scott in the meat section suggests amnesia as disjunctive affect. Viewers respond positively to Scott's excess (his riff on the crazed vet stereotype), his on-screen audience's lack of response (they're stunned and frightened "rednecks," easy targets), and his ken-doll good looks, made more charming by his facial scars and the new ear-necklace he's made for himself. A spectacle of remembering-as-forgetting, the scene refigures persistent identity as pathology. It's better to forget.

TEMPORAL DISLOCATIONS

In *Jacob's Ladder*, Jacob Singer (Tim Robbins) is another Vietnam veteran whose memory has been "cleared" by the government. Directed by Adrian Lyne (whose work tends to the sensational, including *Fatal Attraction* in 1987 and *Lolita* in 1997) and written by Bruce Joel Rubin (whose sensibility is explicitly melodramatic, shown in *Ghost* in 1991 and 1993's *My Life*), *Jacob's Ladder* plays fast and loose with both temporal and emotional coherence.[27] Jacob's drama is organized around white, middle-class masculine anxieties concerning race and sexuality, as these threaten his identity. Like *Universal Soldier*, *Jacob's Ladder* opens with a stock Vietnam War scenario, delivering to audience expectations in order to thwart them in unnerving ways. Images and sounds of choppers signal the standard U.S. technological incursion, a jungle backdrop the primitive wildness of an elusive enemy. Cut to a squad of marines resting in a clearing, smoking dope, and joking about Jake's bodily dysfunctions (he's off in the bush with diarrhea). When Jake returns to the group, a black man baits him: "Jerking off again, huh Jake? Come over here and jerk on this. Come choke my black rooster, please?" Jake's good-natured response suggests that the banter is routine, but it also establishes the film's concern with masculine identity, as it is determined culturally through race, sexuality, and power inequities. Jake says, "Ain't got a fucking tweezer, man," and the predominantly white squad laughs at his score, his ability to hold his ground against a conventionally threatening black masculinity.

This bit of dialogue gives way immediately to the primal battle scene that will be recalled, by various characters, throughout the rest of the film. Hit hard by enemy fire, the men scatter, alternately spewing automatic weapons fire in return and running pell-mell through the jungle. At this moment of attack, the soundtrack fades from external gunfire to an internal silence, as Jake staggers through the bush. Suddenly he wakes on a rocking New York City subway car, Camus's *The Stranger* clutched prominently in his hand. He looks up to read two overhead advertisements, "New York may be a crazy town, but you'll never be bored. Enjoy!" and "HELL: That's what life can be, doing drugs . . ."

Like *Universal Soldier*'s initial set of images, this early sequence assumes audience familiarity with the conventions of Vietnam War movie iconography. Jake's flashback is a hell from which he cannot escape: like most movie veterans, he suffers visibly, with sweaty brow and eyes popping, trapped in his own body. Disoriented, Jake exits the train at the next stop, but not before he spots another man asleep, with a strange, darkly fleshy, tail- or penis-like protuberance visible from under his coat. Jake jumps at the sight. Disheveled and clearly afraid, he's now revealed to be different from standard-issue movie veterans. No tough guy, he's a mailman who reads Camus, a former graduate student whom his fellow marines called "Professor"; Jake has a soft, unassuming presence.[28] And he becomes increasingly frightened by what he's remembering, which is, as it turns out, the course of his death. By film's end, all events are resituated as occurring at the instant of his death; he's bayoneted by a U.S. soldier and dies in country, and all that occurs stateside is his flash forward, his imagining alternate futures that never take place in the film's reality. Jake's story unfolds for us as a series of temporally and materially ambiguous images: where, when, and even *who* he is at any given moment is generally not cued by previous or subsequent images.

One of the most explicit and recurring situations for Jake is his sense of displacement, signaled by his racial environment. Further, his trepidation is repeatedly projected onto the nonwhite bodies with whom he interacts, his black marine buddy, his New York-based Latina lover, Jezzie (Elizabeth Pena), and the head-spinning demons who populate his nightmares. All of his interactions with these characters are eventually exposed as visceral effects without stable identificatory ground: Jake's memory, his sense of himself, is a delusion, his ostensible subjectivity a narrative trope that allows us to hang our audience identification on a protagonist.

Jake's attempts to trace a direct line between his memory of Vietnam and the two "presents" he appears to inhabit are consistently foiled by stories, told by his friends and Jezzie, that conflict with his own. Moreover, his most crucial, foundational experience is officially denied: he's informed by the government that he was never "in Vietnam." His lawyer explains to Jake, "It means that you and your buddies are wacko, that you were discharged on psychological grounds after some war games in Thailand." Obviously, Jake's memory is erratic even by standards set by the fictionalized hysteria of other sensational Vietnam War texts; his remembrance evolves as flashbacks within flashbacks, a network that remains difficult for us to parse. When he confronts the state's formal erasure of his ordeal, he lacks legal and narrative recourse. And yet, for all the film's fucking with temporal structures, it does come to a fairly finite end: Jake dies, ascending to heaven by a stairway, guided by his already-dead son Gabe (played by Macaulay Culkin). Jake's death, then, seems to grant him a measure of reconciliation (he's guilty about the traffic accident that killed Gabe) and Hollywoodish spiritual transcendence (unlike, say, Luc Devereaux, who is left on the ground in a long overhead shot, abandoned by his past, and unresolved). But just as he's headed toward his bright light, Jake is snapped back, dragging us with him, to Vietnam. We see his bloody body on a gurney in an emergency medical tent, and then a written epilogue that asserts, "It was reported that the hallucinogenic drug BZ was used in experiments on soldiers during the Vietnam War. The Pentagon denied the story."

The film's accusations stand, sort of, with this final sentence: the Pentagon is evil. But we already knew that.

What makes *Jacob's Ladder* intriguing is not its indictment of the military or civilian government for abuses of the "boys," but the film's implication that nonlinear memories count as resistance—against the U.S. government, against the march of history, against the national mythologies that prescribe coherence and victors and happy endings. This is only an implication in a film that makes the protagonist's sad and lonely death (by "friendly fire," or rather, "friendly penetration," no less) its climax, but it's a powerful one, entangling collective memories and identities in representational bodies that are increasingly tenuous and immeasurable. This is a movie about borderless bodies and the crisis that these pose for enduring identities, Van Fraasen's genidentities that persist over time.[29] The incessant, hectic multiplicity of Jake's lives, deaths, and selves offers no redemption, no movement toward a singular, stable self. Instead, his nightmares remain fraught with bodies consuming, twisting, spinning, fucking, and dying. His demons are rampant and raging, in continual pain, without evident origin or merciful end. And he's malleable and ineffectual before them: it's like he's malleable and ineffectual before them: it's like he's ravished by them. Grossberg's description of postmodernism's "affective epidemic" approximates Jake's perpetual deterioration: "everyday life as a series of trajectories or mobilities which, while apparently leading to specific concerns, actually constantly redistribute and disperse investments" (Grossberg 284). Ouch.

Jake's chaos is a function of such illusory motion, the trajectories that lead nowhere, the dispersion of investments. His disembodiedness (his deadness) is displayed for us (until the revelation at the end) as too many selves, an abundance of material existences that won't cohere. And, given the film's interest in masculinity as a set of codes and expectations that can't be met, it's not surprising that Jake perceives his nightmares and flashbacks as signs of his impotence, his wartime experience repressed but uncontrolled. His unmistakable horror at the undefined penis thing under the subway sleeper's coat, combined with the film's bit of dialogue about jerking off, suggests that Jake's "coming home" anxieties have everything to do with a destabilizing of raced and sexed identities during the war. What will he find in the world? What will he be in the world? And where is he in the world?

In one of the film's postwar narrative lines, Jake is living with Jezzie, his volatile, sexy coworker at the post office. Their relationship is apparently predicated on sex, specifically her "heat" and his inability to understand it. At first they joke about his having "sold his soul" for a "good lay" (making her a devil or part of a bargain with same). But her sexuality (or more precisely, his relation to it) becomes increasingly threatening over the course of the film. When they go to a party (at her urging; he's a bookworm who'd rather stay home), he's alarmed to see her dance wildly and lasciviously with a dark-skinned man. The scene is soon out of control: Jake sees terrifying flashes of dead animals in between blurred images of Jezzie and her partner, and he finally falls out upon witnessing the partner's transformation into a beast, with a reptilian tail that she caresses and then rides like a huge cock. When Jake awakens, he's burning with a fever so high that Jezzie must force him into a tub of ice water: the whole episode has been a dream, but she's torturing him just the same. Jake screams.

The film continues to structure sexuality as dichotomies of race and class, where the only good, nonthreatening sexuality is nonsexuality between nonbodies, that is, white, middle-class, frigid bodies. So, Jezzie and Jake's working-class life is compared to a parallel narrative track, in which Jake is married to his wife from before Vietnam—the blond, bland, icy Sara, with whom he has three blond, bland children, one being the previously mentioned Gabe—in this plotline resurrected. (Sara's longest scene with Jake runs about two minutes, and in it she complains that the bedroom is too warm, asking him to turn on the air conditioner: both his women want to make his body cold, to kill him.)

The character who connects and also disconnects the two narrative threads is Louie (Danny Aiello), Jake's chiropractor, repeatedly shown in angelic backlighting. Between stories, Jake visits Louie, who adjusts his back with loud, violent cracks, while dispensing romantic and domestic advice. Each crack represents an adjustment of time, such that Jake enters a different plot with each visit. This device suggests that there is a link between Jake's body and his temporal placement, that his identity is determined between the two. He is, like Luc and many other Vietnam War film veterans, a victim of a duplicitous and incompetent command structure; but Jake's alternating life strands offer a peculiar way to rethink identity as it is produced in and out of time. Jake is out of place not only in country (where he's too dorky, not gung ho enough to survive) and in the world (where again, he's too trusting, too jealous, too scared, not paranoid enough), but also in his own body, which is, after all, not his, only borrowed for the duration of the film time, our time for watching him gyrate and worry. The dominant metaphor in the film is the violation and abuse of Jake's body; everyone in the film gets a piece of him: he's downed by the deadly fever, a hit-and-run driver, a car bomb, and a crew of faceless monster-doctors (including one with a face, Jezzie) who begin to cut into him while he's strapped down in some hospital basement of his mind.[30] "This isn't happening!" he screams as the doctors' masks loom over him. "Let me out of here!" A male surgeon replies, "There is no out of here. You've been killed. Don't you remember?"

"This isn't happening." "Don't you remember?" Caught in a loop of subjectivity, Jake cannot "remember" because the film is only marking an instant, a nonmovement in a terminal ever-present. The declaration of Jake's nonexistence—"You've been killed"—unsettles linear time, dissolves this instant into a past tense that consists of a series of moments, each fractured and folded into the ones before and after it. Jake's internal crisis is performed for viewers—us and the doctors who stand in for us, waiting to get at him with their knives—who sit in an operating theater from which there is, indeed, no "out of here." There's no escape because this space and time are the same, an instant unchanging for us, left behind and past, familiar and repeated. Cornelius Castoriadis writes that the characteristics of being in space are the "same as the ones we attribute to time: the unfolding of otherness, the deployment of alterity, together with a dimension of identity/difference (repetition)."[31] When Jake is denied "alterity," when all he sees is sameness and the end of time in this instant, the narrative breaks down and the fiction of his identity turns excruciatingly clear. Not only is he unable to be "out of here"—as he *is* the "in here," it's his dream we and he are witnessing, absolutely and unchangeably—but everyone he encounters from here on, *we* now know, is inside his dream, is, in effect, him. Difference becomes a matter of narrative convenience, a "serialized sense" revealed as "affective epidemic." Does Jake's instant of recognizing or, alternately, imagining an "out of here," continue past its instant-ness, grant him proper movement? Jake, who has not endured, has no genidentity, cannot conclude; rather, he "has been killed," before he woke on the subway, before his story began; he has "been killed" before, interminably, always, now, and here.

The film's incongruous stories intersect and conflict to produce Jake's identity as an effect that remains irrecuperable even in his death. Embodiment assumes faith in spatial limits and sensate boundaries, and serves as the underlying fiction for *Jacob's Ladder*, whose temporal confusions construct a narrative that won't cohere. Such incoherence, as Timothy Corrigan points out, characterizes contemporary media consumption as well as production, as such consumption in turn reflects identity constructions. Channel and web surfing, fast forwarding and internet linking, scanning, filing, and deleting: these activities reorder narrative and time, such that Joe Consumer is "reflected in that experience as always potentially a discontinuous or fragmented subjectivity, without centered or stable position, a discursively mobile identity."[32] Such disruption of domestic time and space (watching television, jacked in to the internet) infuses us with a sense of simultaneous control and passivity, a desire to make sense of what occurs, to apply narrative, to find order. Desire is used to identify RTR victims Luc and Scott in *Universal Soldier* (they become their last living memories). Here desire is more amorphous, not a drive but a retreat. It turns out that Jake wants to dissolve into his dead son's world, never to come home, and in that sense, he effects agency and the film delivers a (generally dissatisfying) resolution.

Jake hears "the truth" (one of them, anyway) from a doctor who was involved in the drug testing program, a doctor significantly named Newman, a self-described "hippie scientist" who says he developed the aggression-inducing hallucinogen called "the ladder" to be used by the U.S. on its own men. This is the drug that we see in action in the film's first scene, when Jake's squad seems to be assaulted by the enemy: here he learns that they attacked each other. On hearing this news, Jake can only die. His passivity is determined by his lack of memory: he can only take what he's told is his past and his motivation, as he has none of his own that he can trust or hold onto beyond three or four minutes. "No one can remember that night," he says, referring to other vet buddies he's tracked down. "I get flashes but they don't make sense. What happened? Was there an offensive?" Newman can't answer him, because Newman is his dream explicator. And the movie doesn't let up on this point of confusion, as it doesn't give up what did happen. Even its final lapse into mushy father-son hand-holding remains nonsense. We see flashbacks that might locate the forgotten narrative in particular bodies: Jake is stabbed by a fellow GI in one of them, supported by the closing epigraph on drug experiments. But no one admits this, and the film has so many stories that never come together that temporal stability and fixed identity seem forever remote, pretty-to-think-so fantasies.

A question frequently asked by viewers of this film is precisely this: "What happened?" for audiences who have learned to expect government deceptions and revisionist histories, one ending makes sense; Jake's pursuit of the conspiracy against him and his fellow marines is never so conventionally hard and noble as those vengeance plots enacted by Norris or Stallone. In its patrilineal discontinuity (father and son are reunited, but father follows son into death) and its hysterical masculine body, *Jacob's Ladder* controverts the legacy of vigorous, masterful soldier-boy heroes who remain available even in the most desperate and angry Vietnam War texts. Here, the hero's body is soft and afraid, never avenged, only beaten and violated into oblivion. Castoriadis writes that "we cannot consider one temporality as the only originary or authentic one" (64). Reminded of his possible, unconfirmable past by a guy named Newman, Jake becomes old and new at once, authentically inauthentic, and looks beyond the horizon of masculine archetypes into some other time.

"NO JUSTICE, NO PEACE"

Cultural assumptions of authenticity and identity are pressed further into temporal trouble by *Boyz N the Hood* and *Dead Presidents.* Focused through an opposition between individual identity and social conformity (that is, the fundamental and irresolvable tension for democracy), both films are organized around questions of gender and class differences, national boundaries, and institutionalized aggressions. At first, this organization in *Boyz* seems to delineate a conventional generational conflict and resolution. When young Tre Styles tells his daddy that he's considering joining the military to get out of South Central Los Angeles, Furious (Laurence Fishburne) brings the boy up short: "Don't never go in the army son. Black man's got no place in the army." Given the ongoing immediacy of hip-hop's east-west splits and alliances; persistent fallout from the 1992 LA uprising, the O. J. Simpson verdicts, and other police and legal system abuses; and the state's use of prisons, the war on drugs, and black market guns to contain the underclass, Furious's assertion continues to resonate across U.S. black communities. As he goes on to describe the socioeconomic conditions that led to his own tour in Vietnam— his wife was pregnant, he was seventeen and without skills—we see father and son on a fishing trip, one of the film's precious few respites from the drivebys, helicopters, searchlights, and sirens that comprise Tre's daily life. By linking memories of the Vietnam War with images of current and expanding militarism in South Central, the movie renders a continuum of oppression, resistance, and identification, creating an "affective epidemic" that is grounded in historical events and dead bodies. As Ruth Wilson Gilmore observes of this milieu, "There is a war on," a war that is premised on social and economic imbalances, exacerbated by the fact that the "state is equipped, with both weaponry and consent, brutally to police the crisis at every step of the way."[33]

It's a crisis that *Boyz* and *Dead Presidents* situates as a not-quite-organized revolt against a homogenous national identity. Where *Boyz* uses war veteran Furious to teach Tre about black political and economic crises, the Hughes brothers' *Dead Presidents*, based on several of the oral histories in Wallace Terry's *Bloods*, is set during the war, following young veteran Anthony's increasingly traumatic and abortive efforts to "be a man" in country and at home. (Anthony is played by Larenz Tate, who was the sociopathic stone killer O'Dog in the Hughes's *Menace II Society* [1993], here transformed to the "sweet" character who can't catch a break.) Both films explore the relationship of black masculine identity to national mythologies. Homi Bhabha writes that it is through a "syntax of forgetting—or being obliged to forget—that the problematic identification of a national people becomes visible. This is again the moment of anteriority of the nation's sign that entirely changes our understanding of the pastness of the past, and the unified present of the will to nationhood."[34] *Boyz* offers a streetwise, if melodramatically heightened, realism; *Dead Presidents* is more visibly and formally surreal, but effects a similarly streetwise, insider's knowledge (in part introduced by the period soundtrack, in part through language and gesture). Both movies use their versions of realism, gleaned in part through their makers' deep research into classic Hollywood cinema, to stage political imperatives and secure audience identifications. And both movies resist the "syntax of forgetting" by literalizing the past, rearticulating it as visible, visceral memory and identity.

At the time of *Boyz*'s theatrical release, the New York Times praised its "gritty peek into a facet of life to which virtually no white audiences have been privy—and that a fair number of black middle-class viewers will find alien as well."[35] Constructing a class and race-based distance between film and viewers, the piece (obnoxiously) asserts the text's strangeness as a measure of its truthfulness. Manthia Diawara makes a similar point when he writes that *Boyz* exemplifies "the new realism" of black filmmaking, its representation of "the existent reality of urban life in America" again determined by its subject matter more than technique, that previously unseen "reality."[36] Stressing connections between representation and experience, between representation and its meanings, Diawara's use of the term realism preserves authenticity as an effective strategy for discursive intervention and political activism. The same can be said for *Presidents*, which, for all its color, flash, and athletic camerawork, is even more dead-on in its depictions of savage violence and its emotional costs.

In this context, where realism assumes a political edge, to argue for *Boyz*'s or *Presidents*'s postmodernism might seem counterproductive. As Henry Louis Gates Jr. writes, there is a certain irony inhering in the moment when, just as African American subjectivity is forcefully asserted, theorized, and represented in mainstream venues like multiplex theaters, "our theoretical colleagues declare that there ain't no such thing as a subject, so why be bothered with that?"[37] *Boyz* asks precisely this question, as does *Presidents*, in a different way. In doing so, the films challenge the assumed relation between memory and national identity. For if, like *Universal Soldier* and *Jacob's Ladder*, these films are concerned with temporal designations and disruptions of identity, they also, quite unlike the white movies, harbor no nostalgia for pre-war narratives of the national subject, domestic order, or political and economic security. The past that Luc and Jake desire so fervently just doesn't exist in the black films. The war has never been over, it just comes back to the hood. While *Boyz* and *Presidents* are emphatic in asserting that as Gates says, "You can't opt out of history," they also make clear that "history" is not a separate category of experience, done and gone, but perpetual, recirculating, and referential (Gates 37). Diawara's reading of *Boyz* names its challenge to dominant narratives (in which black subjects had no voice or identity) as a reformulation of subjective coherence (necessary for the overdetermined codes of "realism"). But while it adheres to a variety of realistic narrative regulations, the film also questions "realism" as a representational mode (whom does it represent, and to what ends?) and as a product of and means to social justice.[38]

Bhabha encourages a rethinking of nationalism, attending to its "temporal dimension," which displaces the "historicism that has dominated discussions of nation as cultural force." He writes, "It is the mark of the ambivalence of the nation as a narrative strategy—and an apparatus of power—that it produces a continual slippage into analogous, even metonymic, categories, like the people, minorities, or 'cultural difference,' that continually overlap in the act of writing the nation" (292). *Boyz* contends with "writing the nation" in a specific context (during the summer of 1991 in California, then immersed in cultural conflicts, Gulf War parades, and mass media replays of the Rodney King beating video). That the only information we have about Furious's past is his service in Vietnam (and his divorce from Tre's mother) makes this moment integral to our understanding of his character. The casting of Fishburne resonates further, recalling his role as the heartbreakingly young soldier, Mr. Clean, in *Apocalypse Now*. As the fourteen-year-old Fishburne observes in his

1978 interview in Fax Bahr and George Hickenlooper's documentary of the making of *Apocalypse Now*, *Hearts of Darkness: A Filmmaker's Apocalypse* (1990), his part was "about the kids over there, snatched up and kinda used as cannon fodder for this war." Amen to that. *Apocalypse Now*, through its well-timed deaths of Clean and the only other black character, Chief (Albert Hall), names the U.S. mission in Southeast Asia for the racist project it was. These two characters must die before the transport boat reaches Kurtz's compound in Cambodia, for as the only black men on board, they would have seen the racist basis of Kurtz's insanity, whereas the white guys can marvel at his appreciation and control of the natives and even try going native themselves. June Jordan indicts *Apocalypse Now* for "wallowing" in its conventional narrative of the white man trapped in a savage heart of darkness: "Said European will collapse, there, into a nigger version, as it were, of his true, more virtuous, and lighter/whiter self. Hence it is never the white colonialist who is the savage or the barbarian. Rather, it is the savage and/or barbaric surroundings of the white man that will compel his untoward display of a nigger identity: i.e., acting out his 'dark' emotions/thoughts, et cetera. Extraordinary."[39]

What's quite extraordinary indeed is the fixed familiarity of this scenario in so many narratives. The history of "Vietnam" is relentlessly white, relentlessly concerned with the search for an identity worth recovering (Haile Gerima's *Ashes and Embers* [1983], Doug McHenry's *Jason's Lyric* [1994], Preston Whitmore III's *The Walking Dead* [1996], and Mario Van Peebles's *Panther* [1996] are all notable exceptions, focused on sympathetic black veterans). No "minority" narrative could sustain this fantasy of pre-war unity and stability, a desire that Corrigan calls "the nostalgia for history" (10). In white war stories, institutionalized racism (the kind that drove the war against "gooks" and "slopes," after all: see *Full Metal Jacket* for a grueling examination of this indoctrination process) is ritually transformed into individual struggles, such that protagonists, white and black, learn to appreciate each other's strengths in the field. These familiar images—in *Platoon*, *Flight of the Intruder*, *84 Charlie Mopic*, for examples—address racism only as it has an impact on white characters. If *Universal Soldier* and *Jacob's Ladder* agonize over the decimation of national identity and idealism by delving into progressively incoherent personalities wounded by the war, *Boyz* and *Presidents* argue that their primary identificatory traumas begin at home.

When Tre's white schoolteacher instructs her class of young black and Latino students about the Pilgrims and Thanksgiving, for instance, their bored faces indicate that this "history" has nothing to do with them. And when Anthony and his buddy Skippy (Chris Tucker) decide to enlist in 1968, they do so choosing to resist their going-nowhere futures in the Bronx, and choosing to ignore the histories of black men who were cast aside after serving in Korea, like Anthony's father and his mentor Kirby (Keith David). Looking to become "men," they have no options.

Rather than a retread collective memory, then, *Boyz* offers an oppositional "report from the front." The war in the hood occurs daily and variously. Mike Davis suggests that the "militarization of city life so grimly visible at street level" and ignored by "urban theory" is always already revealed in "Hollywood's pop-apocalypses and pulp science fiction [which] have been more realistic, and more politically perceptive, in representing the programmed hardening of the urban surface in the wake of the social polarizations of the Reagan era."[40] *Boyz*'s opening scene makes street-level violence immediate and visible to anyone. When Tre and his friends inspect a local murder site, marked by police tape and bloodstains, the camera closes on a series of smiling Ronald Reagan posters, shot full of holes, assertions that the real enemy is not some alien (though with Reagan this point might be argued), but internal, one of us, not incidentally, just like in the Vietnam War movies.

On its release, *Boyz* was subsumed under the gangsta subgenre, due to its "from the street" attitude and graphic displays of violence, and news-reported for the ostensible violence that erupted outside theaters where it was playing. Like most war movies, *Boyz* offers violence that is at once repulsive and celebratory, awful and titillating. And in its treatment of black-on-black youth violence, the film's most self-conscious, precarious, charismatic, and potentially revelatory character is not Furious or Tre, but Tre's childhood friend, the reluctant gangsta Doughboy (Ice Cube). Doughboy is the representative angry young man, resisting white authority, getting by however he can, given the economics of the hood. The ritualistic rerouting of his frustrated resistance as intraracial violence is *Boyz*'s target (its famous first shot, a zoom to a stop sign on a South Central street corner, comes under a scroll of statistics and a soundtrack extolling the inner city's "body count"). Doughboy is caught in a nonspace, between the poles of experience, wise and naïve, embodied by Furious and Tre. As the oldest son in a fatherless household, Dough-boy is simultaneously berated by his mother and responsible for his slow-witted brother, a football star named Ricky (Morris Chestnut); he is afforded neither Furious's moral authority nor Tre's luxury of indecision.[41]

Doughboy is at once dissident and vulnerable, torn between the violence that makes his reputation in the hood (and so keeps him alive) and the desire to be rid of such prescriptions. As charismatic as Doughboy is in this position, however, as bell hooks observes, the character replays familiar stereotypes, exploiting "the commodifi-cation of blackness and the concomitant exotification of phallocen-tric black masculinity."[42] When Ricky is murdered by a gangbanger, Doughboy has no option but to seek retribution: it's the code, it's the rules of war, just as if he were in a declared war zone, just as if he were Furious back in the 1960s. But at the same time, Doughboy is acutely aware of the cycle of violence that ordains his own death by film's end. Though viewers can respond positively to Doughboy's bru-tal shooting of the killer (he cuts him down in a parking lot, then approaches him and shoots the villain in the back while he lies on the ground, defiant to the end, just like any respectable battlefield enemy), Doughboy himself is less than enthusiastic. He illustrates the sense of limits and frustration common for any soldier: the rush of murder is momentary, the day-to-day reality is tedious and unnerv-ing. After he shoots the shooter, Doughboy tells Tre the next morn-ing, "I don't even know how I feel about it man. The shit just goes on and on." A war story for sure. And with that, Doughboy crosses the street, looks back at the camera/Tre, and fades away literally, as a screen title informs us that he dies "two weeks later."

Ice Cube's "authenticating" presence grounds *Boyz*'s interroga-tion of identity as performance. Even as the film's promotional ma-chinery posited Singleton as a genuine homeboy, his description of the project's origins speaks more precisely to processes of imagina-tion and production. *"Boyz* is a good story," he says, "a real story, and they wanted it. It's that simple" (Bates 16). It is and it isn't "that simple." "They" would be a varied group, studio suits and viewers, all apparently responding enthusiastically to this exotic drama of masculine anxiety and resolution.[43] The realness of the story is a question; what's definitely real is product, and marketing campaigns for so-called hood movies (or some hip-hop CDs) are typically predi-cated on a deliberate confusion between real and sensational. Keeping it real means, in some corners, telling an audience what they already know, no matter the source of that knowledge. Conflating gangsta identity and violence, mainstream press coverage of black media and celebrities reveals an anxiety about visibly aggressive black bodies that appears to conform to expectations and so, sell records and tickets.[44] As Tricia Rose puts it, reporting of this kind "is always/already positioned as part of images of black violence and within the larger discourse on the black urban threat" (135).

This larger discourse is good at forgetting. As *Presidents* argues, the black vets who were forgotten and displaced after Vietnam, have every right to be furious, but the right only makes the forgetting harder to take. Anthony spends about twenty minutes in Vietnam in the film (his transition is marked by a nifty dissolve, from his running through Bronx backyards after stealing a last night with his girlfriend Juanita, to his running through a firefight in "Quang Tri Province, 1971"). After a horrific couple of tours on a recon squad (including a scene where he has to kill his own friend, suffering after being castrated in the bush), Anthony returns home pissed off and virtually unemployable (except for a job slicing and dicing in a butcher shop, very appropriately bloody work). Unable to support Juanita and their daughter, with a second child on the way, Anthony desperately plans the robbery of an armored truck, with Juanita's politically schooled (through a group modelled on The Black Panthers) sister, Delilah (N'Bushe Wright), Kirby, Skippy (now a junkie and Agent Orange victim), their demolitions expert buddy Jose (Freddy Rodriguez), and a psychopath they befriended in country, Cleon (Bokeem Woodbine).

The scheme involves their disguising themselves in whiteface, which makes for perhaps the most striking image in a film full of striking images. Facing down the guards, the crew is undone by their tenacity, and the robbery turns ugly and violent (they kill a few guards and a passing policeman, Delilah is killed). Jose, the giddy firebug, loads too much explosive into the mix and blows the truck all over the street; the fiery bills floating to the ground are metaphorically perfect and recall the film's opening credits sequence, which features close-ups of burning bills. As Anthony is carted off to jail at film's end (Cleon is also arrested, Kirby killed, and Skippy overdoses while watching Al Green on television), it's clear that he never had a chance, that he was forgotten and forgot himself. Defined by the "larger discourse," Anthony is a threat that is never quite internal, but close enough to ensure the discourse's repressive tactics. *Boyz,* like *Presidents,* complicates the discourse's formulaic opposition by making visible multiple victims, sources, and frames within conventional masculine codes of loyalty and honor. *Boyz's* and *Presidents'* references to "Vietnam" recover a history of racial conflict that organizes what Michael Rogin calls "the distinctive American political culture" (511). In this distinctive context, the soldiers Furious, Anthony, and Doughboy, are all good at what they do, methodical and thoughtful about their responsibilities. But their skills and experience also put them at a loss in their hoods turned war zones. Obliged and unable to forget their training, they offer possibilities for diverse and, ideally, antinational identities. "To be obliged to forget—in the construction of a national present—is not a question of historical memory; it is the construction of a discourse on society that performs the problematic totalization of the national will" (Bhabha 311).

To "perform" this problem of a unified will is to begin to challenge it and the imagery that sustains it. Resistance to a national will advances another way to conceive identity; if Jake, Luc, or Ron Kovic of *Born on the Fourth of July* is compelled to resist only when confronted by extraordinary betrayal and the loss of a promise made to him (the national narrative of identity and privilege is revealed to be a lie), the route to resistance is much plainer for Anthony, Doughboy, or Furious Styles. The national narrative has never spoken to the post-Vietnam War generation's needs or desires. Doughboy never imagines he has options: every event in his short life informs him that he'll be dead before he's twenty-five, including the murder of his nonbanger brother, Ricky. There's no romantic illusion for him, no escape to a job or the military or college (though Tre does get out). Doughboy/Ice Cube's very existence—as character, persona, celebrity, authentically inauthentic pose—controverts and intervenes in the "larger discourse" even as it verifies the discourse's worst nightmares. Complicating the stereotype of the threatening black male, Doughboy/Ice Cube is desiring, vulnerable, imaginative; he embodies a compelling identity that contradicts the legacy of what legal scholar Patricia Williams has termed "black antiwill." She writes that

> one of the things passed on from slavery, which continues in the oppression of people of color, is a belief structure rooted in a concept of black

(or red or brown) antiwill, the antithetical embodiment of pure will. We live in a society where the closest equivalent of nobility is the display of unremittingly controlled willfulness. To be perceived as unremittingly without will is to be imbued with an almost lethal trait.[45]

Boyz and *Presidents* expose this oppressive "belief structure" as it supports a national identity premised on black subjection and abuse and the fiction of antiwill used to justify it. Furious revises the notion of antiwill in his resistance to official narratives of compliance and "democracy," the "spectacular demonologies" promoted by the Vietnam War era, Reagan-Bush, and now Clinton, administrations.

Furious's lecture to Tre and Ricky on the importance of black enterprise demonstrates his faith in an economic black will and willfulness. Here he proposes yet another battleground. Standing in front of a billboard advertising "Seoul to Seoul Realty," Furious argues that oppression cannot be solved by intraracial violence. However, the sign itself signals ambivalences and appropriations. The use of "Seoul" as a synonym for "soul" confuses black and Korean identities, and even unites them as they share oppressions within and by the dominant culture. Furious cites the economic valence of Korean communal identity, exhorting the boyz to fight the influx of guns and drugs, condoned and supported by existing power structures (in short, keep the neighborhood black) by emulating the Korean landowners' economic militancy (read: capitalism). In accepting yet another culturally ordained opposition, between Asians and blacks, one exploited by U.S. policy-makers following the 1992 uprising, Furious appears to be realistic (at least the neighborhood folks are impressed and convinced by his wisdom).

But the film's resolution is less convincing, leaving Furious out of the frame that Tre and Doughboy fill with such enormous pain and resilience, sharing their brotherhood against the odds that would overwhelm them. For all his wisdom, Furious remains immersed in the apparatus that has conditioned him. It is Doughboy's death that resonates finally, the film's memory of him marked by an ironic recuperation, when a last inscription that reads "Increase the peace" appears under Ice Cube's "How to Survive in South Central." This coda, displaced out of (the film's) time, imagines effective movements and identitites.

NOTES

1. See H. Bruce Franklin's convincing discussion of this image as it has been translated by U.S. media, to demonize the North Vietnamese (*The Deer Hunter* [Michael Cimino 1979]) or glorify Loan (*The Nam* comic book), in "From Realism to Virtual Reality: Images of America's Wars," in *Seeing Through Media: The Persian Gulf War*, eds. Susan Jeffords and Lauren Rabinovitz (New Brunswick, N.J.: Rutgers University Press, 1994), 25–44. What's remarkable about *Universal Soldier*'s revision of the image is that the evil is carried out by tall, blond, Aryan-ish Lundgren, not U.S.-born but acting here as the ultimate U.S. fighting man (certainly he has achieved a more effectively "American" accent than his fellow nonnative English speaker, Van Damme).

2. Michael Rogin, "'Make My Day!' Spectacle as Amnesia in Imperial Politics, The Sequel," in *Cultures of United States Imperialism*, ed. Amy Kaplan and Donald E. Pease (Durham, N.C.: Duke University Press, 1993), 525, 524. Further references will be made parenthetically in the text.

3. The USA Network's edited version of Stone's *Born on the Fourth of July*, usually broadcast on Independence Day, includes this difficult "Fuck you!" scene, but censors these profanities. So, the rhythms of the language, violence, and imagery are considerably altered, as Cruise and Dafoe yell at each other, "Screw you!" Much of the ugliness of the exchange is nevertheless sustained, if in a different form, in part because the actors' mouths don't match the words coming from them; viewers can't help but know the fact that "Fuck you!" is the "real" language, and the censorship becomes its own narrative (based on the question, perhaps, concerning what is at stake, in repressing language, memory, or emotion).

4. Elizabeth Traube, *Dreaming Identities: Class, Gender, and Generation in 1980s Hollywood Movies* (Boulder, Col.: Westview Press, 1993), 40. On the MIA plot(s), see also H. Bruce Franklin, *M.I.A., or Mythmaking in America* (Brooklyn, N.Y.: Hill Books, 1992).

5. As it has been shaped and popularized in numerous vintage-1980s MIA fictions (including *Uncommon Valor* [Ted Kotcheff 1983], *Missing in Action* [Joseph Zito 1984], and *Rambo: First Blood Part 2* [George P. Cosmatos 1985], not to mention Ross Perot, star of his own 1992 presidential campaign, which was partially premised on find-the MIAs rhetoric, and reportedly the model for the hyperconservative financier in *Uncommon Valor*), the term "MIA" refers to a by-now predictable distrust of powers that be, voiced by a spectrum of disenfranchised characters, ranging from conservative to liberal.

6. Yvonne Tasker, *Spectacular Bodies: Gender, Genre, and the Action Cinema* (London: Routledge, 1993). Further references will be made parenthetically in the text.

7. For more on culturally conditioned masculinity and built, muscled, active, and diversely represented bodies, see also Aaron Baker and Todd Boyd, eds., *Out of Bounds: Sports, Media, and the Politics of Identity* (Blooming-

ton: Indiana University Press, 1997); Susan Jeffords, *Hard Bodies: Hollywood Masculinity in the Reagan Era* (New Brunswick, N.J.: Rutgers University Press, 1994); Alan M. Klein, *Little Big Men: Bodybuilding Subculture and Gender Construction* (Albany: State University of New York Press, 1993); Peter Lehman, *Running Scared: Masculinity and the Representation of the Male Body* (Philadelphia: Temple University Press, 1993); Donald M. Lowe, *The Body in Late-Capitalist USA* (Durham, N.C.: Duke University Press, 1995); Pamela L. Moore, ed., *Building Bodies* (New Brunswick, N.J.: Rutgers University Press, 1997); Fred Pfeil, *White Guys: Studies in Postmodern Domination and Difference* (London: Verso, 1995); Robyn Wiegman, *American Anatomies: Theorizing Race and Gender* (Durham, N.C.: Duke University Press, 1995); and Sharon Willis, *High Concept: Race and Gender in Contemporary Hollywood Film* (Durham, N.C.: Duke University Press, 1997).

8. For perceptive, concise accounts of these debates, see, for instance, James William Gibson, *The Perfect War: The War We Couldn't Lose and How We Did* (New York: Vintage Books, 1986); and George C. Herring, *America's Longest War: The United States and Vietnam, 1950–1975*, 2d ed. (New York: Alfred A. Knopf, 1979, 1986). For a somewhat less concise version, see Stanley Karnow, *Vietnam: A History* (New York: Penguin Books, 1984).

9. Scott and Luc's reunion must simultaneously represent and deny the homosocial male couple. As soon as it draws the unisols' rigid identity parameters, the film goes on to pathologize and undermine them, individually and in relation to one another. Luc and Scott go through the standard motions of homoerotic and phobic penetrations (using state-of-the-art weapons, of course). The erotic charge of their encounters, however mediated by Ronnie's (Ally Walker) romantic alliance with Luc, is both passionate and harrowing. Their fights are filmed so that they appear intimate and specific, with the requisite thrusting and grunting.

10. The movie's initial excess (killing off the protagonists) puts a darkly comic spin on the action genre's ritually violent openings: the credits "Jean-Claude Van Damme" and "Dolph Lundgren" appear over their dead faces as they're zipped up in the body bags. Their antagonism then becomes a matter of good and bad outlines. As Luc's "original," nice boy identity reemerges during the film, he loses the trappings of his mechanical, reconstituted "self," the video-camera eye piece, robotic glare, and Desert-Stormish uniform (he strips naked at several points in the film, in efforts to "cool down" his fast-idling system, offering several looks at his well-muscled, hard ass). In contrast, Scott's self-recovery reinforces his supermilitarism, with the addition of a second grisly necklace, this time made of the ears of U.S. authorities and civilians who get in his way, whom he considers "traitors." As the film grinds into high-action gear, its overlay of identities onto indefatigable, enhanced bodies leads to a narrative struggle between the vets' unisols' wasted selves (they're programmed to kill) and signs of national and social "progress" (Luc reads on a cigarette pack that "smoking is hazardous," and makes it his mission to stop Ronnie from smoking).

11. And Scott, ironically, is right to want to kill everyone around him, for as Rambo has already told us in *First Blood*, "There are no friendly civilians."

12. Nirvana, "Come as you are," *Nevermind* (Geffen, 1991). The hook in Nirvana's song refers ironically to romantic notions of memory as a site for secured identity. The verse lyrics collapse "friend" and "enemy" in the same addressee, and "come as you are" emphasizes both the shifts in and the ever presentness of identity.

13. One process of forgetting is circumscribed by the film's own "forgetableness," say, its brief theatrical run. This movie will not, we might imagine, resonate deeply in a broad cultural consciousness, in the ways that *Rambo* and *Platoon* continue to do.

14. Lawrence Grossberg, *We Gotta Get Out of this Place: Popular Conservatism and Postmodern Culture* (New York: Routledge, 1991), 224. Further references will be made parenthetically in the text.

15. Dana Polan, "Postmodernism and Cultural Analysis Today," in *Postmodernism and Its Discontents: Theories, Practices*, ed. E. Ann Kaplan (London: Verso, 1988), 53. Polan also describes the bifurcation of "everyday life" and academia that is generated by "postmodernist discourse," as such discourse "becomes a way for the academic to insist again on the rich difficulty of difficult art," thus reasserting a familiar and conservative intellectual hierarchy (50).

16. Linda Dittmar and Gene Michaud, "America's Vietnam War Films: Marching Toward Denial," in *From Hanoi to Hollywood: The Vietnam War in American Film*, ed. Linda Dittmar and Gene Michaud (New Brunswick, N.J.: Rutgers University Press, 1990), 9.

17. Rick Berg and John Carlos Rowe, "The Vietnam War and American Memory," in *The Vietnam War and American Culture*, ed. Rick Berg and John Carlos Rowe (New York: Columbia University Press, 1991). Further references will be made parenthetically in the text.

18. Body Count, "Body Count Anthem," *Body Count* (New York: Sire Records, 1992).

19. Examining time and narrative, Baastian C. Van Fraasen writes that "two events are incompatible only if, first, incompatible events are involved, but second, these incompatibles inhere in the same subject. This second point requires a relation between these two events—genidentity, the relation of involving the same enduring subject—which is by no means derivative from merely qualitative characteristics." "Time in Physical and Narrative Structure," in *Chronotypes: The Construction of Time*, eds. John Bender and David E. Wellbery (Stanford, Calif.: Stanford University Press, 1991), 30.

20. Judith Halberstam, "Imagined Violence/Queer Violence: Representation, Rage, and Resistance," *Social Text* 37 (1993): 189.

21. The "Cop Killer" controversy blew up when enjoined by vocal Hollywood conservative Charlton Heston (presently, in 1998, the National Rifle Association president), who claimed Ice T was inciting violence against the police, rather than reporting the rage felt by disenfranchised, urban, black and Latino youths who are routinely harassed by the police. Ice T suggested that performative violence need not be confused with actual violence, using Schwarzenegger as his exhibit A. See also Tricia Rose's discussion of the controversy's relationship to the LA uprising, in her *Black Noise: Rap Music and*

Black Culture in Contemporary America (Hanover, N.H.: Wesleyan University Press, 1994).

22. Van Damme is publicly fine with his gay audience (as he understands them as stereotypes). See for instance, his interview with Stephen Rebello: "It doesn't disturb me that I have gay fans. Maybe they like me because gay people love beauty in general. They have a high level of taste." "The Eight Million Dollar Man," *Movieline*, August 1994, 82.

23. Fred Pfeil, "From Pillar to Postmodern: Race, Class, and Gender in the Male Rampage Film," *Socialist Review*, Special Issue: *Media as Activism* 23, no. 2 (1993): 146.

24. Susan Jeffords, *Hard Bodies*, 24.

25. In part this deconstruction of hard-bodied identity reflects the fallout of Reagan Era economic and social policies, and the disintegration of progressive U.S. history (for example, the much-rehearsed narrative of Generation X's downward mobility).

26. While Scott serves as the unredeemable, willfully misremembering perfect product of military culture—much like Sean Penn's Sergeant Meserve in *Casualties of War* (Brian DePalma 1991) or Adam Baldwin's Animal Mother in *Full Metal Jacket*—Luc represents that culture's volatile imperfection, unable to remember what happened.

27. Rubin's films—*Ghost*, directed by Jerry Zucker, and *My Life*, which Rubin directed—are particularly adept at portraying pathos through dead and dying characters. Investigating the relationships between time, identity, and mortality, they both take intensely sentimental routes, ostensibly as ways to consider the limitations and possibilities in the lives of male protagonists (Patrick Swayze and Michael Keaton, respectively). But both films insist on the maudlin, very visibly teary burdens borne by the female partners (Demi Moore and Nicole Kidman). Both women end up doing severe (and typically "female") penance for their partners' inabilities to comprehend the emotional work of relationships over time, until it's "too late" (Swayze is murdered and comes back as a ghost to avenge his death and protect Moore from seduction by his killer; Keaton learns that he's dying of a dread disease but makes his memory/life into a series of videotapes for the couple's unborn child). I'd add, in the context of the racism exhibited in *Jacob's Ladder*, that both of these films deploy racial stereotypes as supporting characters. Swayze returns to Moore through the medium of Whoopi Goldberg (who won a Supporting Actress Academy Award for her performance; shades of Hattie McDaniel in *Gone With the Wind*, or Cuba Gooding Jr. in *Jerry Maguire*, also winners for playing emotional mentors to stiff white folks). And Keaton comes to understand his "pain" and to reach out to his long-suffering wife, following the holistic ministrations of Dr. Haing S. Ngor.

28. Rubin's published screenplay reads at this point, "It is surprising that he's wearing a mailman's uniform. He doesn't look like one." Bruce Joel Rubin, *Jacob's Ladder* (New York: Applause Books, 1992), 2.

29. Jake's amorphously situated body is related to the "body without organs," as described by Gilles Deleuze and Felix Guatarri in *A Thousand Plateaus: Capitalism and Schizophrenia*, trans. Brian Massumi (Minneapo-

lis: University of Minnesota Press, 1987). Scott Bukatman elaborates, writing that the singular Body Without Organs "is the state in which we aspire to dissolve the body and regain the world," in surfaces and desires, certainly an aspiration that might pertain to Jake, so overrun by bodies with no borders. *Terminal Identity: The Virtual Subject in Postmodern Science Fiction* (Durham N.C.: Duke University Press, 1992), 328.

30. When Lieutenant Ellen Ripley (Sigourney Weaver), in *Alien³* (David Fincher 1992) tells a startled fellow prisoner that the monster is "in the basement," he tries to set her straight. "This whole place is a basement," he sneers. But Ripley understands the way that her movie is working: "It's a metaphor," she assures him, leading him out of the frame.

31. Cornelius Castoriadis, "Time and Creation," in *Chronotypes*, 63.

32. Timothy Corrigan, *A Cinema Without Walls: Movies and Culture After Vietnam* (New Brunswick, N.J.: Rutgers University Press, 1991), 29.

33. Ruth Wilson Gilmore, "Public Enemies and Private Intellectuals: Apartheid USA," *Race & Class*, Special Issue: *Black America: The Street and the Campus* 35, no. 1 (July-September 1993): 74.

34. Homi K. Bhabha, "DissemiNation: Time, Narrative, and the Margins of the Modern Nation," in *Nation and Narration*, ed. idem (London: Routledge, 1990), 310.

35. Karen Grigsby Bates, "They've Gotta Have Us: Hollywood's Black Directors," *New York Times Magazine* (14 July 1992): 40. Further references will be made parenthetically in the text.

36. Manthia Diawara, "Black American Cinema: The New Realism," in *Black American Cinema*, ed. Manthia Diawara (New York: Routledge, 1993), 25.

37. Henry Louis Gates Jr., "The Master's Pieces: On Canon Formation and the African American Tradition," in *Loose Canons: Notes on the Culture Wars* (New York: Oxford University Press, 1993), 36. Further references will be made parenthetically in the text.

38. Tre's story, told to his father, about a sexual encounter with a local girl, is relevant here. The film shows the story, with Tre's voice-over, but nothing in the rest of the film supports its truthfulness. The standard realism of the representation is recontextualized by other events.

39. June Jordan, "Beyond *Apocalypse Now* (1980)," in *Civil Wars* (Boston: Beacon Press, 1981), 173–74.

40. Mike Davis, *City of Quartz: Evacuating the Future in Los Angeles* (New York: Vintage Books, 1992), 223.

41. Ice Cube, an LA hardcore gangsta rapper, was initially with NWA, whose "Fuck Tha Police," off *Straight Outta Compton* (Priority Records 1988) set some parameters for socially conscious angry rap, West Coast style. Cube's solo records, such as *AmeriKKKa's Most Wanted* (Priority 1990), *The Predator* (Priority 1990), and *Lethal Injection* (Priority 1993), situated him as a regional storyteller, an authentic, experienced voice from South Central, defying an oppressive state. He has since gone on to appear in mainstream movies like *Anaconda* (Luis Losa 1997) and wrote and directed his first feature, *The Players Club*, in 1998.

42. bell hooks, "Reconstructing Black Masculinity," in *Black Looks: Race and Representation* (Boston: South End Press, 1998), 102.

43. For discussions of the film's sexism, see Lisa Kennedy, "The Body in Question," and Michele Wallace, "*Boyz N the Hood* and *Jungle Fever*," both in *Black Popular Culture*, ed. Gina Dent (Seattle, Wash.: Bay Press, 1993). Both writers point out the stereotypical images of women, as "hos," mothers, junkies, and good girls, in recent films by young black men. Kennedy writes, for example, "(Word to the brother: I will not have some twenty-three-year-old manchild in Lala land telling me I must forego a career to be a good mother, that it's my responsibility to the embattled black family, just because he made a moving film)" (110).

44. See, for instance, the 2 November 1993 *Newsweek* cover story, some time before Tupac and Biggie's murders, featuring Snoop, then just arrested on murder charges (which he went on to beat). The headline reads, "When is rap 2 violent?" Tom Morgenthal's sidebar story, inside, "The New Frontier for Civil Rights," suggests that "rap is a wake-up call for the crisis of black-on-black violence"; the story opens with this invocation: "This is a battle for hearts and minds, just as in Vietnam. And we, who think of ourselves as the good guys, are losing or have already lost" (65). Young black urban youth, it would appear, have become so other that they're comparable to the Vietnamese whom the U.S. could never get their minds around.

45. Patricia J. Williams, *The Alchemy of Race and Rights: Diary of a Law Professor* (Cambridge, Mass.: Harvard University Press, 1991), 219.

TWO

TRACERS

4

"THIS MOVIE IS A THING OF MINE":
HOMEOPATHIC POSTMODERNISM IN
MICHAEL HERR'S *DISPATCHES*

Brady Harrison

Is that you, John Wayne? Is this me?

           Gustav Hasford, *The Short-Timers*

You know he heard the drums of war when the past
was a closing door.

           The Clash, "Sean Flynn"

Dispatches has become, among scholars, a touchstone for postmodern writing. From all the works he could choose as an exemplum of such writing, for example, David Herman sets Michael Herr's book against Virginia Woolf's *Orlando* as a means to distinguish between modern and postmodern writing.[1] Philip Beidler, in *Re-Writing America: Vietnam Authors in Their Generation*, characterizes *Dispatches* as a "postmodern triumph of journalism and art."[2] Fredric Jameson similarly places it in elite postmodern company with E. L. Doctorow's *Ragtime* and William Gibson's *Neuromancer*, and describes Herr's account as a "great book on the experience of Vietnam."[3] I concur with their assessment of the text's importance,[4] and I am interested here in further exploring the *type* of postmodernism Herr practices. He engages in a homeopathic postmodernism; in *Dispatches*, he turns the simulations of the postmodern age against themselves.

Herr concerns himself with screens and simulacra; he asks us to see *Dispatches* as a film instead of a book. Attuned to Hollywood's constructed images of battle and to the countless reels of combat footage broadcast throughout America during the war, *Dispatches* asks that the *reader,* a seasoned viewer of cinema and television screens, construct a motion picture screen to capture Herr's projections of Vietnam. In the postmodern culture of simulations, Herr creates his own remarkable simulacra to push through the glut of media images, to establish hyperimages that will survive the eye and mind-numbing assault of televised carnage. In order to describe his homeopathic form of postmodernism, I read *Dispatches* against the work of two leading theorists of simulations, Fredric Jameson and Jean Baudrillard: in contrast to their assertions that simulacra nullify affect and efface historicity, Herr invests his simulacra with political force and generates his striking simulations to reconnect us to the war's "secret history," the *death* obfuscated under Orwellian press conferences, "facts," and Hollywood simulations. Casting his colleague Sean Flynn as his paradigmatic postmodern image, a "subjectivity" that is already overconstructed by Hollywood, Herr valorizes simulacra as a means to reclaim subjectivity and as a way to achieve historical depth.

Baudrillard and Jameson, of course, hold different positions on simulacra and historicity. In "Forget Baudrillard," Baudrillard argues that "history has stopped meaning, referring to anything—whether you call it social space or the real. We have passed into a kind of hyperreal where things are being replayed *ad infinitum*."[5] Today, saturated with screens, "models" and diverse binary codes (DNA, question/answer, two-party politics), we exist in a space where the "real" has been reproduced, digitized, and simulated into extinction. For Baudrillard, postmodernism produces ennui, a sense of political paralysis, "irreversible coma" ("Forget," 68).

Jameson, offering a less nihilistic view of the postmodern, argues that our entry into "a whole new culture of the image or the simulacrum" has induced a "weakening of historicity, both in our relationship to public History and in new forms of our private temporality. . . ." (*Postmodernism,* 6). At the extreme of this paradigm, we lose historical depth and know only "pop history," or "our ideas and stereotypes about the past" (*Postmodernism,* 25). Characterized by "pastiche" and "historicism, namely the random cannibalization of all styles of the past" (*Postmodernism,* 18), the "Third Machine Age" becomes increasingly dominated by simulacra, the slow death of history and the "real." Nonetheless, though he views postmodernism as "the purest form of capital yet to have emerged, a prodigious expansion of capital into hitherto uncommodified areas" (*Postmodernism*, 36), Jameson rejects a wholly pessimistic view of the culture of simulacra:

> In a well-known passage Marx powerfully urges us to do the impossible, namely to think [the historical development of capitalism] positively *and* negatively all at once; to achieve in other words, a type of thinking that would be capable of grasping the demonstrably baleful features of capitalism along with its extraordinary and liberating dynamism simultaneously within a single thought, and without attenuating any of the force of either judgement. (*Postmodernism*, 47)

Jameson's dialectical assessment of the postmodern seems to me to be most in the spirit of Herr's critical yet positive use of simulations. Generating images of Vietnam that seize upon and then distort contemporary images of the war, Herr calls into being the Baudrillardan "hyperreal," a postmodernist screen projected with simulations rather than representations.

In order to establish what I mean by postmodernist screen—in order, in other words, to delineate the type of surface, not space, that Herr works on and not in—I need to argue with Jameson's sense of "hyperspace" in *Dispatches*. To do so, it's worthwhile to quote some of the same excerpt from Herr that Jameson focuses on in *Postmodernism, or, The Cultural Logic of Late Capitalism:*

> Some of us moved around the war like crazy people until we couldn't see which way the run was even taking us anymore, only the war all over its surface with occasional, unexpected penetration. As long as we could have the choppers like taxis it took real exhaustion or depression near shock or a dozen pipes of opium to keep us even apparently quiet, we'd still be running around inside our skins like something was after us, ha, ha, La Vida Loca.
>
> In the months after I got back the hundreds of helicopters I'd flown in began to draw together until they'd formed a collective meta-chopper, and in my mind it was the sexiest thing going; saver-destroyer, provider-waster, right hand-left hand, nimble, fluent, canny and human; hot steel, grease, jungle-saturated canvas webbing, sweat cooling and warming up again, cassette rock and roll in one ear and door-gun fire in the other, fuel, heat, vitality and death, death itself, hardly an intruder.[6]

Jameson, pointing to the "extraordinary linguistic innovations" (44) in this passage, argues that Herr captures American technomachinery *"in motion"* through a "hyperspace" that transcends "the capacities of the individual human body to locate itself, to organize its immediate surroundings perceptually, and cognitively to map its position in a mappable external world" (44). Where I would like to differ with Jameson, however, is to suggest that the "new machine" (45) is not a machine but a monstrous cyborg, and also to suggest that the chopper is not a "real" chopper occupying three dimensional space, but a simulacrum, an image "hundreds" of times removed from any one referent.

Herr's "creature" transmogrifies "real" choppers with wired-in crews and wired-on gunners into a grotesque network of circuits and flesh pulsating with an orgasmic fury of gunfire and rock and roll. The cyborg, a fusion of flesh and technology, takes on simultaneously a (mock-)erotic and (mock-)biblical status as a giver and taker of life (an ironic version of Baudrillard's theory of binaries) and therefore exerts little claim on the "real." Representation—the "natural" link between the referent and the sign—gives way to distortion, and in Baudrillardan terms, the meta-chopper is a second-order simulation: "it masks and perverts a basic reality."[7] Further, the cybernetic organism renders moot the argument that hyperspace disrupts the body's ability to locate itself since the "creature" already refuses to distinguish the body from the machine. Herr's cyborg belongs less to the register of fact than to that of science fiction (though he abandons this register almost as soon as he employs it in another postmodern disruption of narrative forms), and therefore the hyperspace of the "real" becomes a different "hypersurface" of the fictional.

The meta-chopper passage not only establishes Herr's interest in manipulating the "real,"[8] it also signifies early on in *Dispatches* his privileging of filmic images. Recalling the helicopters that skimmed him over the "surface" of the war, he synthesizes the meta-chopper from "hundreds" of mental pictures: each image maps itself over the last until what he describes exists only as a complex, bristling cyborg-imago. This collective image cannot be reconstructed into the "real," but alters continually like a kaleidoscope pattern—the image will always be an image, always be a simulation. If the authentic helicopters collapse into an image, then the terrain and space around it likewise lose "real" depth, becoming two dimensional with the illusion of three dimensions. As media(ted) subjectivities, we often see images as if they were photographs or, if they move, as motion pictures. There can be no movement through hyperspace, but only across the proper surface for images: a screen. As Herr remarks, "this movie is a thing of mine" (222), and in this context we can only understand the cyborg as a projected motion picture or video image.

Herr's impulse to imagize—to transform the "real" into screen images—can be seen in another spin he gives to the helicopter-as-simulation. Recalling that "loose policy" was to shoot anyone who ran from a gunship, Herr quotes a pilot on "air sports": "Nothing finer, you're up there at two thousand, you're God, just open up the flexies and watch it pee, nail those slime to the paddy wall, nothing finer. . . ." (65). Picking up on the technological glee and phallus worship in the pilot's account, Herr converts "real" firepower into a cinematic simulation: "Nothing like it ever, when we caught a bunch of them out in the open and close together, we really ripped it then, volatile piss-off, crazed expenditure, Godzilla never drew that kind of fire" (65). The reference to the famous Monster-that-Stomped-Tokyo (and, more recently, New York) recasts the attack into a brief motion picture, and the pilot's already glamorized representation of combat transforms into a B movie with overdone special effects. Herr's language captures some of the fluidity of film and his simulation criticizes the brutal, senseless power of American technology: Godzilla, an icon of the atomic bomb, signifies death on a massive scale and the ironic monster reference reminds us that what the pilot's really talking about is killing people.

The screen, as Baudrillard argues, signals a move from the real to the hyperreal. The real exists apart from us, at a distance, a little unknown but still imaginable. As Herr points out, Vietnam in 1963 barely existed for many comfortable, secure Americans: "a dead American in the jungle was an event, a grim thrilling novelty. It was spook-war then, adventure; not exactly soldiers, not even advisors yet, but Irregulars. . . ." (52). For American civilians, Vietnam could be forgotten or fantasized about as if it were a space like someone else's house at night. We know the real from experience without seeing it too closely, without interacting with it. By the time Herr went on assignment in 1967, "Vietnam was perceived as a living-room war by those of us who used to watch the instant replay on television."[9] Once captured on film and beamed all over the United States, the war became obscene, in Baudrillard's sense, too close: "Obscenity begins when there is no more spectacle . . . no more illusions, when everything becomes immediately transparent, visible, exposed in the raw and inexorable light of information and communication."[10] We lose all distance and the violence of the war projects from the screen into the eyes, now known, no longer imaginable, but in our faces at 6:00 P.M. The "over-proximity" of Vietnam in America magnifies, clarifies, and transforms the real into the hyperreal. On the one hand, we could argue that the death rolls and images of combat helped fuel the antiwar movement in the U.S. On the other hand, the war trudged on for over a decade, with the images pouring out over America every evening. The war became one of the longest running shows on television.

The hyperreal, through the sheer repetition of images "more-visible-than-visible" (*Ecstasy*, 22), loses meaning, induces media glut and numbness. The daily combat footage makes the images transparent, as if nothing or no one were there to see. Moreover, the grunts on the television screen are no more "real" than the grunts in any Hollywood movie: habituated to screens as (primarily) the surface of the fabricated, the medium itself impedes affect, an impassioned response to overexposed violence. As Jameson remarks, in a culture of "gleaming" surfaces, "emotional reaction to the world disappears."[11] Just as important, an emotional reaction to the flow of images may not be possible. The news reels, decontextualized, edited, fragmentary, narrated, contain information that cannot be processed, show events that we fear, repress, don't know how to understand. Even as an eyewitness, Herr recalls that "the problem was that you didn't always know what you were seeing until later, maybe years later, that a lot of it never made it in at all, it just stayed stored there in your eyes" (20). Against the overwhelming and dulling effusion of violent simulacra, he looks for a way to make what is seen meaningful.

By incorporating filmic images as part of his narrative strategy, he attacks, even as he inscribes them, the very communication processes of the screen media that render violent images, for some, empty and meaningless. But Herr does not assert the primacy of representations of the real as a means to reconnect subjects to their emotions. In a culture suffused with cinematic codes and deluged with information systems and technologies, the real will not return. Against the proliferation of desensitizing simulacra, Herr creates more potent and memorable simulations like the cyborg. Further, as in the case of the meta-chopper, Herr parodies his image even as he constructs it by making it an opiated sexual fantasy: in this way, he problematizes the codes that go into the creation of any image, any process of representation or simulation.

David Herman, in his reading of *Orlando* and *Dispatches*, also suggests that Herr problematizes the making of representations, and this leads him to a fascinating, if different take on Herr's postmodernism. As Herman argues, in "*Dispatches*, there is no question of perpetually adjusting representations to reality. There is merely the interminable analysis of representation itself" ("Modernism," 183). This analysis leads Herr to create a postmodern text where "representation enjoys an unmediated relationship with reality" (186): "if, for modernism, utopian hopes are spawned by the conflict between word and thing, postmodernism bases the idea of Utopia on a strange new materiality resident in words themselves" (177). As I read Herr, the "real" cannot be retrieved; we exist in the hyperreal. What's more, he places his faith not in a "materiality resident in words," but rather in language-based simulations, projections that lack materiality but that nonetheless connect us, as I shall explore in more depth below, to truths about the war. If I don't accept, as a matter of theoretical consideration, that any form of "representation" stands in a one-to-one relationship with any form of lived experience, I nonetheless agree with the spirit of one of Herman's conclusions. Following Jean-François Lyotard's formulations on dissent in *The Postmodern Condition*, he asserts that Herr's postmodernism calls for (and offers) "local acts of responsible representation" (186). Herr presents his work in opposition to the war—and to the media's and U.S. government's renderings of the war—and seeks a new mode of writing to tell his readers about Vietnam.

The presence of the screen, Herr's synthesis of the filmic with the journalistic, signifies the creation of a new postmodernist narrative form, a form capable of communicating the death and chaos of Vietnam.[12] Jameson sees some of this at work in *Dispatches:* "This first terrible postmodernist war cannot be told in any of the traditional paradigms of the war novel or movie—indeed the breakdown of all previous narrative paradigms is, along with the breakdown of any shared language through which a veteran might convey such experience, among the principle subjects of the book and may be said to open up the place of a whole new reflexivity" (*Postmodernism*, 44–45). Jameson does not elaborate on his reading of the text, but Herr's book does indeed look back upon (and through) earlier narrative forms and its own narrative strategies. From here, I consider how the theoretical problems of screens and simulacra impact upon individual subjectivity in *Dispatches;* I turn, in other words, to one of the primary targets of Herr's narrativity: the "John Wayne" metanarrative.

In Baudrillard's pataphysical "science fiction,"[13] the presence of simulacra signals the death of subjectivity; while we can reject the triumph of the object over the subject as premature and totalizing, we can say that the presence of simulacra signals the fluid, partial objectification and commodification of the subject. Although many factors and forces construct subjectivities, the gaze of the "viewer" at the "film" initiates one of the most profound mediations between subject and object precisely because simulations seem so invitingly "real": the hypnotic allure of motion pictures compels the subject— as Woody Allen playfully suggests, in *The Purple Rose of Cairo,* when Tom Baxter fulfills Cecilia's desire and "steps" from the "screen" into the "theater" and she then returns with him to the "screen"[14]— to identify with the object. This willing objectification, in the postmodern, entangles the increasingly decentered subject in an always expanding repertoire of cinematic narrative codes, images, scenes, gestures, and fragments of dialogue that intervene in cognition, perception, and behavior. The subject becomes like the object. Simulations, then, function as supplements to and substitutes for knowledge.

In the case of Vietnam, the objectification of the subject even impedes the acquisition of knowledge since Hollywood action films supply the subject with codes and perceptions for violent situations she or he has never or rarely experienced. As Herr remarks, "A lot of things had to be unlearned before you could learn anything at all, and even after you knew better you couldn't avoid the ways in which things got mixed, the war itself with those parts of the war that were just like the movies . . . just like all that combat footage from television" (226). Given the profound lack of political, cultural, linguistic, and geographical knowledge on the part of most Americans about Vietnam, the matrix of simulacra pre-inscribes ways of thinking and acting that deflect or mediate learning. Moreover, the problem for Herr is that American film images—mass produced in Hollywood— are often violent, jingoistic, and racist. As Jameson remarks, "this whole global, yet American, postmodern culture is the internal and superstructural expression of a whole new wave of American military and economic domination throughout the world. . . ." (*Postmod-*

ernism, 5). Alert to the potential violence of simulacra, Herr criticizes the media saturation that inhibits knowledge and contributes to American hatred, violence, and death.

Herr's share in the writing of the screenplay for *Full Metal Jacket*—his transition to Hollywood is, after all, a natural, if ironic one[15]—leads him, I think, to overestimate the dramatic appeal of Gustav Hasford's *The Short-Timers:* "I knew I was reading an amazing writer. He was telling a truth about war that was so secret, so hidden, that I could barely stand it."[16] Nonetheless, the riddle that Hasford's "Cowboy" poses—one of the epigraphs to this essay—brilliantly expresses the hold of John Wayne on the imagination and behavior of American soldiers in Vietnam. Some grunts, once in uniform, emulate the most powerful image of a soldier in the culture and sometimes cannot distinguish themselves from the heroes they want to be. Herr concurs:

> I keep thinking about all the kids who get wiped out by seventeen years of war movies before coming to Vietnam to get wiped out for good. You don't know what a media freak is until you've seen the way a few of those grunts would run around during a fight when they knew that there was a television crew nearby; they were actually making war movies in their heads, doing little guts-and-glory Leatherneck tap dances under fire, getting their pimples shot off for the networks. (225)

Transposing their faces to scenes from the movies, the grunts act out power fantasies: they see themselves as John Wayne wiping out "the Indians/the Gooks," risking their lives for the camera.[17] Larry Heinemann, attesting to the centrality of Hollywood in Vietnam, includes a reference to the star of *The Green Berets* in the "Glossary" to his novel, *Close Quarters:* "Wayne, John—Movie actor; nickname for anyone who acted foolishly macho brave. Always derogatory."[18] (This claim contradicts Herr's observation, but we cannot totalize the war experience; at least some grunts saw the danger of "John Wayne.") The John-Wayne-Grunt, modeled after a simulation ("the Duke") of a simulation ("John Wayne") of an obscure reality (Marion Morrison), is a perfect simulacrum: an image that "bears no relation to any reality whatever" (*Simulations,* 11).

Loren Baritz sums up the influence of film images on ways of understanding the lived experience of combat:

> It is astonishing how often American GIs in Vietnam approvingly
> referred to John Wayne, not as a movie star, but as a model and a stan-
> dard. . . . Nineteen-year-old Americans, brought up on World War II mov-
> ies and westerns, walking through the jungle, armed to the teeth, search-
> ing for an invisible enemy who knew the wilderness better than they
> did, could hardly miss these connections. One after another said, at
> some point, something like, "Hey, this is just like a movie."[19]

In the culture of the war, the "real" imitates simulacra. The narrative
codes of action films merge with the codes for interpreting lived experience, thereby breaking down the boundaries between the "real"
and the imaginary. Waiting at a battalion aid station for a medevac,
a marine remarks, "I hate this movie" (*Dispatches*, 203). While the
marine ironically juxtaposes his own suffering with the simulated
violence of films, Herr recognizes the profound media acculturation
that makes such a remark possible and he seizes the idea, asking
rhetorically: "Why not?" (203). As he argues:

> Even the correspondents had seen too many movies, stayed too long in
> Television City, years of media glut had made certain connections diffi-
> cult. The first few times that I got fired at or saw combat deaths, nothing
> really happened, all the responses got locked in my head. It was the same
> familiar violence, only moved over to another medium; some kind of
> jungle play with giant helicopters and fantastic special effects, actors
> lying out there in canvas body bags waiting for the scene to end so they
> could get up again and walk it off. (225–26)

The projected image inscribes itself, as Foucault would say, in "the
nervous system, the temperament,"[20] mediating the individual's understanding of her or his own experience, constructing subjectivity.
The power of simulation engraves itself in bodies and memories, and
the myth of the hero defeating the enemy/the oppressor projects
back off the screen and into the "real."

The rhetoric (one we are all now familiar with, so one which I
will be brief about) of this police/soldier-hero epic finds its concrete
political expression in the Vietnam era in John Kennedy's insistence
that Americans "pay any price, bear any burden, meet any hardship,
support any friend, oppose any foe to assure the survival and the success of liberty." As Philip Caputo remarks in *A Rumor of War*, many
Americans bought into this rhetoric: "War is always attractive to

young men who know nothing about it, but we had also been seduced into John Kennedy's challenge 'to ask what you can do for your country' and by the missionary idealism he had awakened in us."[21] Just as Kennedy's speeches sought to legitimate American intervention, John Wayne movies performed the imaginative equivalent in the popular consciousness, continually reinforcing the metanarrative of the hero winning freedom for the "oppressed." As Caputo suggests, this American epic claims its legitimacy from post-World War II technopower: "America seemed omnipotent then: the country could still claim it had never lost a war, and we believed we were ordained to play cop to the Communists' robber and spread our own political faith around the world" (xiv). While Herr picks up on a similar cultural belief—"There is a point of view that says that the United States got involved in the Vietnam War, commitments and interests aside, simply because we thought it would be easy" (101)— the problem for him (and for Jameson and Baudrillard) becomes that this simulation-enhanced metanarrative confuses, constructs, and simulates subjectivity and historicity.

Saturated by doublespeak press conferences, "facts," and "Vietnam stories," Herr's new narrativity develops from the realization that "conventional journalism could no more reveal this war than conventional firepower could win it, all it could do was take the most profound event of the American decade and turn it into a communications pudding, taking its most obvious, undeniable history and making it into a secret history" (234–35). Herr's move to capture the freaky-spooky, otherside-of-the-worldness of the war is to record as if on film, but in words, an eyewitness-reporter account, to present junkiedom Vietnam as a wired documentary of grotesque and bizarre images that will survive the assault of one more headline or another one-minute reel on the evening news. He's after the *meta-image,* a chilling simulacrum to emerge from all other words, photojournalism, and conventional television: "in the back of every column of print you read about Vietnam there was a dripping, laughing death-face; it hid there in the newspapers and magazines and held to your television screen for hours after the set was turned off for the night, an after-image that simply wanted to tell you at last what somehow had not been told" (235). Herr, seizing the metaphor of the screen, wants the death face to be the one filmic image we know and remember about the war. He wants his simulations "to report meaningfully about death, which of course was really what [the war] was all about"

(231). Conscious of the negative power of simulacra, Herr seeks through his simulacrum to reconnect us to history, the overwhelming and abiding truth about Vietnam: death. Just as important, Herr's eerie image of the mocking, bleeding skull evokes an emotional response; the simulation seeks to reconnect us to our feelings in the face of perpetual violence and seeks to tell us the meaning of all the other simulacra of the war.

As part of the narrative strategy of his new form, Herr blurs the distinctions between his life as a freelancer for *Esquire* and his movie-material role as a "war correspondent." The malevolence of the jungle, the spookiness of the highlands, the ghostlike ability of the NVA to vanish after a battle, and the stoicism of the Vietnamese peasants in the midst of violence and cruelty all contribute to the disruption of Herr's sense of self: "Talk about impersonating an identity, about locking into a role, about irony: I went to cover the war and the war covered me. . . ." (20). Surrounded by the destabilizing intensity of Vietnam, Herr parodically sees himself as a simulation, as a character in a film narrative:

> The war made a place for you that was all yours. Finding it was like listening to esoteric music, you didn't hear it in any essential way through all the repetitions until your own breath had entered it and become another instrument, and by then it wasn't just music anymore, it was experience. Life-as-movie, war-as-(war)movie, war-as-life; a complete process if you got to complete it, a distinct path to travel, but dark and hard. (68)

While Herr takes seriously the hyperreality of war, the proximity and absolute clarity of death, he also lampoons the "haunting romance" of his job as one of "Those Crazy Guys Who Cover The War": "In any other war they would have made movies about us too, *Dateline: Hell!, Dispatch from Dong Ha. . . .*" (202). Herr oscillates between the morbid and the ironic to parody the effects of media saturation on subjectivity: where John Wayne projects off the screen into the consciousness of the grunts, Herr offers us an ironic alternative to undermine the hold of simulacra on Americans. Herr pushes his text-as-film narrativity to its greatest degree in "Colleagues."

By converting photojournalists like Dana Stone and Tim Page into cinematic simulations of themselves, Herr problematizes the status of journalists as recorders of reality: "we have all been com-

pelled to make our own movies, as many movies as there are correspondents, and this one is mine" (202). "Colleagues" opens with a
simulation of a simulation, a brief clip from the (clichéd) reporter-
at-the-front movie genre,[22] that ironically positions Herr and his
friends as conscientious, courageous men getting "the story" to "the
world." Herr casts his colleagues in this manner in order to offer
parodically an antithetical movie hero to John Wayne. The juxta-
position, at the beginning of this paper, of quotes from Hasford and
the Clash set in opposition to the gun-toting, macho hero, a camera-
toting "connoisseur" of war: Sean Flynn.[23] In Herr's life-as-movie,
Flynn is a perfect simulation of a simulation of a simulation: "Sean
could look more incredibly beautiful than even his father, Errol,
had thirty years before as Captain Blood. . . ." (6). A lead actor in Italian movies himself, Flynn exists already as a film image; and even
the grunts, without knowing him, respond to his starlike charisma:
"Flynn was special. We all had our movie-fed war fantasies, the
Marines too, and it could be totally disorienting to have this out-
rageously glamorous figure intrude on them, really unhinging, like
looking up to see that you've been sharing a slit trench with John
Wayne. . . ." (209).

Herr, incorporating the exaggerated superlatives of tabloid journalism, parodies the falseness of the grunts' adoration of John Wayne
since Flynn actually hides in trenches while "the Duke" jumps into
and out of holes on the set. Further, in contrast to John Wayne's ethic
of wiping out the "Cong" in *The Green Berets*, Flynn isn't into work
at all: "I have pictures of Flynn but none by him, he was in so deep
he hardly bothered to take them after a while" (273). As a dope-
smoking star of the subculture of reporters, Flynn parodies his media
image by refusing to turn his camera on the grunts: he won't turn
them into simulations. Further, he subverts the image of the hero-
as-leader in the fight for liberty by refusing to "shoot" with either a
camera or a gun. Flynn seems not to have any "politics" other than
riding through Southeast Asia on his Honda (admittedly, a politics of
a bizarre leisure class), and in this way, he refuses to act out the violence of simulacra.

Flynn's prominence in *Dispatches* suggests, if not a postmodernist reclamation of subjectivity, at least a parodic stance toward it. If
subjectivity is always mediated by images, then Flynn, more than
any other of Herr's colleagues, is in control of his image, his positioning as a simulation. Herr finds a pose, a response to the media, in

Flynn's glamour and indifference: "all of [the movie business] was finished for Flynn, the dues-paying and the accommodations. . . ." (210). As a product of a Hollywood environment, Flynn reverses Herr's and the grunts' formulation of life-as-movie into movie-as-life: he exists beyond media acculturation. Flynn cannot be overcoded by cultural narratives into seeing himself as a simulation since he already knows what it means to be an image: "Definitely off of media, Flynn; a war behind him already where he'd confronted and cleaned the wasting movie-star karma that had burned down his father. Insofar as Sean had been acting out, he was a great actor. He said that the movies just swallowed you up, so he did it on the ground. . . ." (273). In a tentative way, he asserts a degree of control over his subjectivity. For Herr, the new hero must embrace the media, work through it to become a simulation, and then emerge, if only in a postmodern zone, self-aware of how the culture intervenes in his or her sense of self and experience.

As a form of resistance to the imagizing of subjectivity, Flynn's journey through images and out into a heterotopian zone—a place somewhere between an authentic country (Vietnam) and another world (a movie set)—is not without problems. Herr wants an antihero, but he finds one in an educated, hip, white, famous American—all the qualifications of the all-American hero. That Flynn could be all these things, but still not be a hero could be part of Herr's point. Even so, as a laconic connoisseur of the war, Flynn avoids the complex, Foucauldian network of military power and knowledge that continually seeks to legitimize the myth of the hero. He is not obliged to follow orders, to go on missions, to endure the thousand regulations that hold many of the grunts in a highly surveilled subject position. Moreover, he is not constrained by the even greater network of education and economic privilege that forced some to go to war while others avoided conscription. Free to pursue the war at his leisure, Flynn experiments with his own subjectivity in his own way and in his own time. Herr's antihero moves from one privileged position (son-of-movie-star/movie-star) to another (anti-movie-star). At the same time, to dismiss Flynn as just another example of the rich and famous showing us how to be would be to miss the force of Herr's simulations. Herr focuses on Flynn not only because they were friends, but also because Flynn's story is really a story about death: "the ground swallowed him up . . . he and Dana had gone off somewhere together since April 1970, biking into Cambodia, 'presumed captured,' rumors and long silence, MIA to say the least" (273). At some level, all Herr's simulations point to the death in Vietnam.

Herr's strategy of turning simulacra against simulacra approaches Jameson's notion of homeopathic engagement with the postmodern: "To undo postmodernism homeopathically by the methods of postmodernism: to work at dissolving pastiche by using all the instruments of pastiche itself, to reconquer some genuine historical sense by using the instruments of what I have called substitutes for history" ("Regarding Postmodernism," 59). Curiously, if Jameson does not apply this logic to *Dispatches* himself (and so I read Jameson *contra* Jameson), the concept describes Herr's strategies; he uses simulations not to erase history, but to achieve a clearer, deeper sense of it. Jameson, who valorizes the energies and utopian vision of modernism over postmodernism, argues that "modernism, for example, was an experience of nascent commodification which fought reification by means of reification, in terms of reification. It was itself a gigantic process of reification internalized as a homeopathic way of seizing this force, mastering it and opposing the result to reifications passively submitted to an external reality" (60). Since he distrusts postmodernism, he cannot quite bring himself to say that the postmoderns have achieved similar effects on as wide a scale:

> I am wondering whether some positive features of postmodernism couldn't do that as well: an attempt somehow to master these things by choosing them and pushing them to their limits. There is a whole range of so-called oppositional arts, whether it's punk writing, or ethnic writing, which really try to use postmodern techniques—though for obvious reasons I dislike the term technique—to go through and beyond. (60)

Herr's book—a movie, a Hendrix riff, and a spliff all in one—fits this definition of "oppositional arts" and seeks "to go through and beyond" simulacra.

In the postmodern, as *Dispatches* attests, we are overcoded, spectacularized, objectified, awash in simulations. These simulations intervene in our subjectivities, provide us with knowledge and modes of expression and behavior. Given, then, the fragmentation of subjectivity that accompanies the mass production and dissemination of images, we stand in some degree of alienation to ourselves: we act and think in ways that come not only from lived experience but from screens. Through his life-as-movie, Herr attempts to lessen the measure of this alienation. He asserts that we need to adopt a degree of ironic self-awareness. If we create our own simulacra, cast ourselves as simulations, we construct our own screens upon which to experiment with our own subjectivities and to project what we consider to be most crucial in our experience.

Through his homeopathic approach, Herr doesn't want to "dissolve" simulations but rather attack those who control them. As he argues, during the Vietnam War, simulacra were used to efface history:

> Somewhere on the periphery of that total Vietnam issue whose daily reports made the morning papers too heavy to bear, lost in the surreal contexts of television, there was a story that was as simple as it had always been, men hunting men, a hideous war and all kinds of victims. But there was also a Command that didn't feel this, that rode us into attrition traps on the back of fictional kill ratios, and an Administration that believed the Command, a cross-fertilization of ignorance, and a press whose tradition of objectivity and fairness (not to mention self-interest) saw that all of it got space. (231)

Although Herr condemns the media's reiteration of Command doublespeak, and condemns Washington's and the Pentagon's influence on the simulacra of the war, their ability to shape history to their own vision and goals, he retains a grudging admiration for the power of simulations. A film junkie, steeped in a culture of films and images, he criticizes the postmodern and exploits the potency of simulacra to construct subjectivities and to present history.

We can use the concept of a homeopathic engagement to clarify the differences between Baudrillard's and Herr's postmodernism; since I have taken up Baudrillard's theory of simulacra and historicity throughout this chapter, I would like to close with a brief consideration of what he says about the Vietnam War. In *Simulations*, he argues that the war is a "simulacrum of a struggle to death" (68). In Baudrillard's theorizing, where even power is a simulacrum— "power, too, for some time now produces nothing but signs of its resemblance" (45)—the massive carnage of Vietnam becomes trivialized, the unquantifiable trauma part of some near empty game: "Ultimately this war was only a crucial episode in a peaceful coexistence. It marked the advent of China to peaceful coexistence" (67). He also writes that "the intolerable nature of this bombing [of Hanoi] should not conceal the fact that it was only a simulacrum to allow the Vietnamese to seem to countenance a compromise and Nixon to make the Americans swallow the retreat of their forces" (69). While Baudrillard, it seems to me, is perfectly correct in his insistence that simulacra *can* nullify historicity, I would argue that here he has been seduced by his own theorizing into effacing the complex history of Vietnam. His almost casual remarks omit any detailed interpretation of the shifting political allegiances between Washington-Beijing-Moscow and gloss over the political contestation of the war both in America and among the U.S. armed forces in Vietnam. What we could take as a slogan of Baudrillard's—"the simulacra win out over history" (*Simulations*, 100)—could be true if we believe it; Herr, through his simulacra, insists that we might resist the death of historicity.

In one rather startling instance, Baudrillard and Herr echo each other's thinking about simulations. At the beginning of *Simulations*, Baudrillard evokes as his paradigm of the simulacrum, "the Borges tale where the cartographers of the Empire draw up a map so detailed that it ends up exactly covering the territory. . . ." (1). In a moment that Baudrillard might take as an example of how events duplicate themselves, at the beginning of *Dispatches*, Herr selects the same Borgesian notion as his paradigm of simulation: as he looks at a deteriorating colonial map of Vietnam, he realizes that "we also knew . . . for years now there had been no country here but the war" (1). Yet Herr's war-as-simulacrum explicitly reconnects us to historicity, reminding us of the (post-) colonial context of the war. He also gives the map-as-simulation a further spin when he recalls that "it had been a matter of military expediency to impose a new set of references over Vietnam's older, truer being. . . ." (97). In a Baudrillardan moment, Herr suggests that the U.S. created Vietnam as a simulacrum, a deliberate effort to erase it geographically as well as militarily. But against this simulation, he offers a more potent one, one calculated to tell once again the history of the war and its death.

In Herr's narrativity of the text-as-film, all of Vietnam becomes a heterotopian zone of hyperreality. As the ultimate simulation against simulation, Herr projects Vietnam as a movie set. As Flynn remarks, "the whole country" should be called "LZ Loon": "Loon was the ultimate movie location, where all of the mad colonels and death-spaced grunts we'd ever known showed up all at once, saying all the terrible, heart breaking things they always said, so nonchalant about the horror and fear that you knew you'd never really be one of them no matter how long you stayed" (253). Loon is the home of death, a place where Americans and Vietnamese die all the time. More comfortable with the grunts in the field than with Command officers and their briefings—their "informational freak-o-rama[s]"—Herr takes seriously a marine's plea: "you go on out of here you cocksucker, but I mean it, you tell it" (223). Through his simulations, the it he tells is the suffering, terror, and death of the war. Although Vietnam may only be available to us through Herr's simulacra, he reconnects us to our fears and emotions and tells the war's secret history.

NOTES

1. David J. Herman, "Modernism versus Postmodernism: Towards an Analytic Distinction," in *A Postmodern Reader*, ed. Joseph Natoli and Linda Hutcheon (Albany: State University of New York Press, 1993), 177. All further references to this work appear in the text. When necessary, the short form, "Modernism," will be used.

2. Philip D. Beidler, *Re-Writing America: Vietnam Authors in Their Generation* (Athens: The University of Georgia Press, 1991), 265. He goes on to make the remarkable claim that "as fully as for any Vietnam author in the generation of the war, in the work of Michael Herr, the re-writing of America becomes a conscious revision of nothing less than the idea of *writing itself* considered at the very limits of textual understanding at large" (264). For Beidler's earlier take on *Dispatches*, see his *American Literature and the Experience of Vietnam* (Athens: The University of Georgia Press, 1982).

3. Fredric Jameson, *Postmodernism, or, The Cultural Logic of Later Capitalism* (Durham: Duke University Press, 1991), 44–45. All further references to this work appear in the text. When necessary, the short form, *Postmodernism*, will be used.

4. For another take on Herr's work and postmodernism, see Thomas Carmichael, "Postmodernism and American Cultural Difference: *Dispatches*, *Mystery Train*, and *The Art of Japanese Management*," boundary 2 21 (1994): 220–32. Calling his choices "eccentric," Carmichael selects *Dispatches* as a key postmodernist text and argues that "it is ultimately Jim Jarmusch's *Mystery Train* and Michael Herr's *Dispatches*, in their self-conscious acknowledgment of Asian difference, that urge us to recognize the ways in which the American rewritings and appropriations of the sign of the other are also modes of comprehending, in a particularly postmodern sense, one's lived relation to the world" (232).

5. Jean Baudrillard, "Forget Baudrillard," in *Forget Foucault*, trans. Phil Beitchman, Lee Hildreth, and Mark Polizzotti (New York: Semiotext(e), 1987),

69. All further references to this work appear in the text. When necessary, the short form, "Forget," will be used.

6. Michael Herr, *Dispatches* (New York: Avon, 1977), 7–8. All further references to this work appear in the text.

7. Jean Baudrillard, *Simulations,* trans. Paul Foss, Paul Patton, and Philip Beitchman (New York: Semiotext(e), 1983), 11. All further references to this work appear in the text.

8. A number of scholars have noted the blending of fact (the "real") and fiction (the "not real") in *Dispatches.* I'm interested here in the differences between the "real" and the "hyperreal." For scholars on the mixing of journalism and fiction in Herr's book, see, for example: Philip H. Melling, *Vietnam in American Literature* (Boston: Twayne Publishers, 1990), 68; Evelyn Cobley, "Narrating the Facts of War: New Journalism in Herr's *Dispatches* and Documentary Realism in First World War Novels," *The Journal of Narrative Technique* 17 (1987): 97; and Dale W. Jones, "The Vietnams of Michael Herr and Tim O'Brien: Tales of Disintegration and Integration," *The Canadian Review of American Studies* 13.3 (1982): 309.

9. J. Hoberman, "Vietnam: The Remake," in *Remaking History,* ed. Barbara Kruger and Phil Mariani (Seattle, Wash.: Bay Press, 1989), 176.

10. Jean Baudrillard, *The Ecstasy of Communication,* trans. Bernard and Caroline Schutze, ed. Slyvere Lotringer (New York: Semiotext(e), 1988), 21–22. All further references to this work appear in the text. When necessary, the short form *Ecstasy,* will be used.

11. Anders Stephanson, "Regarding Postmodernism—A Conversation with Fredric Jameson," in *Postmodernism/Jameson/Critique,* ed. Douglas Kellner (Washington: Maisonneuve Press, 1989), 45. All further references to this work appear in the text. When necessary, the short form, "Regarding Postmodernism," will be used.

12. For more of Herr's experiments with postmodern narrative forms, see his *Walter Winchell* (New York: Knopf, 1987). As Herr explains in the "Preface" to his novel about the famous gossip columnist and journalist: "Even though *Walter Winchell* is based on the life of a real man and often uses his actual words, it's a fiction, and it's in prose. So it must be prose fiction. You could call it a screenplay that's typed like a novel, that reads like a novel but plays like a movie" (v).

13. See Douglas Kellner, *Jean Baudrillard: From Marxism to Postmodernism and Beyond* (Stanford, Calif.: Stanford University Press, 1989). Kellner succinctly and ironically critiques the more speculative, Alfred Jarry-like metaphysics of Baudrillard's *Les strategies fatales:* "One cannot help but wonder what it was that led Baudrillard to conclude that objects now reign supreme, and that we should submit to their dictates and laws. Was his word processor (if he has one) taking over his thought processes? Or was his television set controlling his imagination? Did his car, as on an episode of the old *Twilight Zone* television series, start driving him one day?" (167).

14. Allen, in *post*modernist, intertextual fashion, borrows the gag from Buster Keaton's modernist classic, *Sherlock Junior* (1924), where Keaton beams himself from the "theater" into the "screen."

15. See Gustav Hasford, *The Short-Timers* (New York: Bantam, 1979), and Stanley Kubrick, Michael Herr, and Gustav Hasford, *Full Metal Jacket* (New York: Knopf, 1987). The fact that Herr coscripted, with Kubrick and Hasford, the screenplay for *Full Metal Jacket* seems natural since Hasford pays homage to *Dispatches* at the beginning of *The Short-Timers.* Hasford quotes: "I think that Vietnam was what we had instead of happy childhoods." Further, Hasford jokes intertextually, putting the anonymous, wounded grunt's line, "I hate this movie" (*Dispatches*, 203) into Joker's mouth during basic training: "I think I'm going to hate this movie" (4). Beyond this, the brilliant scene where a "combat" camera crew pans along a wall filming the grunts while (invisibly) Kubrick's camera crew tracks along behind them suggests at least some of Herr's parodic interest in simulations of simulations of simulations.

16. Michael Herr, "Foreword," *Full Metal Jacket* (New York: Knopf, 1987), vi.

17. I find an interesting spin on the influence of American war movies on individual subjectivity in Bao Ninh's compelling *The Sorrow of War*, trans. Phan Thanh Hao, ed. Frank Palmos (New York: Riverhead Books, 1993). Kien, the North Vietnamese protagonist, recalls how watching a film (presumably *Apocalypse Now*) after the war transports him back to the battlefields: "I am watching a U.S. war movie with scenes of American soldiers yelling as they launch themselves into combat on the TV screen, and once again I'm ready to jump in and mix it in the fiery scene of blood, mad killing, and brutality that warps the soul and personality" (47).

18. Larry Heinemann, *Close Quarters* (New York: Penguin, 1977), 348.

19. Loren Baritz, *Backfire* (New York: William Morrow, 1985), 51–52. Quoted in Hoberman, 177.

20. Michel Foucault, "Nietzsche, Genealogy, History," trans. Donald F. Bouchard and Sherry Simon, in *The Foucault Reader*, ed. Paul Rabinov (New York: Pantheon Books, 1984), 82.

21. Philip Caputo, *A Rumor of War* (New York: Ballantine, 1977), xiv. All further references to this work appear in the text.

22. At the beginning of "Colleagues," Herr seems not to have in mind an obvious, if ironic inspiration for his clichéd movie clip: Errol Flynn's film, *Objective Burma* (1945), directed by Raoul Walsh. As Flynn leads his men, à la John Wayne, on a special mission in the jungle, Henry Hall, playing a war correspondent, goes along, recording his own and the men's feelings and opinions about the war and the Japanese. The reporter in Herr's film "clip" more closely recalls "Papa" Hemingway in his famous-journalist-in-Spain-and-France role. Not surprisingly, like many Vietnam era writers, such as Tim O'Brien, Herr refers directly to Hemingway on a number of occasions (22, 137, 244, 279).

23. The song "Sean Flynn" comes from the Clash's *Combat Rock* (1982). The Clash, in their postpunk phase, show a great deal of fascination for American sixties politics. For example, "Straight to Hell" chronicles the hardships of Ameí-Asian children born in Vietnam. More remarkably, the song that follows "Sean Flynn," "Ghetto Defendant," features Allen Ginsberg giving a stertorous "hooked-on-megalopolis" rap.

5

RITES OF INCORPORATION IN *IN COUNTRY* AND *INDIAN COUNTRY*

Tony Williams

Whether one likes it or not, this particular era is supposedly "post-modern," necessitating some form of understanding and engagement with a notoriously elusive discourse. As a term, postmodernism contains conceptual associations questioning presupposed ideas concerning notions of culture and history. Formerly secure methodologies of literary fidelity and historical veracity now undergo reexamination. Since the Vietnam War is often described as the first postmodern war, lacking supposedly secure epistemological foundations of earlier conflicts, it is crucial to understand how certain texts negotiate specific meanings against the background of a cultural phenomenon questioning the very concept of veracity and historical understanding.

As Fredric Jameson states, "History is what hurts, it is what refuses desire and sets inexorable limits to individual as well as collective praxis."[1] The vast majority of seventies texts accepted the pain. In an era smarting from the historical blows of Watergate and the fall of Saigon, several literary works attempted to fill a void political and public institutions preferred to leave empty. Such examples include Ron Kovic's *Born on the Fourth of July* (1976), Charles Durden's *No Bugles No Drums* (1976), Philip Caputo's *A Rumor of War* (1977), Larry Heinemann's *Close Quarters* (1977), and Gustav Hasford's *The*

Short Timers (1979). The decade also saw the appearance of several films critical of the war, such as Robert Aldrich's Vietnam Western allegory *Ulzana's Raid* (1972), Henry Jaglom's *Tracks* (1977), Ted Post's *Go Tell the Spartans* (1978), and Sydney J. Furie's *The Boys in Company C* (1978). These works all share common traits of anger at deceptive national myths and a willingness to face the agony of historical trauma.

However, the late seventies and eighties saw the appearance of certain texts, both literary and cinematic, that began a process of de-historicization leading to the Reagan era's Ramboesque follies. Films such as *The Deer Hunter* (1978) and *Apocalypse Now* (1979), pulp literature such as the *M.I.A. Hunter* series, and the magazine *Soldier of Fortune* revealed a process of disavowing Vietnam's historical significance. They attempted to repress features, Michael Clark notes, of disturbing analogies "between the violence of the war and the ordinary forms of social interaction" turning "the memory of Vietnam into an image of historical disruption and social disintegration."[2]

During the eighties a postmodernist current resulted in certain particular inflections appearing within varied modes of representations. I wish to show how two specific works, Philip Caputo's *Indian Country* and Bobbie Ann Mason's *In Country*, bear the marks of such inflections. As eighties works they differ from each other in both form and style. Despite utilizing common themes of PTSD and veteran social alienation in different ways they reveal common characteristics. *Indian Country* exhibits a third-person narrative style leading toward a definable textual closure involving personal redemption. Bobbie Ann Mason's *In Country* engages in a more self-reflexive literary style contrasting with the more male-oriented canon of Vietnam literature. However, both novels end in a particular way utilizing a certain type of transcendental conclusion designed to elide the painful memory of historical fact. They form a useful comparison to each other as diverse voices of second-generation Vietnam literary narratives.

Set in the early eighties both novels exhibit definite postmodernist tendencies. They attempt denial of traumatic historical pain and memory, repressing (though not entirely) conflicts and contradictions central to the historical experience of U.S. involvement in Vietnam. Both seek to incorporate their main characters within a transcendental community. Vietnam becomes a distant signified overwhelmed by a bombardment of signifiers from a contemporary corporate culture aiming to suppress painful historical memories a generation after the conflict.

Caputo's *Indian Country* differs from the author's other works (*A Rumor of War*, *Del Corso's Gallery*, and *Horn of Africa*), which exhibit dominant marks of historical pain whether quasiautobiographical or fictional. In contrast, *Indian Country* attempts to disavow historical trauma by recourse to a *Bildungsroman* motif, discredited in key examples of seventies Vietnam literature. *In Country* also *appears* to question Vietnam literature's dominant male trajectory. It uses a self-reflexive narrative mediated by a female protagonist who attempts to negotiate her identity and heritage through a now diffuse mire of personal memory. A *Bildungsroman* motif operates but via a different gendered trajectory. Although these two works appear diverse, they are linked by recourse to a predominant "rite of incorporation" within their specific frameworks attempting to negotiate and disavow the pain of historical memory. By using the *Bildungsroman*, both narratives fall into the realm of a postmodern pastiche form characterized by Fredric Jameson. He sees this as

> an elaborated symptom of the waning of our historicity, of our lived possibility of expressing history in some active way. It cannot therefore be said to produce this strange occultation of the present by its own formal power, but rather merely to demonstrate, through these inner contradictions, the enormity of a situation in which we seem increasingly incapable of fashioning representations of our current experience.[3]

Both *Indian Country* and *In Country* demonstrate this attempted repression of historical conflict. They are works illustrating Jameson's "waning of historicity" thesis influenced by a particular postmodern moment.

Postmodernism is a difficult and elusive term, capable of many definitions. As Jim Collins points out, there is "no short definition of *postmodernism* that can encompass the divergent, often contradictory ways the term has been employed."[4] Postmodernism is really a problematic—what Victor Burgin defines as "a complex of heterogenous but interrelated questions which will not be silenced by any spuriously unitary answer."[5] It is opposed to many tenets of modernism, particularly those involving artistic self-enclosure and separation from a wider social audience. Postmodernism also questions

modernism's supposedly rigid barriers between high art and popular art.

With their various depictions of television, malls, and McDonald's encroaching upon the consciousness of their individual protagonists, both *Indian Country* and *In Country* reveal certain postmodern
tendencies within their respective narratives. Both Chris Starkmann
and Sam Hughes live in a culture exhibiting a proliferation of endlessly circulating signs associated either with information explosion
or identical simulacra of corporate businesses in a geographically diverse American landscape (McDonald's, Burger King, Waldenbooks,
Wendy's, Kmart, Wal-Mart ad nauseam). In both novels these features
frequently function as signifiers of diffusion attempting to erase historical pain.

Postmodernism may contain critical elements involving paradox,
irony, and contradiction, especially in alliance with movements such
as feminism acting as a much-needed "political conscience," according to Laura Kipnis.[6] Yet, as Linda Hutcheon remarks, postmodernism is an evenhanded process since it "ultimately manages to install
and reinforce as much as undermine and subvert the conventions."
The mere appearance of female narration and mergings between history and subjectivity, high and low culture is not enough. What needs
interrogation is how each particular narrative handles the contradictions within its textual formations, especially those involving history and memory. Postmodernism belongs within contemporary debates concerning the nature of representation in historical writings.
But, as Hutcheon further points out, "the postmodern appears to coincide with a general cultural awareness of the existence and power
of systems of representation which do not *reflect* society so much as
grant meaning and value within a particular society."[7]

The concept is double-edged, liable to contamination as well as
progressive usage. Hutcheon notes that postmodernism involves some
sort of complicity with motifs within the dominant culture. But this
complicity does not necessarily entail any oppositional directions.
This particular mode of complicity inevitably conditions both the
radicality of the kind of critique offered and the possibility of suggesting change.[8] It manipulates but does not transform signification.
It disperses but does not (re)construct the structures of subjectivity.[9]
One must investigate how each work uses and interrogates the very
notion of whatever postmodernity it chooses to engage with (whether
conscious or unconscious). There are many postmodernisms, legiti-

mizing as well as subversive.[10] But the difference between recognizing the influence of contemporary modes of thought, power, and domination (while also engaging in subversive analysis) and falling into
dangerous complicity may be very thin, as to be almost nonexistent.
Rather than dedoxification and denaturalization, ideological entrapment may result.[11]

By concentrating on *Indian Country* and *In Country*, I wish to
show how the blurring of boundaries between the historical and the
fictional postmodern, exhibits no progressive structure of meaning.
Instead, in Linda Hutcheon's words, they reveal western capitalism's
cultural power to normalize (or "doxify") signs and images, "however
disparate (or contesting) they may be."[12] While postmodern culture
cannot escape implication within contemporary economic and ideological moments, there may be elements within the cultural terrain
seeking to overpower potentially critical motifs within the text and
reincorporate them within the dominant mainstream. One such
element is a "rite of incorporation" motif used by both Caputo and
Mason.

Each novel exhibits a particular mythic "rite of incorporation" in
the conclusion, a rite containing conservative recuperative elements.
Both works promise a mythic incorporation back into the community. But this occurs at the cost of renegotiating the historical contradictions of a conflict originally causing individual disorientation. In
both cases, contradictions are not handled as continuing strategies
for interrogating the war's disruptive implications upon the community. Instead, these contradictions become ultimately subjected to
textual closure. By means of particular negotiations, the novels emphasize an elaborate form of ideological commodity exchange value
over and above the historical use value each work should have. *Indian Country* and *In Country* are novels whose authorial voices are
textual productions of eighties commodity aesthetics existing within
a postmodernist framework.

W. F. Haug points out that the commodity aesthetic originates in
an immanent contradiction between use value and exchange value
whereby monopoly capitalism inflates the "phantasmal" world of
commodity appearance thus overdetermining social perceptions.[13]
The individual ostensibly reads these novels for their use value in
terms of understanding generational perspectives concerning the
returned veteran. Naturally, historical understanding is important.
But this is the bait whereby exchange value predominates over use

value. *Indian Country* mediates the historical traumas of survivor guilt and PTSD within a specific literary negotiation whereby Chris Starkmann's condition becomes exclusively understood in terms of a conservative Oedipal trajectory motif. This occurs by demeaning the novel's potentially progressive use of disturbing factors of race and gender. In *In Country*, Sam Hughes's generational attempt to understand the significance of an old conflict becomes overwhelmed by a particular ideological direction. It results in a ritualistic fetishizing process concluding at the Washington Vietnam veterans memorial. The rites-of-incorporation motif in both novels represents an eighties ideological exchange value.

Although Haug's findings originate from studies of German postwar, commodity, seventies culture, they are also applicable to eighties America. Haug's work developed at a time when American consumerism and popular culture dominated a country desiring to forget the historical trauma of the thirties and forties. Commodity capitalism formed an exchange value designed to negate the memory of historical pain. New German cinema directors such as Fassbinder and Wenders exposed an American consumerism (including movies) operating as an affluent signifier of exchange value overwhelming and denying the presence of disturbing aspects from the recent past. The eighties era saw a similar exploitation boom within America. A commodity culture proliferation of malls, Hollywood Reaganite entertainment. VCRs, MTV, and multinationalism presented an explosion of signifiers affecting both historical memory and generational perspective. Although the historical pain negotiated by postwar Germany and post-Vietnam America is different, the effect of commodity culture proliferation is the same—the loosening of historical memory, and its eventual disavowal. Against this background both novels reveal the operation of a particular rite of incorporation, offering a mythic transcendence as a means to alleviate historical pain.

These rites of incorporation resemble rituals described by the anthropological investigations of Arnold Van Gennep into magical and religious ceremonies determining individual fusion into the community.[14] They perform a similar function in both novels. In *In Country* Sam's Cawood Pond initiation forms the major crux of the novel. She attempts to incorporate elements of her father's Vietnam experience within a different cultural and historical terrain. The experiment fails. But it leads to her uncle Emmett's successful rebirth at the end of the novel. *Indian Country* concludes with Chris's quasi-mystical baptismal ceremony. He atones for survivor guilt by spiritually fusing with his deceased Indian blood brother, Bonny St. George. Despite the different structures of these novels, the various rites of incorporation function in terms of Haug's definition of an ideological exchange value offering integration within a particular historical simulacrum. Far from being progressive, or even parodic, they illustrate the specific operations of a conservative postmodernist commodity aesthetics cannibalizing history for consumer appeal. They thus resemble Jameson's definition of the pastiche characterized by superficiality and lack of appropriate historical awareness. These novels attempt to repress (though not entirely) historical conflict and contradiction in favor of mythic narrative invocation. The project is explicit in *Indian Country* and implicit in *In Country*. Both works deal with issues concerning race and gender. They reflect the presence of contemporary voices demanding recognition and some form of negotiation. But the manner of negotiation is extremely problematic resulting again in the "same old story" of ideological incorporation.

The two books form interesting counterparts. Despite *In Country*'s feminist overtones, the novel is really as contaminated as *Indian Country*. Functioning as Reaganite ideological exchange-value formations, these novels reaffirm previously discredited master narratives offering readers no insights into history or the desperate plight of postwar America. They also reveal the tendency of motifs from previously discredited ideological master narratives to again re-emerge and dominate the present. This feature parallels the return of *The Green Berets* (1968) motifs within Vietnam movie narratives generated within the Reagan era, such as the *Missing in Action* and *Rambo* series. Both novels actually reveal the operations of an ideological nature that bear a certain resemblance to the activities of eighties Hollywood narrative structures.

Indian Country bears particular marks of a cinematic resolution paralleling contemporary Hollywood's recourse to an Oedipal trajectory hostile to progressive depictions of race and gender. *In Country* also exhibits cinematic features. It acknowledges cinema's role as a dominant feature in its protagonist's life. This is not surprising. Most twentieth-century novels, whether high cultural or popular, generally show some familiarity (and sometimes, usage) of the cinematic medium. However, literary appropriation may either be "against the grain" or unthinkingly reflect mainstream ideology. In neglecting the historical by relying on secondary forms of representations, a novel may appropriate the pastiche baggage of a corporate commodity structure promoting ideological attempts to disavow disturbing echoes of the past.

In contrast to World War I, Vietnam was a war involving cinematic interpretation. Critics such as Paul Fussell, Loren Baritz, Christopher Metress, Philip Melling, and Kali Tal convincingly demonstrate these connections. James Jones noted the deceptive nature of cinematic devices both in novels and critical reviews.[15] Melling also notes the dangers inherent in this type of representation.

> The use of film as a means of exploring culture has created an outlook that is governed by myth and conjecture. In the photographic negatives of military intelligence and the cinematic text of the Hollywood film, the audience is instructed through the use of signs, each of which is a visual allegory and directs the observer to think about the world in a stereotyped way. Film is not simply a medium of information but a vast repository of ideology and bias.[16]

Melling notes certain cinematic features in both *Indian Country* and *In Country* that lend themselves to a barren postmodernist exchange value. Both Chris and Sam live in a world of popular culture and frequently encounter contemporary signifiers such as media references. However, although this may accurately reflect the worlds they live in, the respective encounters are never directly interrogated, re-evaluated, or used in the progressive parodic or ironic dimensions of Nigel Williams's *Star Turn*.[17] Whereas Williams both inscribes *and* de-doxifies his modes of representations, finally revealing them as ideological creations, Caputo and Mason merely inscribe. Such cultural referents only influence the minds of their respective protagonists. They never lead to a radical questioning of their very mode of inscription. In contrast to *Indian Country*, Sam Hughes may attempt some engagement but she never realizes the signifier's manipulative functions. The cinematic references are pastiche formations. They are symptomatic of a contemporary simulacrum situation making characters and culture devoid of historical meaning. Both Chris and Sam *see* in a particular way. In a chapter appropriately entitled, "Seeing Vietnam," Melling refers to traits applicable to *Indian Country*.

> In the predetermined language of a "well-plotted motion picture," the prevailing ideology is "faith in dramatic convention." Things "happen"

in motion pictures. There is always a resolution, always a strong cause-effect dramatic line, and to perceive the world in those terms is to assume an ending for every social scenario. . . . There are no bit players in Hollywood politics: everyone makes things "happen."[18]

Indian Country's, Hollywood Oedipal structure would appear, on first sight, to be a postmodernist parody if the text did not convince the reader that the author takes the whole thing seriously. *Indian Country* narrates the story of Christian (Chris) Starkmann. Repressing survivor guilt following his Vietnam trauma of causing the death of his unit by inaccurately giving the wrong firepower coordinates, Chris now lives in the wilds of Minnesota with his wife, June, and two daughters. One daughter is June's by a former marriage. The novel gradually charts his mental disintegration as he undergoes the deep pain of PTSD and growing family alienation. Haunted by memories and the ghosts of his former Vietnam buddies (similar to the titular character of Heinemann's *Paco's Story*), Chris exhibits violent tendencies that resemble motifs in Gothic male melodrama. He displays deep misogynistic jealousy and hatred toward June. The novel moves towards a climactic resolution when Chris realizes the source of his trauma. It lies in his guilt over causing the death of his adolescent Indian companion, Bonny St. George, in Vietnam. Concluding scenes see Chris's solitary baptismal redemption in a wilderness stream, making peace with both himself and his deceased companion. This is the novel's rite of incorporation.

Indian Country offers a textual resolution displaying a particular form of exchange value in negotiating the historical pain of Vietnam. The novel emphasizes male guilt and misogyny and moves toward a conservative Oedipal resolution designed to disavow and overpower potentially disruptive factors of gender and race. Chris's inherent misogyny toward June denotes Caputo's deep inability to comprehend the changing nature of sexual relationships during previous decades. Instead, *Indian Country* views June through a male typological framework. She is there in the novel, less as a person in her own right, but more as a victimized subordinate heroine of Gothic narrative. Chris's increasing resentment toward her and his daughters reveals male insecurity within the narrative. But this motif never becomes fully acknowledged or even engaged with. Instead, the novel moves exclusively toward male resolution.

Similarly, Bonny St. George represents another *type* familiar in

American literature—the dark ethnic male companion. The historical racial aspects of the Vietnam conflict, involving the disproportionate recruitment of ethnic minorities, become elided within this classical master narrative representation. While *Indian Country* may occasionally recognize disturbing historical features, these become overwhelmed by traditional cultural motifs. These motifs enter the narrative, not to blur boundaries between high and low culture in a progressively postmodernist direction, but rather to nullify memories originating from historical pain and eventually achieve a conservative ideological resolution.

Indian Country attempts to negotiate its historical aspects by presenting them novelistically as archetypal elements needing traditional resolution. Ironically, the simulacra territory of corporate capitalism is the only world within the novel not threatening to Chris: "He [Starkmann] did not feel in enemy territory in Burger King, or in McDonalds, Wendy's, Kentucky Fried, Mr. Chicken, Mr. Donut, the Holiday Inn, Day's Inn, Quality Inn or Best Western. These places were neutral territory, where no one cared who you were or what you'd done."[19]

These worlds are free from the conflicts concerning gender and race that the novel attempts to disavow. *Indian Country* instead moves toward *Christ*(ian) Starkmann's spiritual odyssey. The analogies to a particular cinematic use of *Bildungsroman* and *Platoon*'s *Chris*/ Taylor are certainly not difficult to see. Caputo's novel relies upon the male epistemological terms of a detective thriller. Chris's survivor guilt become dehistoricized and engulfed within elements from conservative features of male melodrama. In addition to these male Gothic literary antecedents, *Indian Country* contains contemporary cinematic parallels to the eighties avenging patriarchal slasher figure intent on punishing females. Throughout the novel, the reader experiences a "will he? wont he?" effect. Starkmann may either commit suicide or attempt "disciplining" his family like Jack Torrance in *The Shining*.

Indian Country appears very much a conscious imitation of Raymond Bellour's classical Hollywood Oedipal trajectory thesis. For Bellour, all Hollywood narratives move toward a patriarchal resolution involving male dominance and female subordination. Any narrative exhibits certain differences. In *Indian Country*, the elements of difference involve historical trauma, gender (June), and race (Bonny), initially causing disruption to the status quo. According to Bellour's thesis, disturbing elements within the narrative become contained and resolved at the film's climax, no matter how arbitrary the mode of resolution. *Indian Country*, thus moves toward a climax denying potentially disturbing issues raised by race and gender to resolve monolithically the trauma of its male protagonist by granting him spiritual cleansing and baptism. The novel ends in a transcendental conclusion.

Indian Country's male, guilt-ridden text is an ideal example of Susan Jeffords's "remasculinization" thesis and is evident in works such as Oliver Stone's *Born* on *the Fourth of July*. These texts recognize male trauma but usually restore some form of phallic authority at the climax, thus disavowing the traumatic factors of historical and gender breakdown that caused the original crisis. Although containing socially relevant features, such as Chris's post-Vietnam syndrome, fragmentary family relationships, and survivor guilt, Caputo's novel drowns them in a quasi-masochistic emphasis upon masculine regeneration. In contrast to *A Rumor of War*, whose seventies narrative trajectory contained both a recognition of cultural conditioning and eventual political awareness of its consequences, *Indian Country* returns to old master narratives validating Starkmann's individual unawareness. Complicit both with the Oedipal trajectory and motifs familiar from Leslie A. Fiedler's *Love and Death in the American Novel*, Starkmann's revolt is a petulant rebellion against his father, involving a sublimated homoerotic desire for union with his Indian friend, Bonny George. In the opening wilderness scenes, Starkmann submits to his father's demands that he attend divinity school: "Christian gave in, a surrender that forced upon him a recognition of how tightly he remained in his father's thrall, and gave rise to a secret desire to commit a liberating apostasy" (38).

It is not accidental that Bonny George taps his shoulder at that particular moment. Defying his father, Starkmann will "light off" for the Vietnam wilderness with Bonny. But this Huck later betrays his Jim. He misreads coordinates, causing napalm to drop on his unconsummated love. Finally, forgiving himself, realizing that his enlistment was really an act of revenge against his father, Starkmann undergoes an individualistic baptismal rebirth in the waters from which Bonny once rescued him.[20]

The novel thus attempts to disavow Vietnam's historical associations in favor of an individualistic male melodramatic format. Potentially disruptive issues concerning gender and race appear as elements of difference. But in the novel's final scenes they become inserted into a male traumatic framework moving toward resolution within a spiritual rite of incorporation. The climax concentrates exclusively upon Chris's male regeneration. June and the daughters are absent. However, despite the climax's intention, the veteran never returns fully to the mythical claws of the American Eagle. The reader senses repressed elements within this textual closure and the arbitrary nature of its intended resolution. However, their presence is not enough to regard the novel's position as containing any positive hegemonic clash of discourses. *Indian Country* attempts to diminish socially valid aspects of veteran trauma and to disavow history. Its conclusion reveals the novel's impoverished structure. Aiming to bury a painful past in a pastiche formation containing classical, transcendental, and popular cultural motifs, the work really belongs in the conservative wing of postmodern discourse. It fails to confront the implications of past and present in a critical manner. The individual *Bildungsroman* conclusion contains traditional "Band-Aid" male bonding motifs.

In Country's Sam Hughes searches for the historical meaning of a war that killed her father. He is the novel's "unknown soldier" whom Sam attempts to recover from secondary sources—oral and personal. Like Caputo, Mason recognizes contemporary veteran problems such as Agent Orange, marital relationships, impotence, and self-destructiveness. But her use of a problematic *Bildungsroman* motif overwhelms a potentially interrogative treatment of these features. Living in Kentucky's rural Hopewell, Sam probes in vain for knowledge. All available sources—Uncle Emmett, his veteran buddies, her mother now living in Lexington, her father's letter, his diary, history books, high school records, and covert television references to the "War" (such as *M*A*S*H**)—prove no help. Sam faces a more problematic situation than Chris Starkmann. He lived through the historical period and had the appropriate gender for *Bildungsroman* recuperation. Her world resembles Baudrillard's simulacrum in which access to the real appears impossible.[21] For Sam, living in 1984, Orwell's work is "just a book I had to read in English"[22]. Commenting on Joan Rivers substituting for Johnny Carson, Emmett notes, "It's a re-run. Nothing's authentic anymore" (19). The nearest Sam and Emmett get to Vietnam is watching *M*A*S*H** reruns. She lives in a world of McDonald's, MTV, remakes of original classical narrative movies such as *The Thing* and *Invasion of the Body Snatchers*, and imaginative simulations of Vietnam. As in *Indian Country*, the soulless, reproducible world of McDonald's is the new ahistorical wasteland for Hopewell's Vietnam veterans (58).

There appears to be no access to a reality or to any dialogical referent in her world. In the following conversation with Emmett, Sam confesses her inability to comprehend Vietnam's historical significance. No contact occurs between the generations concerning war's brutal reality.

> ". . . I can't really see it," Sam said. "All I can see in my mind is picture postcards. It doesn't seem real. I can't believe it was really real."
>
> "It was real all right. You don't want to know how real it was."(95)

Here, the male asserts knowledge of the real while Sam searches for it in vain. This very factor should lead us to consider what form of postmodernism operates in *In Country*. Although the novel attempts to rewrite the *Bildungsroman* format, inserting a female subject who questions male assertion of knowledge and female passivity, Mason's project collapses at the conclusion, when Sam witnesses Emmett's solitary epiphany: "Silently, Sam points to the place where Emmett is studying the names low in a panel. He is sitting there cross-legged in front of the wall, and slowly his face bursts into a smile like flames" (245).[23]

Despite her questioning throughout the novel, at the climax Sam becomes reduced to female passivity witnessing (like Mary Magdalene and countless archetypal successors) male regeneration. This ending is neither positive nor utopian since it reaffirms traditional gender roles the novel attempts in vain to interrogate. The rite of incorporation is for "men only," overwhelming other contesting discourses.

While readers may identify with Sam as a representative of the eighties generation searching for Vietnam's historical significance, her very entrapment in popular culture simulacra raises serious doubts. Although written in a traditional sequence involving search and discovery, its flirtation with postmodernist concepts of historical erasure and simultaneity make *In Country* open to the type of criticism Brent Whelan makes of Ken Kesey's work. Speaking of Kesey's distortions, of "repressing linear temporality and thus historicity, in favor of an all-embracing simultaneity," he notes that in the accompanying historical erasure, "the swallowing up of the past by the present moment, is of course, a familiar typos in American culture and has not surprisingly appeared in the corporate culture that has followed American economic hegemony across the globe."[24] Sam's immersion in the present moment of her culture diffuses any radical attempt to achieve the historical consciousness she seeks. Although Kesey and Mason differ stylistically, both are victims of a contemporary conservative discourse denying historical reality for its own recuperative ends. In Mason's case, pop-cultural, ahistorical immersion anticipates the novel's eventual use of its own rite-of-incorporation motif.

The dominant discourse remains one where the male lays claim to transcendental knowledge. A one-sided activity occurs within this text. Sam consistently encounters denial of her quest from the male members of her world.[25] Eventually disgusted with her father's diary and Emmett's possible involvement in masculine atrocities, Sam decides to undertake a pastiche "regeneration through violence" quest by "humping the boonies" in Cawood's Pond.[26] That quest also ends in failure. Despite Sam's "downhome" feminist feelings, discontent with the male world and recognition of gendered power structures affecting female politicians (208), she does not get any further. As Emmett finally says to her, "I came out here to save you, but maybe I can't. Maybe you have to find out for yourself. Fuck. You can't learn from the past. The main thing you learn from history is that you can't learn from history. That's what history is." He finally states, "There are some things you can never figure out" (226).

Sam's attempted Walden odyssey comes to nothing. Her individual rite of passage actually fails. The novel makes clear that Emmett is the one who will successfully achieve this transition as the final lines (quoted above) reveal. After Sam's failure, the narrative begins to focus on Emmett. He, not Sam, initiates the trip to the memorial. Although the novel promises much concerning the progressive possibility of a female mode of writing that interrogates male postwar experience, certain problematic discourses inherent in the novel undermine these promises. Does Sam actually have to reproduce her father's Vietnam boonie's experience by spending a night at Cawood's Pool? The Walden associations stem from a male writer. Does a female author living in the post-Vietnam world actually have to reproduce past traditional discourses rather than attempting a contestational style confronting gender, tradition, and discourse? The failure of the Cawood Pool episode leads to the successful conclusion of the memorial resolution, both for Emmett and Sam. One signifier with its connotations of a happy ending replaces another. As W. D. Ehrhart notes, the Wall becomes "a moving and inarticulate substitute for accountability," an "intoxicating and misleading artifice" stimulating a quasi-born-again transcendental look on the male hero's face.[27]

Although Sam's very name suggests the novel's potential for raising radical issues of gender ambiguity, these issues never become realized. Susan Jeffords notes that Sam's actual name is ironic since it is a product of the masculine collective.[28] As Emmett undergoes regeneration at the Wall, Sam shares in this incorporation by witnessing the act. She "points to the place" but functions in a subordinate gender-traditional position while Emmett undergoes the rite. Although not eliminated from the final act, like June Starkmann in *Indian Country*, Sam undertakes a "witness" role while the male undergoes physical and spiritual redemption. The novel anticipates her eventual incorporation by identifying her with Radar in a *M*A*S*H* episode dealing with the colonel's death: "she felt it was poignant because Radar had looked up to the Colonel like a father" (25). Radar is, of course, the series' prepubescent male figure functioning as a child in relation to the major characters. While Sam's name suggests gender diffusion, its positive implications are never fully realized due to the character's position in the text and the novel's ultimate emphasis upon exclusive male regeneration.

Both *Indian Country* and *In Country* function as rituals incorporating the individual within the community in similar ways. They attempt to nullify the historical trauma of the Vietnam War by recourse to traditional models similar to those described by Arnold Van Gennep's anthropological research into primitive rites of incorporation. Originally, based on magical and religious ceremonies, these rites take on a psychic, privatized significance for the male characters in each novel.[29] They return home again. The climactic weight of each novel focuses on rites of incorporation that attempt to nullify the trauma of historical pain. In this way, their endings parallel those stereotypical television closures aiming to assimilate the veteran into the never-never world of the happy ending. As Michael Clark notes, "They relegate the specific, concrete contradictions of being a veteran at a particular moment in history to the realm of private experience and personal memory, and they divorce that realm entirely from the forms of social interaction that are represented as permanent and universal." Each concluding image rehearses again familiar images of the veteran "while stripping that character of its vestigial social implications in favor of a pompous rhetoric of existential vision."[30]

The final sentences of each novel make clear these implications.

> Never had the air smelled so good, nor seemed so clear, and the trees appeared to be holding out their arms in welcome. He looked at the world around him as if it had just been created, though he knew it was old and worn, full of death and pain; yet it appeared new to him because he saw it through new eyes, and so it was full of life, renewal and hope. "I forgive you," he repeated. . . . When the echoes died away, he dressed, hoisted his pack, and started walking, though not toward home, he was already there, returned to himself. Home, the place he had not seen or been these many years. *Home.* (Caputo 433)
>
> Silently, Sam points to the place where Emmett is studying the names low on a panel. He is sitting there cross-legged in front of the wall, and slowly his face bursts into a smile like flames. (Mason 245)

Unlike the works of an earlier decade both novels subjugate any possibility for historical use value by emphasizing an inflationary aesthetic mediated by their respective rites of incorporation. They promise investigations of historical memory, contemporary experience, and the interrogative discourses affecting the past's relation to the present. But both *Indian Country* and *In Country* contain a much more mystical aura than that within any religiously dominated society in Van Gennep's works. They eventually move toward a dangerous transcendental exchange value overwhelming much-needed investigations of personality, history, and contemporary society. As W. F. Haug points out concerning late capitalism, "the production of mere appearance is no longer confined to certain places that represent the sacred power, but form a totality of sensuousness of which soon not a single element will not have been subjected to the capitalist process of utilization."[31]

Indian Country presents the process in a more blatant way than *In Country*. It uses those old master narrative codes of masculine regeneration to achieve a conservative climax. *In Country*'s mediation of this process is more indirect. Despite representing the confusing, contradictory commodity, class, and gender relations grounded in postmodern America, *In Country*'s climax forecloses further exploration of the complexities generated by its narrative. The Washington Vietnam veterans memorial becomes a commodity form designed to provide an answer to Sam's and Emmett's historical dilemmas, with the weight naturally loaded in the latter's favor. By its dark mirror like construction the memorial dialectically reflects the observing community's image with the names of those who died for it. The wall's very construction presupposes an interplay of past and present historical memory. It thus contains the possibility of leading the viewer into activating a process of questioning the historical circumstances leading to Vietnam. The novel misses this potential. Instead, *In Country*'s conclusion presents an auratic transcendental climax affirming the masculine bond.

Both *Indian Country* and *In Country* eventually suppress historical pain that moves toward dimensions of individual, solipsistic, realization. Their different worlds of manifold associations seek not to interrogate the past's relationship to the present but to continually circumvent critical judgments as to whether they do provide a relevant historical use-value function. If the reader accepts the mystic claims of each novel's rite of incorporation s/he falls into that unreal relationship of the buyer in our contemporary commodity world accepting empty, spectacular signifiers of illusionary exchange value. Both *Indian Country* and *In Country* offer glittering, transcendental closures that are, in reality, empty vessels. They do not sufficiently interrogate the contradictions of the Vietnam era or the continuing problematic of the veteran's role in a forgetful America.

In contrast to Walter Benjamin's observations concerning the withering of aura in an age of mechanical reproduction, these works present a new form of "aura." It is one offering an idealistic, imaginary exchange value quashing the initial historically governed use value that brought these objects into being in the first place. An escapist, fantastic rite of incorporation appears as a transcendental answer once more, affirming that ritualized aestheticization of politics Benjamin warned against in the thirties.[32] Thus, while old traditions were once drastically affected by historical pain, under a deceptive postmodernist guise the new commodified culture of the nineties attempts to again restore to predominance mythic narratives that provide a dehistoricized aura.

NOTES

I wish to thank Michael Bibby for his helpful comments on different drafts of this article.

1. Fredric Jameson, *The Political Unconscious: Narrative as a Socially Symbolic Act* (Ithaca, N.Y.: Cornell University Press, 1981), 102.

2. Michael Clark, "Remembering Vietnam," *Cultural Critique* 3 (Spring 1986): 76.

3. Fredric Jameson, *Postmodernism, or The Cultural Logic of Late Capitalism* (Durham, N.C.: Duke University Press, 1991), 21.

4. Jim Collins, "Postmodernism and Television," in *Channels of Discourse, Reassembled,* ed. Robert C. Allen (Chapel Hill: University of North Carolina Press, 1992), 327; emphasis original.

5. Qtd. Linda Hutcheon, *The Politics of Postmodernism* (New York: Routledge, 1989), 15.

6. Laura Kipnis, "Feminism: The Political Conscience of Postmodernism," in *Universal Abandon? The Politics of Postmodernism,* ed. Andrew Ross (Minneapolis: University of Minnesota Press, 1988), 149–66.

7. *Politics of Postmodernism,* 1–2.

8. Ibid., 2; also see Hutcheon, *A Poetics of Postmodernism* (New York: Routledge, 1988), 3–21.

9. *Politics of Postmodernism,* 13–14.

10. Ibid., 11–12; *Poetics,* 222–31. Also see Richard W. McCormick, *Politics of the Self* (Princeton, N.J.: Princeton University Press, 1991), 9, 11–12; and Collins, "Postmodernism and Television," 327–31.

11. Rosalind Krauss, "John Mason and Postmodernist Sculpture: New Experiences, New Words," *Art in America* 67, no. 3 (1979): 121.

12. *Politics of Postmodernism,* 7.

13. See Michel Schneider, *Neurosis and Civilization: A Marxist/Freudian Synthesis,* trans. Michael Roboff (New York: The Seabury Press, 1975), 214–19, for a useful discussion of ideas contained in W. F. Haug's *Zur Kritik der Warenesthetik* (1971).

14. Arnold Van Gennep, *The Rites of Passage,* trans. Monika B. Vizedom and Gabrielle L. Caffee (London: Routledge and Kegan Paul, 1960). For the problematic use of such rites in Mason's writings, see Albert E. Wilhelm, "Private Rituals: Coping with Change in the Fiction of Bobbie Ann Mason," *The Midwest Quarterly* 28, no. 2 (1987): 271–82.

15. James Jones, "Phony War Movies," *Saturday Evening Post* (30 March 1963): 64–67. In *From Here to Eternity,* the thirties Warner Brothers social consciousness movies are contributory elements resulting in Robert E. Lee Prewitt's self-destructive naive idealism.

16. Philip Melling, *Vietnam in American Literature* (Boston: Twayne, 1990), 149–50.

17. For the significance of Williams's work as a radical postmodernist strategy, see Hutcheon, *Politics,* 4–6, 161.

18. *Vietnam in American Literature,* 155.

19. Philip Caputo, *Indian Country* (New York: Bantam, 1987), 72. Further references will be cited in the text.

20. For critiques of *Indian Country,* see Sybil Steinburg, review of *Indian Country, Publishers Weekly* (6 March 1987): 104; and Robert H. Donahugh, rev. of *Indian Country, Library Journal* 1 (April 1987): 160, who castigates it for its "melodrama" and "too obvious insights." See also Frank Conroy, "Bringing the Terrors Back Home," The *New York Times Book Review* (17 May 1987): 7. For relevant material on Bobbie Ann Mason see the following: Thomas De Pietro, review of *In Country, Commonweal* (1 November 1985): 620; Lila Havens, "Residents and Transients: An Interview with Bobbie Ann Mason," *Crazyhorse* 29 (Fall 1985): 87–104; Robert H. Brinkmeyer Jr., "Finding One's History: Bobbie Ann Mason and Contemporary Southern Literature," the *Southern Literary Journal* 19, no. 2 (1987): 21–33; Leslie White, "The Function of Popular Culture in Bobbie Ann Mason's *Shiloh and Other Stories* and *In Country,*" the *Southern Quarterly: A Journal of the Arts in the South* 26, no. 2 (1988): 69–79; Michael Smith, "Bobbie Ann Mason: Artist and Rebel: An Interview," the *Literary Review* 8, no. 3 (1988): 56–85; Barbara Henning, "Minimalism and the American Dream: *Shiloh* by Bobbie Ann Mason and *Preservations* by Raymond Carver," *Modern Fiction Studies* 35 (1989): 689–98; Vincent Kling, "A Conversation with Bobbie Ann Mason," *Four Quarters* 4, no. 1 (1990): 17–22; Sandra Bonilla Durham, "Women and War: Bobbie Ann Mason's *In Country,*" *Southern Literary Journal* 22, no. 2 (1990): 45–52; Barbara T. Ryan, "Decentered Authority in Bobbie Ann Mason's *In Country,*" *Critique: Studies in Contemporary Fiction* 31, no. 3 (1990): 199–212; Ellen A. Blais, "Gender Issues in Bobbie Ann Mason's *In Country,*" *South Atlantic Review* 56, no. 2 (1991): 107–08; David Booth, "Emmett's Wound: Grail Motifs in Bobbie Ann Mason's Portrait of America after Vietnam," *Southern Literary Journal* 23, no. 2 (1991): 98–109; Bonnie Lyons and Bill Oliver, "An Interview with Bobbie Ann Mason," *Contemporary Literature* 32 (1991): 449–70; Matthew C. Stewart, "Realism, Verismilitude, and the Depiction of Vietnam Veterans in *In Country,*" in *Fourteen Landing Zones: Approaches to Vietnam War Literature,* ed. Philip K. Jason (Iowa City: University of Iowa Press, 1991), 166–79; Thomas J. Morrissey, "Mason's *In Country,*" *Explicator* 50, no. 1 (1991): 62–64; Dorothy Combs Hill, "An Interview with Bobbie Ann Mason," the *Southern Quarterly* 31, no. 1 (1992): 85–118; June Dwyer, "New Roles, New History and New Patriotism: Bobbie Ann Mason's *In Country,*" *Modern Language Studies* 22, no. 2 (1992): 72–78; Joanna Price, "Remembering Vietnam: Subjectivity and Mourning in American New Realist Writing," *Journal of American Studies* 27 (1993): 173–86; Marjorie Winther, "Malls and Meaning: Popular and Corporate Culture in *In Country,*" *Literature/Interpretation/Theory* 4, no. 3 (1993): 195–220; Yonka Krasteva, "The South and the West in Bobbie Ann Mason's *In Country,*" *Southern Literary Journal* 26, no. 2 (1994): 77–90; and Barbara Tepa Lupack, "History as Her Story: Adapting Bobbie Ann Mason's *In Country* to Film," in *Vision/Revision: Adapting Contemporary American Fiction by Women to Film,* ed. Barbara Tepa Lupack (Bowling Green, Ohio: Popular Press, 1996), 159–92.

21. Jean Baudrillard, *Simulations,* trans. Paul Foss, Paul Patton, and Philip Beitchman (New York: Semiotex[t]e, 1983).

22. Bobbie Ann Mason, *In Country* (New York: Harper and Row, 1985), 8. Further references will be cited inthe text.

23. Although Celicia Tichi places Mason among a new group of contemporary writers in "full revolt against the traditional structure of beginning and middle and end because it is false to their perceptual experience," except for the flashback structure Mason's novel is actually very traditional in form. "Video Novels," *Boston Review* 12, no. 3 (June 1987): 13. Furthermore, although *In Country* bears several traces of the contemporary simulacra world questioning past realities, these are by no means progressive. Andreas Huyssen points out that many postmodernist strategies actually oppose the feminist threat to established cultural traditions. *After the Great Divide: Modernism, Mass Culture, Postmodernism* (Bloomington: Indiana University Press, 1986), 199, 219–20.

24. Brent Whelan, "Further Reflections on Counterculture and the Postmodern," *Cultural Critique* 11 (1988/89): 78.

25. In a rare comment upon motifs in her own fiction Mason states, "The classic quest for the father is one of the oldest themes isn't it? Except it's usually the young man looking for his father." See Wilhelm, 31. This patriarchal slippage and the male transcendental conclusion make questionable Evan Cannon's positive evaluation of Mason's work.

26. On the Cawood Pool episode Mason says, "She sets out to face facts the way Thoreau did not." See Enid Shomer, "An Interview with Bobbie Ann Mason," *Black Warrior Review* 12, no. 2 (1986): 100.

27. W. D. Erhart, "Who's Responsible," *Viet Nam Generation* 4 (1992): 96.

28. Susan Jeffords, *The Remasculinization of America: Gender and the Vietnam War* (Bloomington: Indiana University Press, 1989), 62–65.

29. See *The Rites of Passage.*

30. "Remembering Vietnam," 54, 58.

31. Qtd. Schneider, 215–16. See also Diane Johnson, "Southern Comfort," The *New York Times Book Review* (17 November 1985): 15–17. She links both *In Country* and *The Accidental Tourist* to the current sociohistorical era in a manner that could not be justifiably categorized as an argument for what Thomas Myers calls "a reductive historical consensus." "Dispatches from Ghost Country: The Vietnam Veteran in Recent American Fiction," *Genre* 21 (1988): 424. Johnson's views are extremely pertinent for understanding how Mason's potentially valuable self-reflexive gender strategies become stifled in the novel. "These are in a way Reaganesque dream novels, where the poor are deserving and spunkiness will win. The great works of the past by their form console us for the harshness of human reality that they confront. But perhaps confrontation is not the national mood, and these are books of out times" (17).

32. Walter Benjamin, "The Work of Art in the Age of Mechanical Reproduction," in *Film Theory and Criticism,* ed. Gerald Mast and Marshall Cohen. (New York: Oxford University Press, 1974), 612–34.

6

BRUISED AZALEAS:
BRUCE WEIGL AND THE
POSTWAR AESTHETIC

Eric Gadzinski

Bruce Weigl's Vietnam War poems are a leading example of the American soldier poetry of the war. Primarily consisting of short lyrics employing a spare, unornamented language, this poetry reflects a pragmatic use of form and basic, unreflexive loyalty to fact in tracing the effects of the war's reality on the individual. The character of this poetry's response to what Fredric Jameson has called "the first postmodern war"[1] bears examination for understanding how the term "postmodern" applies to this work and how this work relates to current postmodern aesthetics.

Weigl's poems depict the persistent and unredeemable shock and self-laceration resulting from his experience as a nineteen-year-old infantryman in 1967–68. The poems use a conventional free verse (often in a loose sonnet structure) uncomplicated by experiments in spatial arrangement, syntax, or enjambment, and employ an anonymous, generic American diction undistracted by dialect, neologism, music, irony, or metaphor. This style removes all challenges or mediations to the accessibility of images and incidents and the frankness of the apostrophes they inspire. The depth of these poems is not that of cultural or historical perspective, resolution, or sublime or utopian transcendence, but of the profundity of private pain that echoes from personal contact with the implacable surface of the real. Weigl's work is not strictly autobiographical or documentary, yet his imagined dramas, in serving to capture and convey the authenticity of experience, remain indistinguishable from genuine confession or testimony.[2]

Many of Weigl's poems occupy a postwar space in which memory of the war constitutes a perpetual, self-contained reality that tyrannizes the present. The flat, clinical precision of Weigl's language strips the moment of this crippling encounter to a stark intensity. The title of the poem "Breakdown," for example, signals this approach in borrowing from the vocabulary of pathology to denote crisis and failure, while also alluding to the term used (e.g., in military weapons training, or mechanical engineering) to denote disassembly or anatomy (as in "parts breakdown"). The poem portrays the war's effects in physical terms as producing an inescapable insomnia and opens with the description of "its" incipience:

> With sleep that is barely under the surface
> it begins, a twisting sleep as if a wire
> were inside you. . . .

The poem quickly moves to the source of "it," the image of "strangers with guns," "teenage soldiers glancing back / over their shoulders" before they "squeeze the trigger" at "children trapped in the alley." It hardly matters whether this is a memory of an actual event or an emblematic image of violated innocence. The plausibility of the act is supported by the documentary record, while the validity of the emblem is verified by the testimony of veterans who continue to suffer the horror inflicted by the guilty "strangers" of their teenage soldier-selves on their "trapped" youth.

The poem concludes:

> I am going to stay here as long as I can.
> I am going to sit in the garden as if nothing has happened
> and let the bruised azaleas have their way.[3]

The effort to remain "here," in the "garden" of a present safe from the predation of the past, involves for Weigl an attempt at denial that collapses in the recognition of its pretense, leaving submission to the unresolved, insomniac ache of a wounded spring as the only possible (and far from confident) course.

As in "Breakdown," the theme of many of Weigl's poems is the undeniability of a nightmare reality that absorbs a pastoral present, and the unredeemability of the speaker's "bruise." The poem "Amnesia" (again taking a conceit from clinical vocabulary) provides perhaps the most poignant treatment of this theme (Weigl 53). Here the image of transcendence or release acquires an agonizing power through its unattainability.

The poem begins: "If there was a world more disturbing than this / . . . you don't remember it." This "world" that "swallowed you whole" is a "muggy" jungle "twilight," "effervescent" with rot, where "monkeys / screamed something / that came to sound like words." It is a present "swallowed" by an oppressive past (whose hallucinatory image of a haunted, corrupting obscurity is nevertheless an accurate description of features of the Asian landscape), where animal screams become words and words screams. Again as in "Breakdown," the suffering subject (displaced as "you," the self-as-other, as well as the reader thrust into the speaker's place) attempts a futile denial: "You tell yourself no and cry a thousand days." Finally, however, instead of the submission to the bruise of "Breakdown," the incurability of the bruise is further wrung by the image of a tantalizing yet unreachable solace in death:

> You imagine the crows calling autumn into place
> are your brothers and you could
> if only the strength and will were there
> fly up to them to be black
> and useful to the wind.

The "bruise" incapacitates all power to resist. Neither denial nor performative acts of the imagination have the "strength and will" to prevent the collapse of tenses and persons into the monkey's scream.[4]

Weigl's work has immediate precedents in literary and testimonial responses to the enormities of World War II, such as the Holocaust. His realistic approach has an analogue in Holocaust literature in what Sidra Ezrahi defines as a dominant mode of "concentrationary realism," which uses history as a creative resource but maintains a documentary verisimilitude in portraying the erosion of individual autonomy and integrity.[5] Weigl's theme of the predations of memory is also echoed in Holocaust survivor narratives where, as Lawrence Langer observes (recalling the conceit of "Breakdown"), the inconsolable memory of atrocious reality becomes a continually disruptive "insomniac faculty."[6] In this context, although one must not overdraw the comparison, Weigl's unsleeping, creative yet literal "bruise" can be seen as inhabiting its own version of a *"univers concentrationnaire."*[7]

Julia Kristeva's discussion of the "postwar" aesthetic arising from the Second World War provides perhaps the most useful account for locating Weigl's low key, private, bruised, and bruising lyrics.[8] Citing the work of Marguerite Duras as exemplifying a postwar consciousness uniquely brutalized by the magnitude of the World War's confrontation with the "horror in oneself and in the world," Kristeva defines a "rhetoric of apocalypse" that employs an underrated, nondemonstrative language and a "wealth of images" to present a "raw display of monstrosity" and "follow ill-being step by step, almost in clinical fashion, without ever getting the better of it." This rhetoric strives to "remain faithful to the intensity of horror," and reveals a "pain from which only tension remains," offering "no purification . . . no improvement, no promise of a beyond, not even the enchanting beauty of style or irony that might provide a bonus of pleasure." Concerned with "baring the malady" without "distance or perspective," such writing "does not analyze itself by seeking its sources in the music that lies under the words or the defeat of the narrative's logic," but "encounters, recognizes, [and] spreads the pain that summons it" (223–29 passim). Here,

> Private suffering absorbs political horror into the subject's psychic microcosm. . . . [T]he private domain gains a solemn dignity that depreciates the public domain while allocating to history the imposing responsibility for having triggered the malady of death. As a result, . . . private life . . . is emphasized to the point of filling the whole of the real and invalidating any other concern. (234–36)

Kristeva characterizes the horror at the source of this rhetoric as a "monstrous nothing," where the word "nothing" signifies a "perfect state of disorder," both internal and external, that "blinds and compels one to be silent" (222–24). Her image for this "perfect state," one borrowed from Paul Valery, is a "kiln heated to incandescence" in which "no luminous disparity would remain" (222). This incandescent disorder can be seen in the disorienting "effervescence" of war memory at the center of Weigl's poems. However, the clarity of Weigl's depiction of horror (the murder in "Breakdown," the jungle in "Amnesia," and their ambush of the infectious "you" in both) appears to contradict Kristeva's assertion of such horror's "silence" or "infernal inaccessibility" (258), a contradiction that she seems to admit in maintaining that the postwar aesthetic "encounters" and "recognizes" its pain and provides a "raw display" of monstrosity. In this transparency Weigl is, again, not unique; rather, the notion of silence or inaccessibility that is so much a convention of postwar criticism may indicate critical resistance to the challenge such transparency poses to a traditional positivist and redemptive conception of the human image. As Langer observes of Holocaust testimonies:

> [T]he more we listen, the more evidence we have that the question of inaccessibility may be our own invented defense against the invitation to imagine what is perfectly explicit in the remembered experience before our eyes and ears. . . . We may call it inaccessible, but what we really mean is that it is not discussable. We lack terms of discourse for such human situations, preferring to call them inhuman and thus banish them from civilized consciousness.[9]

As these testimonies and Weigl's poems make plain, horror does not necessarily defeat language. It is both speakable and imaginable. To do either, however, one must relinquish resistance to it and the habits of "civilized" discourse that would silence or conceal the irreconcilable presence of the thing itself. It is quite possible that Duras yields to such critical resistance. However, one must also question if it is rather Kristeva who yields to such defense in designating this rhetoric as wholly a "no man's land of aching affects" that must be "read" for what it cannot say, rather than one, such as Weigl's and that of his Holocaust counterparts, that combines both the crime and its aftermath, bruised affects and the raw display of something we do not wish to see (Kristeva 246). In any event, Weigl's is not the opacity of a "dead" language but the clear, level intensity of a sniper's eye.[10]

While the horror may not be as secret as we would have it, its constraining effects in Weigl's "bruise" bear examination for their relation to the "malady" Kristeva defines in Duras. Duras refuses to "drown suffering in the conqueror's triumph, or in metaphysical sarcasms and enthusiasms, or yet in the fondness of erotic pleasure," but "chooses or yields to the . . . conniving, voluptuous, bewitching contemplation of death within us, of the wound's constancy" (Kristeva 236). The issue of the "voluptuous" in the "wound" is bound up with what Kristeva identifies as the role of "biology" (225). In Duras's woman Kristeva finds "not a repression but an exhaustion of erotic drives," a "basic disconnection" that turns her "only toward the hollow of one's own proper body." Being "aloof" yet "compliant," capable of "ravishment—but not pleasure," she is

> fond of the death she believes she bears within herself. Even more so, such a complicity with death gives her the feeling that she is beyond death: a woman neither gives nor undergoes death because she is part of it and because she imposes it. He is the one who catches the malady of death. . . . A certain truth of feminine experience involving the jouissance of suffering verges, with Duras, on the mythification of the inaccessible feminine. (244–46 passim)

The feminine subject "domesticates" death and expresses suffering through a "frigidity" that "holds back a passion that could not flow," making her remote and unavailable to the "stranger" (i.e., the man) who "lives on the surface" (227, 240).

In Weigl's poems, which also refuse the "conqueror's triumph" (necessarily), and erotic or metaphysical enthusiasms, the speaker does indeed seem to be the guy "on the surface" who "catches" the malady. Reflecting a conventional trope of masculine experience, Weigl's subject does not "domesticate" death, but bears its external weight in a posture of resistance that ossifies into a repressive paralysis. In contrast to what Kristeva defines as Duras's feminine frigidity of exhaustion, Weigl's disconnection, self-absorption, and compliance to the pleasureless ravishment of the bruised azaleas, while parallel, are the function of an enforced impotence. The term "impotence," denoting an essential lack of vigor or ability, is not really accurate to describe the failure of "strength and will" that the "bruise" imposes. Rather, the "scream" of Weigl's poems is that of volatile contents under pressure, burning trapped in the dead armor of war. The masculine subject thus finds himself caught between the dual annihilations of the death posture's rigid desensitivity and the explosion of superheated passion.

These features are most clearly expressed in the poem "On the Anniversary of Her Grace." Here, in a conventional masculine treatment, the feminine represents life, grace, for which the speaker tragically yearns yet fears to touch. The poem opens with a move typical of Weigl, using a natural occurrence, a storm, to signal here the threatening, excessive rise of memory and desire:[11]

> Rain and low clouds blown through the valley,
>
> . . . .
>
> rivers at their high tides too high,
> rain and black skies that come for you.

The drama of the poem is the familiar one of a veteran's return, presented as the troubled recollection of a thwarted reunion. The speaker (now "I") wakes from a "restless night of dreams of her / whom I will never have again" (the insomnia trope) and recalls his past anticipation of "fulfillment" in "a kiss I had imagined / would come again and again to my face." This remembered anticipation is checked, however, by recollection of the corrosive grief and repression wrought by the war: "Inside me the war had eaten a hole." This hole is the access of the irrevocable "place / where they still fell in their blood" and the stoic necessities of survival there. The line, "I could keep the dragons at the gate," a rare excursion into metaphor that exploits an Asian allusion, introduces a litany of defensive skills: "I could paint my face and hide;" "I could not eat or sleep then walk all day;" "I could draw leeches from my skin / with the tip of a lit cigarette / and dig a hole deep enough to save me." Inured to the practice of invulnerability, the speaker finds himself both calloused and frighteningly aware of the flammable vulnerability such callousness contains. That flammability, compounded with the rigor mortis of habitual defense, finally prevents him from leaving his clenched but accustomed "place":

> but I could not open my arms to her
> that first night of forgiveness.
> I could not touch anyone.
> I thought my body would catch fire. (54–55)

The husk acquired in war becomes a brittle tinder of fear, grief, and yearning easily ignited into a self-consuming chaos.

As a pair, this poem and the poem "Amnesia" reveal an anguished predicament that allows neither escape through death nor acceptance through life, but that combines death-in-life with life-in-death. This is not a numbed existence, but one where numbness and vitality continually wrestle in the implacable enclosure with which the war circumscribes consciousness. Where Duras's woman, in Kristeva's construction, is a war bride, death's intimate whose exhaustion makes her a ghost echoing the pain of her murder, Weigl's man remains a hostile prisoner of war pacing the perpetual cell of war's conflicting persecutions. Given this difference, what unites the two in the infectious tension of their detachment, absorption, and ravishment is an exclusive focus on what Weigl calls, in the poem "Elegy," the "black understanding" of those who were "not allowed" to die (Weigl 70).

The determining ground of this understanding appears to be the intensity of horror experienced by individuals made particularly vulnerable through any or all of the factors of youth, self-uncertainty, deprivation, displacement, and rigid or idealistic expectations. Kristeva speculates that apart from the function of "biology," Duras's acute sensitivity to the "malady of death" stems from experience of the Second World War combined with the "strange experience of having been uprooted, a childhood on the Asian continent, the stress of a difficult existence next to her courageous, harsh mother [and] . . . the precocious encounter with her brother's mental illness and the prevailing poverty" (237–38). This combination of war and precocious familiarity with dislocation, emotional and material hardship, mental illness, and parental oppression are also features of the Vietnam soldier's experience.

As Jacqueline Lawson observes, what distinguishes the Vietnam soldier's experience from that of his World War predecessors is its precociousness. The extreme youth and relative psychological immaturity of the Vietnam soldier made the terror and hardships of war and the feelings of confusion, isolation, and betrayal into psychological burdens that were particularly debilitating.[12] Uprooted from "the World" to "the Nam" and back again to the anomie of what Philip Beidler calls a "solitary confinement" in a hostile or indifferent society, the veteran bore unresolved memories of a fantastic, vicious, formless, and purposeless war in which there were "no real points of reference" other than death and suffering.[13] The widespread effect of this war on the teenagers who fought it is expressed through the symptoms of Posttraumatic Stress Disorder, which include a "sudden acting or feeling as if the traumatic event were reoccurring," a "feeling of detachment or estrangement from others," and "hyper-alertness"—symptoms differing from those of World War "combat fatigue" or "shell shock" primarily in the degree of their intensity and pervasiveness.[14] Compounding these difficulties was the failure, perceived by veterans both in themselves and in the culture, of an idealized patriarchal model from World War II. Consisting of a stoic rectitude and heroic self-reliance destined to survive and triumph over a discernible evil, this model was valorized in the Hollywood image of John Wayne and often echoed by the presence of real fathers who were veterans of "the big one." Thus, the failure of "strength and will" in the war's abject "world of hurt" was rendered doubly damning, further magnifying the "bruise" beyond mediation or redemption.[15] Attesting to the war's persistent vividness and formative centrality in veteran consciousness, John Clark Pratt observes that "the war was the most explicit experience we have ever seen,"[16] and Michael Herr concludes from the ruin of adolescence wasted by "something more complicated than death, an annihilation less final but more complete," that Vietnam was "what we had instead of happy childhoods."[17]

Jean Baudrillard and Fredric Jameson echo the salient character of the war's effect on consciousness in their description of postmodern schizophrenia: "the absolute proximity, the total instantaneity of things, the feeling of no defense, no retreat";[18] an experience of "heightened intensity" in which "isolated. . . . material signifiers" bear a "mysterious and oppressive charge of affect" and where there is a lack of a sense of "the persistence of the 'I' and 'me' over time."[19] To the extent that this description proves apt for the hallucinatory, decentering transparency of Weigl's "bruise" one may be justified in labeling it postmodern. Certainly, at a more basic level of definition, the rubric also fits insofar as Weigl's poems are not what John Felstiner has called the "emotionally adequate and balanced" verse characteristic of Second World War poets such as Randall Jarrell and Karl Shapiro.[20] However, the affinity of Weigl's bruise to the Holocaust survivors' "insomniac faculty" tends to invalidate any contention for Weigl's privileged claim to postmodernity in this regard, although it suggests that postmodernity is rooted in a psychic trauma that has its analogues and origins in historical experience.

Kristeva suggests that it is the materiality or physicality of traumatic experience that finally locates work such as Weigl's. Using the Second World War as a benchmark for contemporary history (in which Vietnam, among other "minor" traumas, does not figure), Kristeva posits the absorption of the postwar "abyssal discontent" into the "narrative synthesis" of a postmodern "comedy." In this "new amatory world," the postwar apocalyptic vision has been so "thoroughly investigated" as to become a commonplace—almost a cliché, the ground upon which now plays the "shimmering of artificial amenities" that includes "philosophical mediations as well as erotic protections or entertaining pleasures" and the "distraction of parody" (258–59). This postmodern "shimmering" implies an aesthetic of absence that contrasts with the presence signified by the postwar's "kiln heated to incandescence," and suggests that the postmodern "comedy" emerges as the material immediacy of of such presence recedes. Where the postwar "rhetoric of apocalypse" struggles to delineate the image of an all-consuming, undeniable physical presence, the postmodern "comedy" seems to appear as image-making becomes facile, eminently deniable, no longer accountable to the thing itself, since there is no thing. Rather, the postmodern inherits the desolate mind-scape of postwar destruction without physical memory of its source, and plays in the ashes.

The evidence of Weigl's poetry, however, with its unreflexive "postwar" concentration on the agonized face of the bruise, indicates that the cultural shift Kristeva describes is not monolithic. Instead, Weigl demonstrates that each fresh encounter with horror, for those in its path, defers the playful shimmering of erotic and metaphysical laughter to the ripples of the subsiding wake of the Thing. For those upon whose bodies it is inscribed, such horror can never be so "thoroughly investigated" as to lose its tragic incandescence. The "bruise," the "malady," the "black understanding" of the horror in oneself and the world manifest itself across space, time, and gender. Neither anomaly nor anachronism in our postmodern era, it reappears to trace the monstrous immediacies that our times continue to present, and from which our comedies may distract but cannot escape.

As Kali Tal observes, there is ample reason to view the literature of the Vietnam War within a context of a literature of trauma, connecting veterans to survivors of the Holocaust and Hiroshima as well as to contemporary rape and incest victims.[21] In the poem, "The Impossible," Weigl makes such a contemporary connection, to victims of child abuse, in an allegory of the origin and character of this traumatic aesthetic.[22] Bidden by "Winter's last rain and a light I don't recognize," the displacing release of frozen memory, the poem's speaker recalls "the man who made me suck his cock / when I was seven, in sunlight, between boxcars." The memory is one of a preco-

cious, brutal annunciation that excommunicates—"changing me /
so I could not move among my people in the old way. / . . . . God
could not save me from a mouthful of cum. / That afternoon some
lives turned away from the light"—yet also ordains to lucidity:

> He taught me how to move my tongue around.
> In his hands he held my head like a lover.
> Say it clearly and you make it beautiful, no matter
> what.

In Weigl's ability to do the impossible, to "say it clearly," and in that
of other writers who share the dubious privilege of his aesthetic,
there is a terrible beauty of necessity that gives pause, even as it gives
rise, to our search for amatory distractions.

NOTES

1. Fredric Jameson, "Postmodernism, or the Cultural Logic of Late Capitalism," *New Left Review* 146 (July–August 1984): 84.

2. In a recent interview, Weigl acknowledged his use of fictional settings and incidents yet noted that their apparent verisimilitude often leads readers to inquire or commiserate about the particulars he describes. Bruce Weigl, "Song of Napalm," *New Letters on the Air, Contemporary Writers on Radio,* Kansas City: University of Missouri, 1988, audiocassette. Tim O'Brien provides an illuminating discussion of the use of such creative realism in "How to Tell a True War Story," *The Things They Carried* (New York: Penguin, 1990).

3. Bruce Weigl, *Song of Napalm* (New York: Atlantic Monthly Press, 1988), 47. Further references will be cited parenthetically in the text.

4. The figure of the monkey becomes an especially pregnant symbol of the Vietnam experience in Weigl's poem "Monkey" (*Napalm,* 20), where it carries connotations of a sense-nonsense dilemma, racism, animality, self-displacement, and affliction, and alludes to 1968, the "Year of the Monkey" in the Vietnamese calendar, and also the year of Weigl's tour of duty.

5. Sidra DeKoven Ezrahi, *By Words Alone: The Holocaust in Literature* (Chicago: University of Chicago Press, 1980), 14.

6. Lawrence L. Langer, *Holocaust Testimonies: The Ruins of Memory* (New Haven: Yale University Press, 1991), xv.

7. This term, from David Rousset's Holocaust memoir, *The Other Kingdom,* is cited by Ezrahi in coining the adjective "concentrationary," and denotes the self-contained universe of the camps and of Nazi persecution of the Jews in general. *By Words Alone,* 10. Any comparison to the Holocaust is problematic. The one made here serves merely to draw attention to certain

characteristics of self-containment and realism in traumatic representation. Ezrahi identifies a critical distinction between war experience and the Holocaust in observing that for the soldier, survival remains "at least a logical possibility" that mediates his apprehension of fate (ibid.).

8. Julia Kristeva, *Black Sun: Depression and Melancholia,* trans. Leon S. Roudiez (New York: Columbia University Press, 1989). See "The Malady of Grief: Duras," 221–83. Further references will be cited parenthetically in the text.

9. Langer, *Holocaust Testimonies,* 82, 118.

10. Weigl acknowledges that he "struggles hard" for a "clear, direct language," disdaining the "old diction" that "doesn't work anymore" to "tell the war." Eric James Schroeder, *Vietnam, We've All Been There: Interviews with American Writers* (Westport, Conn.: Praeger, 1992), 191.

11. Weigl has acknowledged the influence of the English Romantics (especially Wordsworth and Keats) on his work. This influence may partly account for his frequent use of emblematic natural or pastoral settings. Schroeder, *Vietnam, We've All Been There,* 184.

12. Jacqueline E. Lawson, "'Old Kids': The Adolescent Experience in the Nonfiction Narratives of the Vietnam War," *Search and Clear: Critical Responses to Selected Literature and Films of the Vietnam War,* ed. William J. Searle (Bowling Green, Ohio: Popular Press, 1988), 27.

13. Philip D. Beidler, *American Literature and the Experience of Vietnam* (Athens: University of Georgia Press, 1982), 9, 164.

14. Joel Osler Brende and Erwin Randolph Parson, *Vietnam Veterans: The Road to Recovery* (New York: Signet, 1985), 102–04.

15. Among many critical discussions of the effects of the John Wayne-World War myth on American attitudes and expectations in the Vietnam War, Lloyd Lewis provides one of the more thorough analyses in chapter 2 of *The Tainted War: Culture and Identity in Vietnam War Narratives* (Westport, Conn.: Greenwood Press, 1985).

16. John Clark Pratt, "Preface," *Unaccustomed Mercy: Soldier Poets of the Vietnam War,* ed. W. D. Ehrhart (Lubbock: Texas Tech University Press, 1989), viii.

17. Michael Herr, *Dispatches* (New York: Avon, 1978), 243–44.

18. Jean Baudrillard, "The Ecstacy of Communication," trans. John Johnston, in *The Anti-Aesthetic: Essays on Postmodern Culture,* ed. Hal Foster (Seattle, Wash.: Bay Press, 1989), 133.

19. Fredric Jameson, "Postmodernism and Consumer Society," in *The Anti-Aesthetic,* 119–20.

20. John Felstiner, "American Poetry and the War in Vietnam," *Stand* 19, no. 2 (1978): 11.

21. Kali Tal, "Speaking the Language of Pain: Vietnam War Literature in the Context of a Literature of Trauma," in *Fourteen Landing Zones: Approaches to Vietnam War Literature,* ed. Philip K. Jason (Iowa City: University of Iowa Press, 1991), 244.

22. Bruce Weigl, *What Saves Us* (Evanston, Ill.: TriQuarterly Books, 1992), 68.

THREE

POST/VIETNAM/MODERN

7

THE POST-VIETNAM CONDITION

Michael Bibby

After our war, the dismembered bits
—all those pierced eyes, ear slivers, jaw splinters
gouged lips, odd tibias, skin flaps, and toes—
came squinting, wobbling, jabbering back.

. . . .

After the war, . . .
will the ancient tales still tell us new truths?
       John Balaban, *Locusts at the Edge of Summer*

ROMANCING THE "TRUE"

The climactic scene in the Quentin Tarantino-Tony Scott film *True Romance* (1993) comes about after the main character, Clarence Worley, played by Christian Slater, arranges to sell a suitcase of stolen cocaine to a big-time Hollywood producer named Lee Donowitz, whose fame seems to rest on his Vietnam War film, "Coming Home in a Body Bag." With his car phone, silk shirts, and vaguely new-age affectations, Donowitz signifies the worst of Hollywood culture. Clarence, who regularly communes with the spirit of Elvis, tells Donowitz several times how much he liked "Coming Home in a Body Bag," explaining that his vet friends thought it was the truest representation yet. As the drug deal unfolds in the suite of a swanky hotel, Donowitz's Vietnam War film is being projected onto a big-screen video monitor, its images sometimes superimposed over the characters of *True Romance* as they build up to its climax of orgiastic violence. The police show up with guns drawn, and then the mafiosi whose coke Clarence stole also show up with their guns at the ready, and everyone starts shooting, while scenes of a Huey hovering over the fields of Vietnam flicker over the violence so that the two films become one, the "crazed expenditure" that the war symbolizes mirrored in the hyperviolence acted out in 1990s Hollywood.[1]

As with other Tarantino films, *True Romance* fetishizes disposable trash culture—the grungy, violent excess of a Hollywood simulacra world where everything is affect and content is merely a vague memory. Its characters constitute nothing so much as an amalgamation of citational gestures. They exist and function less as human beings than as stereotypes, signifiers, depthless affectations, expressive of violence as style. Like *Reservoir Dogs* (1992) and *Pulp Fiction* (1994), *True Romance* seems much less about story and more about hyperreal violence as a stylistic gesture. Its pastiche of 1950s motel architecture haunting 1990s L.A., of Vegas-era Elvis as spiritual guide and B-grade, *Gun Crazy* crime thriller narratives inflecting grunge aimlessness seems to epitomize the depthlessness, ahistoricity, and schizophrenia often cited as indicative of postmodernism.

What precisely "postmodernism" *is* has been the focus of great debate—as can be seen not only by the plethora of books on the subject but as well by the essays in the present collection. The word emphasizes a historicity and pronounces its coming "after modernism." "Modernism" enjoys somewhat more stability in critical discourse, having been the site of a variety of foundational gestures, not least of which was the New Criticism, and thus, has been institutionalized as both a particular set of aesthetic practices and a specific historical period, generally understood to span the late 1890s to about World War II. Postmodernism, however, is often understood loosely as a general cultural condition, sometimes irrespective of a specific historical reference point, some critics arguing that works traditionally understood as both historically and aesthetically modernist—such as Gertrude Stein's *Tender Buttons* or Virginia Woolf's *The Waves*—should be regarded as postmodernist. Although the word "postmodernism" was used as early as the 1870s by the British artist John Watkins Chapman, it only begins to gain currency in the 1950s and only by the 1970s does it enter into the general vernacular and become one of the central problematics of critical discourse. Yet despite attempts to dehistoricize it, "postmodernism" usually designates a historical period, although its parameters have widely varied. Further the term has come to designate not only aesthetic practices but also a range of social, political, and economic conditions specific to the changing shape of late twentieth-century experience.

Some of the key elements that distinguish postmodernism from modernism include a hyperproblematization of representation and a consequent "death of the signified." Where modernism questioned mimesis and the problem of representation, it nonetheless retained a faith in a transcendental signified, in an immutable essence; postmodernism posits a world in which signs beget signs such that no transcendental signified is possible. Modernism deployed multiple perspectivism and ironic relativism in order to reveal the true nature of reality and its underlying metaphysical narrative. Postmodernism, on the other hand, sees multiplicity and irony as ends in themselves, being ultimately suspicious of metanarratives. Where modernism reified the role of the artist and clung to an Arnoldian belief in art's civilizing virtues, postmodernism challenges the notion that the artist can stand outside the world, outside the reach of mass culture, preferring to see all cultural production—from the Picasso in the gallery to motel signs in Las Vegas—as equally valid objects of critical inquiry. Modernism saw fragmentation as a tragic existential condition that must be resisted; postmodernism revels in fragmentation. Where modernism's edict was "make it new," postmodernism has made nostalgia, pastiche, and simulacrum its standards. And where modernism was concerned with immanent meanings and deep consciousness, postmodernism is about the play of surfaces, style, and affect.

True Romance, in other words, seems an ideal example of postmodernist cinema. The particular moment I have chosen to focus on, however, draws our attention to yet another Hollywood genre seemingly emblematic of postmodern American pop culture: the Vietnam War film, and in particular the Rambo-esque B-movie genre of the 1980s, resonant with associations to hyperviolent nihilism and pumped-up fake heroism, a mournful ode to lost masculine virtues, a genre itself only a vague simulacrum of its predecessor, the World War II movie—which thus, echoes *True Romance*'s own self-conscious, ironic stance toward Hollywood and its "crazed expenditures." Ultimately, *True Romance*'s reference is not to the Vietnam War but to a film genre, the scenes of the war superimposed as sheer surface, ghostly tissue over the scenes of graphic gunplay set around a cocaine deal gone bad in a late twentieth-century Hollywood hotel room. Consequently the war registers only as a trace signifying nothing in itself beyond generic conventions and representationality. As yet another simulacrum in the society of the spectacle, the historical war is rendered conspicuously absent by its very enunciation. The Vietnam War doesn't exist as any motivating factor in Tarantino's film—rather, it is invoked both as a gesture toward an implicitly debased genre metaphoric of Hollywood trash culture and as a plot device meant to foreshadow the film's hyperviolent climax. The war has been entirely dissolved, digested, and disseminated as an opportunity for representing spectacle.

Since the mid-1980s—significantly a period in which the Wall was inaugurated and the Reagan Administration sought to rearticulate the Vietnam veteran as an American hero and "remasculinize" the nation[2]—a number of films have similarly cited the Vietnam War as a generic sign of hyperviolence, excess, and militaristic spectacle. These are not war films per se so much as excessive displays of technowar that affect the hypostatized stylistic features of what has come to be known about the Vietnam War. James Cameron's *Aliens* (1986), for example, appropriates the attitude and patois of Vietnam-era, working-class "grunts" for its ensemble of macho "GIs" fighting mysterious and elusive "bugs" in a futuristic, outerspace technojungle. Similarly John McTiernan's *Predator* (1987) puts Arnold Schwarznegger as an ex-Marine mercenary in the jungles of Central America (once considered America's "new Vietnam") against an alien enemy who can blend seamlessly into the environment. Hyperviolent crime films, from the mainstream *Lethal Weapon* series to more "arty" productions such as David Lynch's *Wild at Heart*, feature key characters who, as Vietnam vets, signify aspects of either regenerative or cathartic violence. Such citationality produces what Jean Baudrillard has called a "fatal process," in that "the Vietnam War" becomes a sign pointing only to another sign, an "endless enwrapping of images . . . which leaves images no other destiny than images." The concrete historicity of the war gives way to an extravagant procession, a romancing of the "true," in which the historical war has become nothing more than a sign in the society of the spectacle, a simulation of simulation, "the death sentence of every reference."[3]

It occurred to me, watching *True Romance* on my VCR—in that uniquely postmodern experience of thoroughly fragmented, alienated spectatorship, with its fluid channel shiftings, fast-forwards, rewinds, and freeze-frames—that much the same thing has happened to the Vietnam War in critical and theoretical studies of postmodernity. Few of these studies cite the Vietnam War as historical event, indeed very few acknowledge that it even happened.[4] Yet in cases where some attempt is made to connect the war and postmodernity, the former is presented as exemplifying the latter, such that the Vietnam War is seen as a "postmodernist war."[5] Consequently the longest military engagement in U.S. history and a key conflict of the Cold War era, a decade-long military struggle that profoundly inflected social experience for both Americans and Southeast Asians, and had a critical impact on the global economy, and continues to shape current geopolitical alignments is subordinated by such rhetoric to an effect of a supposedly transcendental cultural condition. As in *True Romance*, it appears as a citational moment expressive of a cultural style.

Perhaps the most famous example of this rhetorical move appears in Jameson's axiomatic essay, "Postmodernism, or the Cultural Logic of Late Capitalism." Discussing Michael Herr's *Dispatches*, Jameson writes:

> The extraordinary linguistic innovations of this work may still be considered postmodern, in the eclectic way in which its language impersonally fuses a whole range of contemporary collective idiolects, most notably rock language and black language; but the fusion is dictated by problems of content. *The first terrible postmodernist war* cannot be told in any of the traditional paradigms of the war novel or movie—indeed, that breakdown of all previous narrative paradigms is, along with the breakdown of any shared language through which a veteran might convey such experience, among the principle subjects of the book and may be said to open up the place of a whole new reflexivity.[6]

Jameson suggests that the Vietnam War cannot be told through any appeal to the grand narratives of modernity, and thus, the subject of Herr's book is less the war and more "the breakdown of all previous narrative paradigms" to account for this war. According to Jameson, this is because the Vietnam War resists the abilities of post-Vietnam War writers to narrate it, because the war maps an ineluctable, fragmented, deterritorialized space.[7] The war *is* the breakdown of the grand narratives so symptomatic of the postmodern; unlike previous wars, the U.S. intervention in Vietnam does not acquiesce to the narrative conventions of heroism, progress, just cause, etc. But is the *war* "postmodernist"? Does thinking the war as "postmodernist" oversimplify and, thus, dehistoricize the relationships between the sociocultural, aesthetic, political, and economic?

To modify the war as "postmodernist" implies that the war is yet another phenomenon of postmodernity. The war, in this sense, is read as exhibiting the traits of a general historical, cultural condition already identifiable. If we can attach a qualification to the name of the war, it must be because that which qualifies it supersedes it, gives it shape, definition, morphological precision. To term the war "postmodernist," then, is to colonize the war under the cultural; to subsume it under a critical sign, a name for the various modes of cultural practices we have come to recognize as the postmodern; to restrict the war under this name; to repress its historicity in the name of a unifying signifier.[8] To do so not only enacts an epistemic violence in the articulation of the name of the Vietnam War, a name that for the U.S., continues to be the always already unrepresentable,[9] but that also threatens to elide the historical conditions under which postmodernity itself to a large extent has been produced. To qualify the Vietnam War as "postmodernist," in effect, is to place the cultural before the historical, to forget the barbarity that Walter Benjamin insisted underwrites any "document of civilization."[10] It is to claim that the various cultural phenomena that Jameson and others claim are symptomatic of postmodernity—the loss of historical sense, the disappearance of the subject, the dominance of the fragmentary—emerge not as an effect of material, economic conditions but preexist these conditions as pure, transcendental superstructure. And just as Jameson points out that the colonization of the real is indicative of postmodernism, his own colonization of a war whose "reality" violently configured late twentieth-century history is itself indicative of theoretical discourse on the postmodern.

The problem of qualifying the war as "postmodernist" is also a problem of conflating "postmodernism" with "postmodernity." Jameson has used "postmodernism" to refer to "a whole set of aesthetic and cultural features and procedures," as well as to refer to "the socioeconomic organization of our society commonly called late capitalism."[11] Yet postmodernity has most often been used to refer to the latter conception rather than the former, where the aesthetic and cultural is considered as articulated within the socioeconomic and historical.[12] As Linda Hutcheon points out, postmodernity "has been variously defined in terms of the relationship between intellectual and state discourses; as a condition determined by universal, diffuse cynicism, by a panic sense of the hyperreal and the simulacrum." And as Hutcheon argues later, to conflate cultural and aesthetic practices with historical conditions tends to dissolve the possibilities for understanding how cultural postmodernism can be both critical and complicitous with the socioeconomic and historical. It is, in effect, to elide the dialectical nature of the postmodern.[13]

If Jameson and others would argue that the postmodern is more than cultural style, but also describes a general cultural condition, I would contend that we must find ways of accounting for how the Vietnam War played a key role in producing the material conditions within which it has become possible to make postmodern culture. The attempt by "developed" nations (France and the United States) over the course of at least twenty-five years to colonize, subjugate, and lay waste to southeast Asia, an attempt that we now often reduce to the name of the Vietnam War, must be understood in relation to the paradigmatic shifts in politics, social life, economy, and philosophy many argue constitute key elements of postmodernist culture. Yet Jameson and other theorists of postmodernism usually gesture to it only in passing, if at all. Indeed, when Jameson comments on Herr in an earlier version of this essay, he does so "in passing" (PNL 84).[14] Thus the war, the range of economic and political configurations that generated and executed the war, the social and cultural forces articulated by the power relations constituted by the war fade away "in passing" as yet one more example of the postmodern condition. It seems inconsistent with the historicist views Jameson elaborates, however, to imagine that the protracted commitment of U.S. industry and the military to the war, its overarching burden on the national economy, the intense political debate the war generated, to say nothing of the seismic impact it had on everyday American lives would not have in some significant sense to be accounted for in any theory of the geopolitical and cultural conditions Jameson and others have described as postmodernity.[15] By using the term "postmodernism" to qualify the U.S. intervention in Vietnam, Jameson and others risk reiterating the Western tradition of making Vietnam a metaphor or allegory for Western history, effacing the nation and people of Vietnam and their history, as well as the material fact of U.S. intervention.[16] Indeed, for many writers, "Vietnam" becomes a metaphor for the deterritorialized space of fragmentary signs we call postmodernism.[17] In a sense, then, the tendency to qualify the war as "postmodernist" risks romanticizing it, giving it a cultural extravagance that ignores or denies its material history, ultimately reifying "postmodernity" as a transcendental historical stage unencumbered by the facts of war, imperialism, and terror. Like *True Romance*'s glib reference to the war as Hollywood B movie, the qualification of the war under the postmodern romances the true. But by reflecting on how the U.S. intervention and the social, economic, and political structures it generated have mapped the terrain for the articulation of postmodernity, we may retrieve the brutality underwriting the imperial metropolitan culture of the late twentieth century. Such an approach asks us to consider not how Vietnam can substitute for developments in Western cultural history—and thus be sacrificed and erased in that metaphorizing violence—but rather how the postmodern reflects the history of Western colonialism, militarism, and economic violence in the post-World War II era.

PERIODIZING THE POSTMODERN

It would be a mistake, of course, to suggest that Jameson's work on postmodernism is ahistorical; indeed, he notes that its appearance "is the internal and superstructural expression of a whole new wave of American military and economic domination throughout the world" (*P,* 5).[18] Concluding this claim, Jameson then states that "in this sense, as throughout class history, the underside of culture is blood, torture, death, and terror" (*P,* 5). Yet Jameson's inability to delineate and concretely account for this "underside" suggests a fatal blindness that haunts his attempts to periodize postmodernity. Indeed, throughout his work Jameson's periodization is elusive and bears careful analysis.

Jameson often situates the emergence of postmodernity in the post-World War II contexts of late capitalism. Following Ernest Mandel's schema for a third stage in the development of capital, Jameson writes:

> Mandel suggests that the basic new technological *prerequisites* of the new "long wave" of capitalism's third stage (here called "late capitalism") were *available by the end of World War II,* which also had the effect of reorganizing international relations, decolonizing the colonies,

and *laying the groundwork* for the emergence of a new economic world system. (*P* xx; emphasis added)

It is significant that Mandel does not postulate a late capitalism emerging full blown out of the wreckage of World War II, but suggests that its "prerequisites . . . were available" by then and that the war's end served to lay "the groundwork" for the new system Jameson would identify as postmodernism. One of the outcomes of World War II's end, besides clearing space for national liberation revolts against the imperial metropolitan powers and precipitating the process of decolonization that the United States engaged most intractably in southeast Asia, would be the production and maintenance of a permanent war economy, which in turn made possible the Vietnam War. Thus the Vietnam War should be more properly understood as part of "laying the groundwork of a new economic world system," by which Jameson means postmodernity. The postmodernity Jameson tends to envision as already recognizable by the time of the Vietnam War might better be understood, then, as being prepared for by the politicoeconomic conditions produced by the Vietnam War. Jameson goes on to elaborate on Mandel further:

> Culturally, however, the precondition is to be found (apart from a wide variety of aberrant modernist "experiments" which are then restructured in the form of predecessors) in the enormous social and psychological transformations of the 1960s, which swept so much of tradition away on the level of *mentalités*. Thus the economic preparation of postmodernism or late capitalism began in the 1950s, after the wartime shortages of consumer goods and spare parts had been made up, and new products and new technologies (not least of those of the media) could be pioneered. On the other hand, the psychic *habitus* of the new age demands the absolute break, strengthened by a generational rupture, achieved more properly in the 1960s. (*P* xx)

Jameson locates the precondition of the general *cultural* conditions for postmodernism and subsequently its superstructural expressions in the 1960s, during the Vietnam War, with its economic base and structure in the 1950s subsequent to post-1945 demobilization and demilitarization. Yet this narrative overlooks the ways in which the military industrialism of World War II was maintained and, indeed, expanded during the fifties—which made it possible to wage war against Vietnam—and neglects to consider how the effects of war-making during the Vietnam era bore directly on the material conditions possible for cultural production. Jameson's schema makes post-modernity coterminous with "postwar," which is always implicitly understood as "post-World War II," always implicitly erasing the Vietnam War. In apologizing for the "Americanocentrism" of this view, Jameson points out that it can be "justified only to the degree that it was the brief 'American century' (1945–73) that constituted the hothouse, or forcing ground, of the new system" (P xx). Here it would seem that Jameson understands postmodernity as post-Vietnam War —the "new system" of postmodern late capitalism is being prepared for during the war. Yet Jameson later also claims that "some radical break" occurred somewhere "at the end of the 1950s or the early 1960s" (P 1), and, as the passage quoted above indicates, that the economic preconditions for postmodernity can be located in the 1950s.[19] But as James William Gibson, Seymour Melman, and, in the present collection, Douglas Kellner, and Chris Hables Gray have argued in varying ways, the political economy of the Vietnam War was consistent with early postwar conditions and did not exhibit a postmodernist break.

In another context Jameson has argued that periodizing should describe a "common objective situation" against which and/or within which "a whole range of varied responses and creative innovations is then possible, but always within that situation's structural limits." Its goal is not so much to imply kinship and uniformity in history as to develop a way of reading the hegemonic and the emergent.[20] It would be hard to imagine, particularly in the "Americanocentric" contexts within which Jameson develops his periodization, a more "common objective situation" than the Vietnam War for U.S. culture. Not only was the U.S. intervention in Southeast Asia the longest military effort in U.S. history, it was also its longest sustained interaction of military, government, and business, and this interaction has radically altered both the United States and global social and economic configurations key to the emergence of those cultural forms commonly recognized as postmodern. To cite just the most obvious of the dread statistics: By 1975 the Vietnam War had involved 2.5 million U.S. soldiers. It killed 58,135 of those soldiers in combat along with 35,000 noncombatant U.S. civilians. It wounded

303,616 more soldiers, 33,000 of whom were paralyzed. According to a 1982 report, 110,000 more died from "war-related" problems after returning to the U.S.—of those, 60,000 were suicides. Outside of the Americanocentric effects of the war, however, the years of U.S. military intervention witnessed the deaths of over 1.9 million Vietnamese, 200,000 Cambodians, and 100,000 Laotians. The war left 3.2 million Vietnamese, Cambodians, and Laotians wounded and made more than 14.3 million more refugees by its end. According to one account, between 1965 and 1973 about one out of every thirty Indochinese was killed by the war.[21] Along with these direct human costs of the war we can cite the massive environmental costs. U.S. intervention involved the use of 15.5 million tons of bombs and munitions in Vietnam, and the spraying of 18 million gallons of poisonous chemical herbicides (including Agent Orange) over the country's forests and farmlands.[22] The direct financial costs of the U.S. intervention, including military and economic aid to South Vietnam, Laos, and Cambodia, was at least $168.1 billion. Add to this the estimated final costs of the war, taking into consideration veterans benefits, interest, postwar programs, etc., and the bill extends anywhere from $350 to $900 billion.[23]

This "crazed expenditure" of human life, national production, and capital clearly would have had a significant impact on the material conditions possible for the production of new cultural forms. As economist Seymour Melman has pointed out: "In the United States from 1951 to the present year [1983], the finance capital allocated to the military functions in this society has exceeded, every year, the net profits of all corporations."[24] James William Gibson sees the conditions of the military economy Melman portrays as having had a direct impact on the deterioration of the U.S. infrastructure and its diminishing role in global markets:

> The rise of the military has had deleterious effects on the American economy. By 1965 many American corporations were emulating the defense contractor practice of "passing cost increases along to price rather than striving to offset them by their internal methods [to increase productivity]." American engineering has also adopted the military practice of designing objects that achieve "maximum" performance (on paper) regardless of costs. Consequently American goods have become less competitive on both domestic and world markets. Industrial decline and

high unemployment in traditional manufacturing areas have become important social problems. Defense expenditures together with interest payments on the national debt (a debt created through past wars and military expenditures) take up more than 60 percent of the federal budget.
Remaining funds are no longer adequate to maintain basic public infra-
structures—roads, railways, water and sewage systems, education and
health care systems, and so forth.[25]

These conditions are precisely those often described in postmodern
studies as central to the postmodern condition: performativity as a
measure of truth; inflation; decaying infrastructure; unemployment;
the waning of American goods on the global and domestic markets.[26]
The enormous burdens of sustaining an exponentially expanding
military economy since the 1950s, along with the consequent imbrication of military economy with civilian economy, should be viewed
as the "prerequisites" and groundwork for that general cultural logic
Jameson, Lyotard, and others identify as postmodernity. And considering how the Vietnam War marked the explosive escalation of the
military-industrial economy and signaled the expansion of the gross
national product, a strong U.S. dollar, and the proliferation of consumer goods so characteristic of 1960s culture, it seems necessary to
consider how the war specifically structured the economic sphere
capable of sustaining those cultural forms unique to post-1960s history. The rise of the current global economy, for example, can be directly linked to the impact on the U.S. economy of the Vietnam War.
Melman points out, for example, that gold reserves in the U.S. Trea-
sury declined by as much as $15 billion from 1950 to 1973 primarily
because of "a massive net accumulation of dollars in the hands of
foreigners as a consequence of foreign military spending by the U.S.
government." Melman also argues that inflation, which has become
common in post-Vietnam U.S. society, has been largely the result of
the "parasitic output" of war-making during the Vietnam era.[27] The
decay of urban environments and the related expansion of an economic underclass that seem inseparable from postmodernity's cultural conditions might also be understood in relation to the war, in
terms of the disproportionate amount the U.S. government spent on
it as compared to the amount spent on economic revitalization and
the so-called war on poverty.[28]

WAR IN THE FILIGREE OF THEORY

In his course summary, "War in the Filigree of Peace," Michel Foucault proposes to develop a genealogy of "war" as an analytical tool for history and social relations. His approach ultimately asks that we consider "war" as not only the violent event that happens "out there"—in a foreign land or on distant battlefields—but also as a general principle for organizing social relations, knowledge, narrative, exposition, argument: the hallmarks of the *civitas*.[29] As Foucault's title suggests, war is worked into the very fabric of "civilized" discourse, in the embellishment that gives that fabric its design. Foucault's suggestions in this summary invite us to reexamine the relationships between war and peace in ways that do not repeat the easy binarism that contains "war" as simply an act of the military and its machinery, the effect of the most obvious plots of political power, a pathology, that thus reifies civilized discourse as the normal and exterior to war, an effect of rational community. Such thinking elides the responsibilities the *civitas* must bear for the naturalization of combat, militarism, and atrocity—the concrete, historical effects of the logic of war. If it is true, as Foucault has argued in another context, that "[e]ven when one writes the history of peace and its institutions, it is always the history of this war that one is writing," then it would seem judicious to consider how the theoretical discourses of postmodernism themselves have been inflected by a war that played a significant role in shaping the history of a generation.[30]

Indeed, an analysis of the rhetorical tropes commonly deployed in the work of writers like Jameson, Lyotard, Baudrillard, and others suggests that the historical experience of the Vietnam era resonates palpably in the filigree of theory. Since the 1970s, for example, theoretical writing has been characterized by the deployment of geographical tropes, a rhetoric of *zones, borders, boundaries, territories.* It would seem reasonable to posit that the appearance of such tropes in theoretical discourse might correlate to the experiences of a period in Western history when geography had become so thoroughly contested and so often illegible, as the grand narratives of the imperial metropolitan's maps became undermined and disarticulated by the colonized. The language of Deleuze and Guattari's *A Thousand Plateaus* powerfully evokes geographical tropes reminiscent of the Vietnam War, where the plateau is described as "a continuous, self-vibrating region of intensities whose development avoids any orientation toward a culmination point."[31] Deleuze and Guattari's description of a "plateau" as "any multiplicity connected to other multiplicities by superficial underground stems in such a way as to form or extend a rhizome" calls to mind stories of the network of underground tunnels in Vietnam used by guerrillas against the United States.[32]

The emphasis on an epistemology of dissent, subversion from within, heterology, and fragmentation in theoretical discourse on post-modernity further suggests both the continuing influence of sixties left politics for western intellectuals as well as the resonance for these scholars of the imagery of anti-imperialist revolution epitomized by the Viet Cong and NLF.[33] One of the more powerful motifs inherited from the Vietnam War experience has been that of the jungle guerrilla as a free-floating agent of subversion—mobile, hard to detect—bedeviling the U.S. military's attempts to stage battlegrounds. Since the war, the trope of the guerrilla appears in a number of theoretical discourses. It can be read in Deleuze and Guattari's theory of the nomad, a mobile, self-contained unit disarticulating the static zones of western culture's narratives of subjectivity.[34] It is also delineated by Paul Virilio's theories of speed and "pure war." Virilio has argued that in postmodernity ruptures of temporality proliferate throughout the globe such that no political state can be said to be static, but is rather always an event. Speed becomes politics and war is about the control of movement and temporality. For Virilio this situation is epitomized by the *maquisard*, who blends into the environment, not unlike a guerilla in the jungle: "he lives then under the cover of grass and trees, in atmospheric vibrations, darkness."[35] Virilio's *maquisard* calls to mind images of the Vietcong, an icon of revolutionary hero-ism for the French left generation of May 1968.

Another compelling trope from the war—the undescribable, in-tense, hallucinogenic chaos the U.S. soldier experiences 'in coun-try"—can also be read in many postmodern studies. Consider the following passage by Jameson:

> In our present context, [the schizo experience of the breakdown of signi-fication] suggests the following: first, the breakdown of temporality sud-denly releases this present of time from all the activities and intentional-ities that might focus it and make it a space of praxis; thereby isolated, that present suddenly engulfs the subject with undescribable vividness, a materiality of perception properly overwhelming, which effectively

dramatizes the power of the material—or better still, the literal—signifier in isolation. This present of the world or material signifier comes
before the subject with heightened intensity, bearing a mysterious charge
of affect, here described in the negative terms of anxiety and loss of
reality, but which one could just as well imagine in the positive terms
of euphoria, a high, an intoxicatory or hallucinogenic intensity. (27–28)

Here the narrative of breakdown Jameson sees as indicative of postmodern discourse mirrors typical narratives of the Vietnam War experience. The scene painted in the first sentence resonates with an image
common to Vietnam War narratives: in the loss of focus brought
about by the breakdown of discernible coordinates in this alien territory, the subject/U.S. soldier is isolated and overwhelmed by the "undescribable vividness" or, we might also say, the "crazed expenditure," "freakyfluky," or "La Vida Loca" of "the Nam." The subject is
engulfed by "undescribable vividness," the overwhelming hegemony
of the signifier, lacerated by a mixture of horror and euphoria, anxiety and intoxication. Jameson's rhetoric resembles Herr's hallucinogenic descriptions of the Vietnam War.

As many historians and critics have pointed out, following World
War II's imbrication of military and industry, the U.S. military became increasingly managerial and corporatist. During the Vietnam
War, the military's emphasis on interpreting numbers (kill ratios,
body counts), its bureaucratic doublespeak and meaningless "information" in its "five-o-clock follies," and its valorization of bottom-
line performance over and against clearly articulated political goals
presages postmodernism's death of the signified, its multinational
corporate values, and its eclipse of knowledge by information. Jean-
Francois Lyotard's description of the postmodern conditions for
knowledge in the post-1945 era demonstrates revealing parallels with
accounts of U.S. military strategies during the Vietnam War. For Lyotard, "[t]he true goal of the system, the reason it programs itself like
a computer, is the optimization of the global relationship between
input and output—in other words, performativity."[36] What characterizes the U.S. military thinking after World War II for historian James
William Gibson is the emphasis on systems analysis, corporatization, and a "production model of war" in which performativity reigns
supreme.[37] As Gibson describes it, the move toward corporatization
in the military stems from the intimate relationships forged between
the military and industry during World War II.[38] The government's

endowment of military contracts to the largest industrial firms led to a virtual conflation of the state, industry, and military. The military, in turn, took on scientistic views of research and production that privileged performativity. Performance was rated by numbers: the body count. Consequently the literal significance of the human body, and by extension subjectivity, collapses into a catalog of integers. According to the logics of the body count, as Gibson has demonstrated, success for the United States in the Vietnam War was measured through the consistent production of high numbers of bodies.[39] It is the number, however, and not the body that, quite literally, counts. The demands of performativity in the Vietnam War set the stage for thinking about the human body less as a (modernist) totality and instead as an empty simulacrum, a sign in which the signified has been eclipsed by its signifier. Furthermore, as Gibson argues, the Cold War mentality that led the United States to Vietnam and structured U.S. military principles during the war was grounded in a faith in Newtonian mechanics inflected by Fordist principles of assembly line production.[40] Gibson quotes Lieutenant General Julian J. Ewell as saying that "In Vietnam, with all its ambiguities, one was dealing with a highly repetitive operation. It was comparable to an *assembly line*, whereas one could visualize a 'western war' as an episodic or climactic affair with periods of low activity."[41] Ironically, Ewell's rhetoric employs tropes now commonly seen in theoretical discourses on postmodernity. The Other (Vietnam) is a space of ambiguities, repetition, whereas "western war" (i.e., modernist) follows the conventions of the grand narratives with episodes and climax. I don't mean to suggest that there is any conscious and simple correspondence between Ewell's rhetoric and that of cultural theorists; rather, I point this out to suggest how these tropes are symptomatic of a general cultural condition that emerges as an effect of the U.S. war against Vietnam. The distinction here, and Gibson's history also implies this, is that the U.S. military sought to impose Newtonian rationalism and enlightenment modernity on the non-Western Other, whereas cultural theorists of postmodernity value the ambiguities of the Other as a means of subverting Western metaphysics from within. Where these views coincide, however, is in their similar portrayal of the Other as the source of ambiguities and a threat to (Western) rationality. In their own ways, each mode of thought colonizes the Other.

One of the key problems Gibson identifies in the French and

U.S. conceptualization of combat in Vietnam was that it imagined "war as a struggle between machines."[42] This view posits machines as units comprised of working parts that necessarily depend for their effectiveness on the sublimation of the parts to the whole. Such a view is macrological, statist, and monolithic. Repeatedly the Viet Minh and later the NLF demonstrated that war could be won through the efficient and persistent array of molecular networks of resistance, that power could be implemented through diverse, contingent, and pragmatic means. This opposition between the macro and the micro, the molar and molecular, recalls a trope dominant in narratives of oppositional struggle since at least the early-1960s: the monolithic, "First World" (i.e., Western), military-state machine versus the small, "Third World" (i.e., Eastern) mobile, nomadic guerilla insurgent. Lyotard's "grand narrative" of postmodernity posits a proliferation of heterological possibilities, an expansion of the sublime, and an insurgent politics of difference as a "progressive" opposition to the official, state-bureaucratic, and scientist conditions of knowledge. This narrative of the nomadic insurgent traversing territories of the monolithic state and fragmenting it from within has become a hallmark of postmodern theory.

We can see this trope play itself out in the move away from a preference for "high" modernist literary practices and its valorization of an elite aesthetics to a celebration of the popular, to mass aesthetics, whether in "kitsch," consumerism, "spoken word" poetry, or in the supposedly democraticizing possibilities of the Internet.[43] Literary criticism in particular, by interrogating the inherently antidemocratic principles of modernist New Critical aesthetics, has dramatically expanded the canon. Such practices must be viewed in the contexts of the post-Vietnam era as the continued efforts of the intellectual left to carry out cultural revolution. During the war, the dominant theory in literary criticism was New Criticism, the critical doxa founded on High Modernist reading practices and inflected by U.S. Cold War ideologies. It was only *after* the student riots, the Free Speech movement, the youth counterculture's celebration of decolonization, race rebellion, the interventions of feminism, Stonewall, May 1968, and the antiwar movement that literary studies turned toward theories grounded in the revolutionary impulses of the Vietnam era.[44] The Maoism of *Tel Quel*, the popularity of Democratic Socialism in America, the rise of Gramsci in cultural studies, the recuperation of such "Third World" philosophers as Frantz Fanon,

C. L. R. James, Amilcar Cabral, and Albert Memmi, for example, point to the influences of the Vietnam era's convulsive encounters with decolonization on a new tendency in theory toward the paracritical, subversive, and insurgent. As Steven Connor has noted, Jean Baudrillard's theories, for example, can be read in part as being motivated by "the hatred of post-1968 French intellectuals for any social movement that even suggests centralized or unified effort."[45]

According to Thomas Docherty, the contemporary interest in postmodernism "dates from 1968, that *annus mirabilis* which is the great '1848' of modern Europe."

> Since the eighteenth century in Europe, it had been taken more or less for granted that knowledge gave an entitlement to legislation. That is, social and political formations were grounded upon a truthful knowledge about the ways of the world. But after 1968, all such knowledges begin to be deemed "local" and specific to the pragmatic necessities of the specific culture from which the knowledges emanate and whose interests they serve. Now, knowledge does not give power; rather, it is utterly imbricated with power from the outset, and is thus not a pure knowledge at all but a practical knowledge, a knowledge whose *raison d'être* is power itself. From 1968, the leftist intellectual begins to be suspicious of a knowledge which will legislate for any culture other than the very culture which produced that knowledge in the first place.[46]

Indeed, although Docherty's historical reference point is the Paris revolts, the *mentalité* he describes expresses the historical experience of the Left in the imperial metropolis faced with the atrocities of the Vietnam War perpetrated under the name of modernity and liberal humanism. The attitude toward knowledge Docherty portrays here is manifestly different from the position of the Left prior to the 1960s, a left that still clung to what might be called the "modernist" certitudes of Marxism, which posited what was essentially a Eurocentric totality—the dictatorship of the proletariat—and which believed that its political system could be legislated with progressive effect for any culture on the globe. In the post-Vietnam era, however, such certainty has been shattered by the very dialectics of anti-imperialist thought. To presume the intellectual leadership for the colonized began to seem like colonization itself. For Virilio, Deleuze, Guattari, Baudrillard, Lyotard, and other influential French theorists of postmodernism, the "guerilla warfare" they sought to wage against Western philosophy, Newtonianism, Cartesianism, and the Hobbesian state, infiltrating these monolithic systems of thought and sabotaging them from within, was articulated in the shadow of the Vietnam War.[47]

According to William Spanos, "posthumanist theory"—by which he means both Heiddegerian poststructuralist and postmodernist theories—was significantly enabled by the experience of the Vietnam War, "by the contradictory spectacle of a brutal intervention in the affairs of a non-European people in the name of (European) freedom."[48] Later he adds:

> What the actual events of this shameful period in American history disclosed more dramatically and forcefully than any other historically specific moment—even that extended period in the nineteenth century bearing witness to the brutalities of slavery and the genocidal practices of Manifest Destiny—is, to use an Althusserian terminology, that the cultural apparatuses, the agencies of knowledge production, were absolutely continuous with the (repressive) state apparatuses; that the American command that wasted Vietnam in trying to fulfill its restricted narrative economy was not purely a military/political command. It was, rather, a *relay* of commands extending from the government through the military/industrial complex to the network of technical advisory agencies (military, political, cultural, social, informational, economic, etc.), and, as the protest movement made clear in exposing the complicity of the university with these commands, especially the institutions of knowledge production. (208–09)

He also notes that theoretical discourses we have come to identify with poststructuralism and postmodernism, articulated by Derrida, Lacan, Althusser, Foucault, Lyotard, and others, "are the discourses that got their historically specific impetus in the period of the Vietnam War" (221).

The relationships of postmodern theory to Heideggerian philosophy detailed by Spanos bear recalling, because they further underscore the epistemic break between Vietnam-era and post-Vietnam critical discourses. It is interesting that, as Spanos points out, the philosophers most often discussed *during* the war among American leftists were French existentialists such as Sartre and Merleau-Ponty, and Christian and Jewish existentialist theologians such as Paul Tillich, Reinhold Niebuhr, and Martin Buber. Such philosophers were well aware of Heidegger's Nazi affiliations, and sixties intellectual circles in the United States tended to ignore him. Yet *after* the war, Heidegger emerged as a powerful influence. It became possible for American intellectuals either to ignore or rearticulate Heidegger's Nazi past only in the post-Vietnam era. The point here is not that Heidegger is "bad," but that what we now have come to regard as a certain poststructuralist orientation in postmodernity has only become possible once America passed through its own twentieth-century infamy. It took the Vietnam War to give rise in the United States to the notion that the Enlightenment project of modernity and humanism could have its own horrors. American intellectuals of the sixties were predominantly humanist, and in a particular sense, modernist. But by the mid-seventies, a Heideggerian "posthumanist" thought emerged and became so closely linked to postmodern philosophy that Spanos actually would substitute the former for the latter term.[49]

Despite the evidence that postmodern theoretical discourses are themselves inflected by the Vietnam War experience, and that postmodernity as a historical condition is concretely related to the war, as I have pointed out, studies of postmodernism almost universally neglect to even mention the war. Spanos points out that "the epochal historical occasion that . . . humanist critique [of posthumanism and postmodernism] 'forgets'" is the Vietnam War, the mass protests it elicited in the imperialist nations, and the resulting exposure of humanism's complicity with the "state apparatuses conducting or supporting the imperialist/racist war in Vietnam" (190). But he might well have lodged a similar attack against postmodern theorists themselves. Indeed, Spanos is one of the few theorists to assiduously retrieve the name of the Vietnam War in the signature of postmodernity. Numerous accounts of postmodernity have also forgotten the war as their epochal historical occasion. Spanos asks, "Why do the American humanists who condemn Heidegger's 'failure to pronounce the name of the Jews' as 'beyond pardon,' fail, in turn, to pronounce the name of the Vietnamese?" (220). But anti-Heiddegerian humanists are not alone in this silence and silencing—American postmodern studies almost universally refuse to pronounce the name of the Vietnamese, or, for that matter, as Simon During points out, the name of all those "other" epochal moments of civilization's brutality upon which one can very clearly demonstrate that postmodernity in the imperial metropolis has been erected.[50]

What During suggests is that "postmodernity" and "postmodernism" cannot be regarded as global theoretical categories in any unified or static sense, but that they must be understood in relation to the global differentials of power that the history of imperialism has made manifest and that continue to organize political economy. America's "postmodernity" has been built upon its postwar neo-imperialism; its "postmodernism" has been made possible within this political economy. And thus, the Vietnam War must be understood as central to that condition. But at the same time, postmodernity might look very different from the perspective of the poet working in Ho Chi Minh City, for whom concepts of, say, virtual reality, society of the spectacle, and multinational economy will necessarily have very different resonances, precisely because they are produced out of specific concrete conditions. To privilege the Holocaust as *the* epochal moment—as many theories of the postmodern do—to trace postmodernity, understood as a "geo-aesthetic" or a "global cultural condition," from this point, it should be said, is to write Euro-American history as global history and, subsequently, to erase or elide all the various histories of those "others" who have suffered their own holocausts at the hands of the imperial metropolis. It is to presume that the systematic slaughter of European Jews, horrific and abominable though it undeniably was, is more definitive of global cultural history than the systematic slaughter of the Chinese by the Japanese during World War II, or of the Armenians by the Turks, the Indians by the British, the Filipinos by Americans—and, of course, the Vietnamese, Laotians, and Cambodians by American and French imperialist intervention. It is to make the Holocaust synecdochic of technologized brutality, which is to subsume and erase all other specific, local experiences of comparable brutalities. And because it is very easy to identify the evil of the Holocaust as German National Socialism, to privilege it thus as the sign of historical evil is to exculpate other imperial metropolitan histories, to "forget" how all such histories are written in blood.

Thus the periodizing of postmodernity becomes crucial, because to place its emergence at the end of World War II is to "forget" the significance of the Vietnam War in the shaping of contemporary history. I would argue that what many read as postmodern in U.S. culture from 1945 to about 1972 is actually the vanguard expression of modernity's demise still not fully articulated to a general cultural condition of postmodernity. Warhol's pop art, McLuhan's "global village," the Situationist's "society of the spectacle" are expressions of the emerging *mentalité* that only after 1972, after the last troop deployments and the escalation of U.S. military withdrawal from Vietnam, have become disseminated as general cultural forms, such that by the 1990s postmodernity typifies advertising, music videos, shopping malls, and the flattening of historicity evident in *True Romance*. According to Steven Connor, "Although the term 'postmodernism' had been used by a number of writers in the 1950s and 1960s, the concept of postmodernism cannot be said to have crystallised until about the mid-1970s, when claims for the existence of this diversely social and cultural phenomenon began to harden within and across a number of different cultural areas and academic disciplines, in philosophy, architecture, film studies and literary subjects."[51] Andreas Huyssen writes that "the term postmodernism only gained wide currency in the 1970s, while much of the language used to describe the art, architecture, and literature of the 1960s was still derived—and plausibly so—from the rhetoric of avantgardism and from what I called the ideology of modernization."[52] Perhaps, as Philip D. Beidler eloquently suggests in his essay in the present collection, the inauguration of the U.S. postmodern might be located in that indelible image of the last Huey lifting off from the embassy in Saigon.

Of course, the vast constellation of discourses, cultural productions, and geopolitical arrangements generally understood as postmodernity cannot be neatly anchored to the Vietnam War nor seen as simply a product of the war. I do not mean to flatten postmodernity under a single historical event. Yet it seems evident that the war has played a much more important role in the shaping of postmodernity than has been previously acknowledged. Further silence on the war in the many historically detailed and philosophically sophisticated discourses on postmodernity produced in the past twenty years suggests deeply ideological investments that require more trenchant interrogation. Any theory of postmodernity that does not adequately account for the war fails to acknowledge in any concrete sense the importance of cold war militarism, the permanent war economy, the most protracted U.S. encounter with postwar decolonization and anti-imperialist struggle, and the long-term effects of the war for contemporary society. The Vietnam War needs to be recognized in postmodern theory not, as in *True Romance*, as another commodity spectacle simply expressing a style or genre, but as the concrete groundwork for late twentieth-century cultural conditions. As the

John Balaban poem in my epigraph grimly reminds us, the war's dismembered ghosts continue to haunt American culture, shadowing
our attempts to go on telling the old tales.

NOTES

1. This phrase was made famous by Michael Herr in his *Dispatches* (New
York: Vintage, 1977).

2. See Susan Jeffords, *The Remasculinization of America: Gender and
the Vietnam War* (Bloomington: University of Indiana Press, 1989).

3. Jean Baudrillard, "The Evil Demon of Images and the Precession of
Simulacra," in *Simulations* (New York: Semiotext(e), 1983).
Discussing *Apocalypse Now,* Simon During makes a similar point to
mine about the emptying of historicity, arguing that the film does not tell
the audience about the Vietnam War so much as it presents a "mere monu-
mentalization of modernism." Its citations of Conrad, Eliot, Frazer, Nietzsche,
and Weston are not about the war but about Western civilization. "The age
of history may disappear into history. Here we catch sight of the way in which
postmodernity consumes history, in the sense of nullifying it. [In *Apocalypse
Now*] [i]t remains an effect rather than an expression or theme." "Postmodernism or Post-colonialism Today," in *The Postmodern Reader*, ed. Thomas
Docherty (New York: Columbia UP, 1993), 453–54.

4. For example, the war is not mentioned in any of the following: Steven
Connor, *Postmodernist Culture: An Introduction to Theories of the Contem-
porary* (Oxford: Basil Blackwell, 1989); Linda Hutcheon, *The Politics of Post-
modernism* (London: Routledge, 1989); Ingeborg Hoesterey, ed., *Zeitgeist in
Babel: The Postmodernist Controversy* (Bloomington: Indiana University
Press, 1991); Linda J. Nicholson, ed., *Feminism/Postmodernism* (New York:
Routledge, 1990); Andrew Ross, ed., *Universal Abandon: The Politics of
Postmodernism* (Minneapolis: University of Minnesota Press, 1988).

5. Although see Chris Hables Gray's essay in this collection, where the
terms "modern" and "postmodern" delineate periods in the history of warfare more than cultural periods.

6. Fredric Jameson, *Postmodernism, or, the Cultural Logic of Late Capitalism* (Durham, N.C.: Duke University Press, 1991), 44–45, emphasis added.
Further references will be cited in the text as *P.* The chapter this passage
has been quoted from, "The Cultural Logic of Late Capitalism," originally
appeared in a slightly different version as"Postmodernism, or the Cultural
Logic of Late Capitalism," *New Left Review* 146 (July/August 1984): 53–92.
References to this version will be cited in the text as PNL. An earlier and
much shorter version of this essay appeared as "Postmodernism and Consumer Society," *The Anti-Aesthetic: Essays on Postmodern Culture*, ed. Hal
Foster (Seattle, Wash.: Bay Press, 1983). References will be cited in the text
as PCS.

7. Yet in discussing Herr in another context, Jameson writes that the

"new language experiment" exemplified in *Dispatches* "does not *express* the nightmare of the Vietnam War, but substitutes a textual equivalent for it." In this sense, then, it is not the *war* but Herr's text that is postmodernist. Earlier in this passage, however, Jameson suggests that the Vietnam War is "postmodern or interventionist warfare." *The Geopolitical Aesthetic: Cinema and Space in the World System* (Bloomington: Indiana University Press, 1992), 43; emphasis in original.

8. For a critique of the ways theorists paradoxically enact the very authoritarianism they would critique by synthesizing a group of positions under the postmodern, see Judith Butler, "Contingent Foundations: Feminism and the Question of 'Postmodernism'," *Feminists Theorize the Political*, ed. Judith Butler and Joan W. Scott (New York: Routledge, 1992), 3–21.

9. Now, however, the Clinton Administration's opening of trade relations with Vietnam suggests that multinational capital has, in fact, finally "won the war." The Vietnamese could withstand the massive technowar waged against them by the U.S. military, but they could not withstand the more insidious and encompassing reach of neocolonialist late capitalism.

10. "There is no document of civilization which is not at the same time a document of barbarism." Walter Benjamin, "Theses on the Philosophy of History," *Illuminations: Essays and Reflections*, trans. Harry Zohn, ed. Hannah Arendt (New York: Schocken Books, 1969), 256.

11. Qtd. Hutcheon, *Politics*, 25.

12. Douglas Kellner and Steven Best, for example, have defined "postmodernity" as a term signifying "an epochal rupture with 'modernity,' conceived as a socio-historical epoch." See Kellner and Best, *Postmodern Theory: Critical Interrogations* (London: Guilford Press, 1991). Also see Kellner, "From Vietnam to the Gulf: Postmodern Wars?," in this collection, n. 2.

13. Hutcheon, *Politics*, 23, 26.

14. Jameson writes, "But as I am anxious that Portman's space not be perceived as something either exceptional or seemingly marginalized and leisure-specialized on the order of Disneyland, I would like in passing to juxtapose this complacent and entertaining (although bewildering) leisure-time space with its analogue in a very different area, namely the space of postmodern warfare" (PNL 84).

15. This is not to suggest, however, that the war constitutes the only major factor in the shaping of the contemporary geopolitical condition. The rise of African American social activism, both in Civil Rights and Black Liberation, which in turn inspired the mobilization of a number of social agents (the Brown Berets, the American Indian Movement, Women's Liberation, Gay Liberation, etc.), must also be seen as another significant factor in the emergence of postmodernity. Just to cite one example of the way race-gender-sexuality activism has led to a new order of social and political life that configures the conditions for cultural production in postmodernism, one might consider the formation and operation of state bureaucracy in the post-1970s: the creation of a new bureaucratic class as a result of Civil Rights legislation; the emergence of new hiring practices across the professions; the production of new art forms generated out of the lived experiences of social policies

related to "the Great Society" programs and changes in welfare. Although considerable attention has been paid to the significance of the social movements of the 1960s in shaping contemporary culture, the Vietnam War remains underexamined. My main goal here is to suggest how the Vietnam War can be seen as foundational to the emergence of postmodernity, rather than an effect of postmodernity.

16. William Spanos also takes note of Jameson's remarks "in passing" that the war was the first "postmodern war": "What Jameson neglects to add is that its postmodernity was determined by one of the relay of 'others' struggling to e-merge from the domination of the imperial cultural and sociopolitical narrative of the collective Occidental subject." *Heidegger and Criticism: Rewriting the Cultural Politics of Destruction* (Minneapolis: University of Minnesota Press, 1993), 305, n. 29. While I agree with Spanos that Jameson's "passing" remark neglects to acknowledge the Vietnamese struggle against U.S. imperialism as central to postmodernity, I would not agree that the war itself, as Spanos indicates, can also be seen as postmodern. Rather I want to consider how the war enabled postmodernity, understood as a general historical condition, a view which would place the war outside or preceding this condition.

17. For examples, see Philip Francis Kuberski, "Genres of Vietnam," *Cultural Critique* 3 (1986): 168–88; and Herman Rapaport, "Vietnam: The Thousand Plateaus," *The 60s Without Apology*, ed. Sohyna Sayres et al. (Minneapolis: University of Minnesota Press, 1984), 137–47.

18. Also see Jameson's "Periodizing the 60s," in *The 60s Without Apology*, 178–209.

19. But Jameson has also written in an earlier version of this essay that postmodernism describes the cultural forms that correlate to the social and economic configurations of a new stage of capitalism that "can be dated from the postwar boom in the United States in the late 1940s and early '50s." He goes on to claim that "[T]he 1960s are in many ways the key transitional period, a period in which the new international order (neocolonialism, the Green Revolution, computerization and electronic information) is at one and the same time set in place and is swept and shaken by its own internal contradictions and by external resistance" (PCS 113). Clearly the 1960s Jameson describes is a period both internally and externally fraught with not only upheavals in the Congo, Indonesia, and the Middle East, but also the U.S. intervention in Southeast Asia.

20. Jameson, "Periodizing the 60s," 178.

21. Reese Williams, ed., *Unwinding the Vietnam War: From War Into Peace* (Seattle: The Real Comet Press, 1987), 7–8.

22. By comparison, six million tons of bombs and munitions were used by U.S. forces in World War II. Williams, 8.

23. Ibid. It should be borne in mind that these figures were compiled in 1982. The recent payments made to Vietnam to settle disputes over the MIA/POW issue no doubt would increase these costs.

24. Qtd. James William Gibson, *The Perfect War: The War We Couldn't Lose and How We Did* (New York: Vintage, 1986, 1988), 451–52.

25. Ibid., 452.

26. For examples, see Fredric Jameson, *Postmodernism;* Jean-Francois Lyotard, *The Postmodern Condition: A Report on Knowledge,* trans. Geoff Bennington and Brian Massumi (Minneapolis: University of Minnesota Press, 1984); Arthur Kroker and David Cook, *The Postmodern Scene: Excremental Culture and Hyper-Aesthetics* (New York: St. Martin's Press, 1986); Andreas Huyssen, *After the Great Divide: Modernism, Mass Culture, Postmodernism* (Bloomington: Indiana University Press, 1986); and Steven Connor, *Postmodernist Culture.* Also see the essays in *Universal Abandon,* especially Stanley Aronowitz, "Postmodernism and Politics," 46–62; Paul Smith, "Visiting the Banana Republic," 128–48; Abigail Solomon-Godeau, "Living with Contradictions: Critical Practices in the Age of Supply-Side Aesthetics," 191–213; and Hal Foster, "Wild Signs: The Breakup of the Sign in Seventies' Art," 251–68.

27. Seymour Melman, *The Permanent War Economy: American Capitalism in Decline,* rev. ed. (New York: Touchstone, 1985), 69, 70.

28. "[A]bout $375 billion worth of effort, extended over a ten-year period, would be required to make the leap forward that is called economic development. But sums of this magnitude were never available through the so-called War on Poverty. . . . From 1965 to 1970, the real war in Vietnam and the paper 'war' on poverty used up, together, $115 billion. Vietnam took 91.7 percent and the 'war' on poverty 8.3 percent." Melman, 121.

29. This heading refers to the title of a course outline by Michel Foucault, "War in the Filigree of Peace," *Oxford Literary Review* 4.2 (1980): 15–18.

30. Michel Foucault, "Two Lectures" in *Power/Knowledge: Selected Interviews and Other Writings, 1972–1977,* ed. Colin Gordon (New York: Pantheon, 1980), 91.

31. Gilles Deleuze and Félix Guattari, *A Thousand Plateaus: Capitalism and Schizophrenia* (1980) trans. Brian Massumi (Minneapolis: University of Minnesota Press, 1987), 22. Also see Herman Rapaport, "Vietnam: The Thousand Plateaus" in *The 60s Without Apology,* 137–47. Rapaport quotes the NLF's Truong Son as explaining how North Vietnamese strategy was to fragment and disarticulate the U.S. military so that it could have no particular focus, no particular "zone" of conflict. As Rapaport further notes, "There is a fluidity of combinative intensities which allows at once for the most primitive and most advanced methods of warfare. The American enemy is on all sides at once, working in all kinds of heterogeneous modes and combining or recombining them at will. The aim is not quick victory, of course, but . . . a 'sapping' which produces a kind of 'quagmire' or sea of disarticulated and hostile activities whose climaxes are never really peaks, but merely plateaus of various intensities which take their toll and then subside" (147, n. 8).

32. Deleuze and Guattari, *A Thousand Plateaus,* 22. Stories of underground tunnels in Vietnam were widely circulated in the press coverage of the war during the sixties and have come to figure in a number of post-Vietnam personal narratives, such as Herr's *Dispatches,* Al Santoli's *Everything We Had* (1981), and Mark Baker's *Nam* (1981), and it has become a

literary trope of post-Vietnam fiction, such as Tim O'Brien's *Going After Cacciato* (1979) and Bobbie Ann Mason's *In Country* (1985).

33. For example, Susan Rubin Suleiman writes that "the choice of models of dissent and heterogeneity over models of consensus and systemic totality . . . are concepts grounded in poststructuralist thought, as the latter was elaborated in France in the 1960s and 1970s by Lyotard, Derrida, Foucault, and others." "Feminism and Postmodernism: A Question of Politics," *Zeitgeist in Babel*, 112. Indeed, Jameson himself has noted that the paradigms of otherness, difference, ideological critique, and the nomadic can be traced to the currency of revolutionary political thought among young intellectuals of the 1960s. See "Periodizing the 60s." Douglas Kellner also notes that Jameson's development as a theorist of Marxist literary criticism "was part of a generational shift, the 'generation of the 60s,' whose members moved to the most radical alternatives within contemporary politics and theory. For Jameson and many of his cohorts this meant a turn to Marxism and in particular to the dialectical versions of Marxism associated with the tradition of European Hegelian Marxism." Douglas Kellner, "Introduction: Jameson, Marxism, and Postmodernism," *Postmodernism/Jameson/Critique*, ed. idem (Washington, D.C.: Maisonneuve, 1989), 9.

34. As Ronald Bogue summarizes it, "[t]he nomadic subject is a point of pure intensity traversing the grid of the body without organs, a mobile locus of becoming commingling identities as it migrates from desiring-machine to desiring-machine." *Deleuze and Guattari* (London: Routledge, 1989), 95.

35. Qtd. Thomas Docherty, "Postmodernism: An Introduction," in *Postmodernism: A Reader*, ed. Thomas Docherty (New York: Columbia University Press, 1993), 20; from Virilio, *L'Horizon négatif: essai de dromoscopic* (Paris: Editions Galilée, 1984), 100.

36. Lyotard, *The Postmodern Condition*, 11.

37. Gibson, *The Perfect War*. See especially 1–27.

38. Gibson situates the genesis of corporatist thinking in the military with Chief of Staff George C. Marshall's decision during World War II to organize military logistics according to corporate models (ibid., 22).

39. Gibson devotes considerable attention to the body count. See *The Perfect War*, especially 111–28.

40. Ibid., 26.

41. Qtd. Ibid., 103; emphasis original.

42. Ibid., 63.

43. Ironically, as many have noted, the Internet, the World Wide Web, and other forms of computer communications networks were initially made possible through military research and development in the Vietnam era.

44. It is interesting to note here that it was after the protests that disrupted the 1968 Modern Language Association convention in New York City, and whose primary agenda was to protest the Vietnam War, that the Radical Caucus of the MLA was formed and the work of canon critique became a professional interest among literature departments in higher education. According to Paul Lauter, who had been involved in the 1968 protests, the Radical Caucus, and Feminist Press, canon critique "emerged in the late 1960s

and early 1970s." See *Canons and Contexts* (New York: Oxford University Press, 1991), 146–48. The impact of such criticism, however, actually became widespread in the 1980s and culminated in the publication of *The Heath Anthology of American Literature* (1990).

Although I am claiming that modernism held sway over left intellectualism during the sixties, Bruce Norton has argued that Jameson's analysis of postmodernism "is a starkly modernist one. . . . With Jameson's intervention a twentieth-century classical sort of Marxism looks in the face of the cacophony of postmodernist and poststructuralist themes . . . and rather than flinching, offers a grand narrative to make sense of it all." "Late Capitalism and Postmodernism: Jameson/Mandel," in *Marxism in the Postmodern Age: Confronting the New World Order*, ed. Antonio Callari, Stephen Cullenberg, and Carole Biewener (New York: Guilford, 1995), 59–60.

45. Connor, *Postmodernist Culture*, 60.

46. Docherty, "Postmodernism: An Introduction," 35, 36.

47. According to Vincent Leitch, "Interest in postmodernism increased from the 1970s into the 1990s, culminating in the fin de siècle. It was during the later phase that postmodernism crystallized as a galvanizing period concept rather than simply a style, a movement, or a particular philosophy." *Postmodernism: Local Effects, Global Flows* (Albany: State University of New York Press, 1996), xii.

48. Spanos, *Heidegger and Criticism*, 200. Further references will be cited in the text.

49. See ibid. 298, n. 2. Explaining his preference for the term "posthumanist," Spanos writes:

> As the editor of *boundary 2: a journal of postmodern literature and culture*, I must acknowledge my contribution to the process that has institutionalized the term "postmodernism." Nevertheless, I have come to realize that this word is misleading and in some ways disabling in its all-encompassing, which is to say dedifferentiating, generality. It obscures, if it does not annul, the fundamental point of departure of the oppositional discourses in question: that they exist to interrogate the anthropological subject; i.e., the discourse of Man. (298, n. 6)

50. Comparing the importance of the name of Auschwitz in Western theory to the total absence of other names that evoke similar atrocities for colonized peoples, During notes that, "Auschwitz resonates for us, not because we are who we are genetically, but because memories of it are constantly circulated orally and in writing." "Postmodernism or Postcolonialism Today," 458.

51. Connor, *Postmodernist Culture*, 6.

52. Huyssen affirms Jameson's "Americanocentrism" when he notes "the specifically American character of postmodernism." He continues: "After all, the term accrued its emphatic connotations in the United States, not in Europe." Huyssen argues that 1960s West Germany was invested primarily in recuperating the leftist modernism of the 1920s, exemplified in the work of

Brecht, Grosz, Adorno, and Benjamin. *After the Great Divide*, 190–91; 195. Ingeborg Hoesterey more emphatically and precisely locates 1976 as the point when "the concept [of postmodernism] acquired almost overnight the identity of an emerging force for a number of communicative systems of culture." "Introduction: Postmodernism as Discursive Event," *Zeitgeist in Babel*, x. Although I remain skeptical about her historicization, Hoesterey's date is not only significant as the year in which Charles Jenck's *The Language of Post-Modern Architecture* first appeared in America, but it is also the first year after the fall of Saigon, the first year of a truly post-Vietnam War era.

8

POSTMODERNISM WITH A VENGEANCE:
THE VIETNAM WAR

Chris Hables Gray

When I was first writing this the Vietnam memorial was celebrating its tenth anniversary. Every day I read about the reading of the names and every day I cried. Polls now show that an overwhelming number of U.S. citizens now think the war was wrong, as do most contemporary academic researchers, although only a minority note that it was morally wrong, as well as politically and militarily unwinnable.[1] I was nineteen in 1972 when I reached the same conclusion after supporting the war for twelve years. The war has always been important to me. Through an accident of personal history I lived in Vietnam as a child and I still remember searching for helmets without holes in the military dump near our compound. It was a relatively peaceful time for recent Vietnamese history; Diem was yet to fall (get pushed) and U.S. involvement was "limited" to money, spies, weapons, and advisors, including civilians such as my father, a highway engineer. Even then I thought of it as *our* war. At my insistence our family had two U.S. Marines off the USS *St. Paul* over for Thanksgiving dinner. For most of my youth my greatest desire was to join the marines, return to Nam, and fight for freedom against the evil commies.

But hundreds of books and several meetings with returning veterans changed my mind about what was best for Vietnam and the U.S., even though my disgust with communism remained. So I went from organizing pro-war speeches at my high school to joining anti-war demonstrations in college. After turning against the war I experienced my own war here at home, as so many others did. I was framed by lying police, chased by rednecks and cop cars, gassed and beaten again and again, and I even watched fellow protesters die. Many nights I camped with the VVAW (Vietnam Veterans Against the War) at Miami and Washington, D.C., having joined that wonderful brotherhood by dint of my two years as a child in Saigon. The movement was my new family and I was estranged from my biological family until my father called me one December, crying in horror at Kissinger's Christmas bombing, to tell me that he too now opposed the war.

So when I argue in my academic work that the Vietnam War was a crucial turning point in the history of war, that it represents the development of postmodern war out of five hundred years of modern war, and that it was all in all a most remarkable and significant conflict, I have to ask myself, am I just reading my own life into my historical analysis?

I don't think so. I know this war. For myself, and everyone of my generation who took a real stand on the war, on either side, we knew then that it was important. Now, with the distance of a few decades, it is clear that the Vietnam War was even more important than most of us thought, because it did mark the end of modern war and, let us be optimistic, perhaps the beginning of the end for war itself.

Here we should pause to consider what is assumed by even saying that we can now imagine an end to war. During most of history, that war was and would be was not a matter for discussion. How to win battles was considered at length, as were the customs and rules of conflict, but war itself was not really debatable. There will be war! Except for a handful of pacifists, war was considered by everyone an inevitable, if unfortunate, result of human nature. During the twentieth century this has changed considerably. Antiwar sentiments have grown immensely, especially since the invention of atomic weapons. Today, the purpose, the form, and even the inevitability of wars, are all challenged on many different grounds. It is a crucial debate. What we call war, and how we define it, will help to determine what, and if, wars are.

Clearly, my decision to call war today "postmodern" can hardly be innocent.[2] For the last half of this century an increasing number of observers have argued that war has been fundamentally changing. The more insightful commentators noted many of the important implications of high technology weapons (war can no longer be total, speed is now more important than courage, industrial virtues outweigh military values) and the permanent military mobilization that has existed since 1945. They have called this new type of war permanent war, technology war, high technology war, technological war, technowar, perfect war, imaginary war, computer war, war without end, Militarism USA, light war, cyberwar, high modern war, hypermodern war, and pure war.[3]

These labels all try to mark how different war is now from World War II, so why choose "postmodern" over the others? Two different arguments convinced me. First, modern war as a category is used by most military historians, who usually see it as starting in the 1500s, when the application of new technologies in the quest for ever more powerful versions of total war first became dominant in Europe, and continuing up to 1945 and Hiroshima. It is obvious that the logic and culture of modern war changed significantly during World War II, especially as total war was no longer possible. The new kind of war, while clearly related to modern war, is different enough to deserve the appellation "postmodern."

Second, even though "postmodern" is a very complex and contradictory term, and even though it is applied to various fields in wildly uneven ways temporally and intellectually, there is enough similarity between the different descriptions of postmodern phenomena specifically, and postmodernity in general, to persuade me that there is something systematic happening in areas as diverse as art, literature, economics, philosophy, and war. Briefly, as I hope to demonstrate below, postmodern war is like postmodernity in that

- it privileges information and its interpretation over all other activities;
- it often prioritizes simulation over substance
- it is presentist (ignoring history as well as considerations for the far future);
- its material context is late twentieth-century technoscience, especially information processing machinery;
- it is an acceleration; and
- it is an epistemological cacophony

One thing almost all postmodern theorists agree about is that there is no pure master narrative in postmodernity, whether it is called capitalism, communism, imperialism, or even Vietnamese nationalism.[4] Ideologies, and all other categories, are contingent, limited, and ultimately contradictory when viewed up close and personal. The bricolage construction of old and new that represents lived reality has come to the fore in the postmodern era, since it is no longer painted over by a sweet simple tale such as "White Man's Burden," "Alliance for Progress," or "National Liberation Front."

POSTMODERN WAR

War is perhaps impossible: it continues
nonetheless everywhere you look.
>   Baudrillard and Lotringer, *Forget*
>   *Foucault/Forget Baudrillard*

Total war itself is surpassed, towards a form of
peace more terrifying still.
>   Deleuze and Guattari, *Nomadology:*
>   *The War Machine*

The assumption of most of the military establishments of the world is that there is now a science of war, mastery of which, especially with the latest weapons, makes victory assured. But this belief isn't held by everyone. Many revolutionary movements and a few established armies (China, Vietnam, Afghanistan) are strongly influenced by the "people's war" approach, which seeks appropriate weapons for the social-political context, instead of just the latest weapons. Within this general framework versions of what war is proliferate incredibly, as do ways of thinking about military threats and how to neutralize them. This proliferation is based on a progression of new information technologies, complex simulations, advancing weapons, and expanding definitions of security. Such ambiguous "progress" is only possible through the replacement of substance with spectacle and simulation, the valuation of information above any other factor or virtue, both in the context of a proliferation of contentious epistemologies. This system is a central engine of postmodernity and it has stimulated other dynamics as well.

Many postmodernists argue that because epistemologies are contested there is an inevitable valorization of difference and multiple subjectivities over illusions of the "whole" man.[5] It is matched by a rejection of any "grand" narrative or completely explanatory totalizing vision of truth in favor of local, limited, and contingent truths, especially those articulated by human bodies, protesting, dying, loving. In Vietnam we can see that the spectacle of TV got out of official control and undermined the war itself, which ended up being fought over perceptions (faked body counts versus images of atrocity and defeat) more than "real" battles. Meanwhile, pure anticommunism floundered in the face of the complexity of the land and people of Vietnam. For the Vietnamese, reunification's aftermath of impoverishment, exodus, and border wars with neighboring Marxist regimes revealed that rather than being "scientific" (and therefore mistakenly assumed to be complete), Marxism was as limited a worldview as any other.

Postmodernism is fragmentation and that is the structure, or better, geography, of postmodern war. There are a whole range of conflicts, often carried out through proxies, human and machine. The idea of war itself has fragmented. Iranians fight holy war with human wave attacks and car bombs; IRA soldiers wage a war of fear in the media; counter- and pro-insurgents and nationalists struggle in dirty wars, secret wars, civil wars all over Asia, Africa, and Latin America. It is a system of contradictions and tensions. Wars are now always a mixture of types always in the context of the nuclear war(s) that can never be fought. There are technophiliaic computer wars, as the Allies fought it in Kuwait, appropriate technology people's war like Afhanistan, and dozens of variations of civil war, from crude gun battles to ethnic cleansing. There are even more ways to wage lower-intensity conflicts that can include terrorism (state or otherwise), economic aggression and espionage, or are even purely rhetorical or even cultural.

This period of mixed forms may not last very long. It is unstable because postmodern war is fundamentally a system of paradoxes. Among the most significant:

- The main moral justification for war is now peace.
- The main practical justification for repression is the fight for freedom.
- To save something, you often have to destroy it, be it a village or democracy itself.
- Security comes from putting the very future of the planet in grave risk.

- People are too fragile for the new levels of lethality; machines are too stupid for the complexity of battle.
- There is a continual tension between bodies and machines. In purely military terms, machines, such as tanks, planes, ships, missiles, and guns, are considered more important than people. But back at home the human soldiers are usually more valuable politically.
- The pace of battle is set by the machines, experienced by the humans.
- Advanced weapons are neither machines nor humans, but both: man-machine weapon systems.
- The "battlefield" is really a *battlespace*. It is now three-dimensional and ranges beyond the atmosphere. It is on thousands of electronic wavelengths. It is on the "homefront" as much as the battlefront.
- The battlespace is also often very constrained. Many targets, even adversaries, may not be attacked. Even in war zones the full fury of postmodern weapons is reserved for special killing boxes, free-fire zones, politically acceptable targets and the actual battle-line, if any.
- Politics are so militarized that every act of war needs political preparation and justification. There is only the most limited war space, where all important decisions are made on military grounds. Wars can only be won politically. Through military means the best that can be accomplished is not to lose.
- Obvious genocide (nuclear war), now that it is technologically easy, is morally impossible. Even barbarities that stop short of Hiroshima or the Holocaust, such as ethnic cleansing and massive famines, are difficult for the world body politic to suffer long.
- The industrialized countries want colonialism without responsibility (neo); they want empire without casualties.
- Some people in the nonindustrial and industrializing regions want Western technology without Western culture; others want both; others want neither.
- Soldiers are no longer uniform. They range from the DOD (Department of Defense) officials in suits to the women doctors at the front lines, with spies, flacks, analysts, commando-warriors, techs, grunts, desk jockeys, and many others besides.
- The traditional "male" gender of soldiers is changing to a more amorphous cyborg soldier whose persona is masculine, status is feminine, and sex and sexual preference variable.[6] In the U.S. women can now serve in almost all the subcategories of postmodern soldier except for the three basics of land combat: infantry, artillery, and armor.

- Civilians, and nature itself, are usually more threatened in battle than the soldiers are.
- New styles of war are invented but old styles of war continue. War itself proliferates into the general culture.

All these contradictions stem from the central problem of postmodern war—war itself. Unless war changes radically, it will be impossible for war and humanity to continue to coexist. Modern war's hunger for totality remains, and yet slaking it with postmodern weapons is exterminism. Weapons, especially CBN (chemical-biological-nuclear), are just too powerful. *And they proliferate even as you read this!* They proliferate not just to more and more nation-states, and inevitably someday soon to nongovernmental organizations, but they proliferate in kind and in power as well.

So the old and conservative discourse of war has forsaken its traditional resistance to new technologies and has become wildly experimental.[7] It has even institutionalized innovation to an amazing degree, seeking ways to keep war viable by creating new weapons to either rationalize battle, or make it so irrational it can never take place. The same military institution may seek to prepare for many different types of war, some of them "imaginary" and even ultimately "unthinkable." War itself militarizes the culture, and to cope, the military of the U.S., for example, abandoned traditional military virtues and replaced them with pseudoscientific techniques and high technology weapons—an approach, by the way, that while poorly suited for Vietnam has advantages for other types of limited conflicts, from invading small countries (Santo Domingo, Grenada, Panama) to set-piece battles against an exposed and incompetent enemy such as Iraq.

To show postmodern war in its specificity, it will help to follow the career of one U.S. soldier from 1946 to 1972. The main features and tensions of the contemporary U.S. approach to war are revealed in Col. David H. Hackworth's life in the U.S. Army, from green recruit to hero to antiwar activist.[8]

Colonel Hackworth joined the army right at the end of World War II and soon found himself under fire from Yugoslav partisans as he patrolled the border with Italy. He was involved in several confrontations with the Soviets at Berlin before going to Korea for his real baptism under fire. The "cold war" was the underlying justification for the permanent military mobilization of which he was a part. It became clear to him even then that the U.S. military's "zero defects" and "New Look" emphasis on replacing men with machines (especially nuclear weapons), and its drive toward making soldiers technologists, would turn it into a careerist bureaucracy. But he thought Korea, a "real" war, would sweep the bureaucrats away.

Korea at first did seem real, like a conventional modern war. But soon, for combatants and observers alike, it began to resemble the Indochina campaign the French were busy losing, rather than World War II. Politics, appearances, rhetoric (in treaties and on TV), and the weapons themselves all applied strange limits to the actual scope of battle, and yet the war also sprawled everywhere, eventually into the streets of the United States. Vietnam, for example, was civil war, small war, anticolonial revolution, communist coup, total war, cold war, peace action, and protest campaign all rolled into one. Korea wasn't quite so elaborate but it was similar in its complexity. Hackworth saw many friends die in Korea learning the lessons of such semilimited wars.

Struggling to fit into the technophile military of the late 1950s, Hackworth mastered anti-aircraft missile technologies and commanded a battery stationed near Disneyland. Later he went to missile school to learn how to use tactical nuclear weapons and then he joined the "Nuke the Pukes" world, as he put it, as the CO (Commanding Officer) of an atomic missile unit in Europe. On returning to the States he qualified airborne in time to help plan for the 101st Division's intervention against the segregationist governor of Alabama, George Wallace, if it was necessary. It wasn't.

Then came Vietnam. At first it seemed a godsend to the combat-obsessed Hackworth. But once there he quickly noticed that the U.S. was losing and concluded that what was needed was a new strategy. From then on, like John Paul Vann, he spent a great deal of time trying to change the U.S. military.[9] Finally, after much bloodshed, he realized that his army couldn't win that impossible war. It was not even fighting to win, he concluded, but rather to test new "Buck Rogers" technoweapons, to get fancy medals and tickets punched for ambitious officers, and to maintain the "war state." Between tours he again prepared for military intervention domestically, this time against antiwar protesters and black militants, by setting up training programs to militarize state and local police departments.

In the end he resigned in protest and moved to Australia where he wrote his remarkable memoirs, a strange mix of war stories, political analysis, and unintentionally revealing psychological insights. Hackworth was a warrior, known as "Sergeant Combat" from the beginning of his career. He did not fit into the postmodern military, useful as he was in combat. He believed more in sexual conquests and effective killing as criteria for judging a soldier's worth than efficient paper shuffling. He wanted to lead men into battle, not become a general. His World War II-inspired dreams of glory were tenacious; it took the Korean and Vietnam Wars to kill them. But once they died he looked with horror at his "work" of preparing for nuclear war and of waging high-tech war against the people, and very land, of Asia.

His personal story is as good an analysis of the postmodern U.S. military as any academic or official study could be. It is not perfect knowledge, but it doesn't claim to be either. It is personal, local, and emotional knowledge and it is very sad and quite true as far as it goes. Colonel Hackworth lived out his career in what we now call history, even if only contemporary history. His experience has to be put in context if the fuller implications of postmodern war are to become clear.

A GENEALOGY OF LITTLE WARS

Between 1492 and 1939 the modern armies of Europe and North America took control of most of the world's land. Resistance to Western expansion was tenacious, often lasting hundreds of years. However, with very few exceptions (Ethiopia, Afghanistan, Japan) the West always triumphed eventually. These wars were marked by the use of surrogate forces, the effective deployment of new technologies, and incredible moral license. Genocide was often the strategy for victory.

But at the end of World War II a sea change took place. Colonialism was suddenly collapsing under political and military pressures that ranged across the spectrum from satyagraha (the "truth force" of Gandhi's independence movement) through voting to violence. Part of this great rollback of colonialism was merely a strategic retreat to neocolonialism. For the West, the indirect economic and cultural domination of neocolonialism, as exemplified by U.S. control of Latin America, had much to recommend it. Most nations either moved into neocolonial relationships or thrust off European sovereignty altogether but only by ceding some measure of control to regional powers or to the so-called second world. The Communist Bloc did not lead countries to liberation, but it helped create some room to maneuver, if not real independence.[10] For a few countries with extraordinary national resources or exemplerary leadership, real autonomy was possible. This is seen most clearly in the case of war. Consider the spectrum of allies that the Vietnamese mobilized for their extended war: Sweden and many other nonaligned nations, China, the USSR, and large parts of the international peace movement. The Vietnamese also perfected the second major style of postmodern war to counter the high-tech approach of the Japanese, French, and North Americans.

While modern war was developing toward total war it was often challenged by "irregular war." When Western armies met each other they fought modern wars, but when they went to war against other people it was a more limited struggle, from the point of view of the Europeans. They called it insurrection, revolution, guerilla war, tribal revolt, rebellion, uprising, police action, little war, imperfect war, colonial war, and limited war. These wars were only little on one side. For the nonindustrialized cultures they were total wars sure enough, often leading to the destruction of whole cultures and the genocide, or near genocide, of entire peoples.

Postmodern war has imposed the framework of "minor" wars onto all conflicts, even those between the great powers. This came as something of a surprise for them at first, and even as late as 1960 they still almost blundered into nuclear conflagration. Eventually they did figure out that their competition had to be controlled below a certain threshold—which they have done, using economics or fighting proxies in regional conflicts. Still, even a limited war can be very bloody. Over two million died in Korea. But considering the butcher's bill of a full war between China and the U.S., it is clear that it was quite "limited" for them both, although not for the Koreans.

But even before Korea, even before World War II, the first postmodern war began when the Vietnamese started their revolution for independence against the French. It was a long war because they then fought the Japanese, then the French again, and finally the Americans and their allies from South Korea and Australia, with a few battles against the British and the Chinese as well, and always fighting against other Vietnamese. What makes this long war so important is that it reversed hundreds of years of European victories. True, indigenous people had won many battles, but they had lost almost all the wars. And, true, Japan had defeated Russia in 1905, but Japan was an industrialized power and it had never been colonized. With Vietnam, a small agricultural country defeated its colonizer and then the most powerful empire in history by framing war in basically political terms.

This was not a totally new strategy. In part, it was George Washington's approach during the American Revolution, something the Vietnamese were well aware of. It also was an approach that drew strongly on the hundreds of years of Vietnamese resistance to Chinese imperialism, and, ironically enough, on the more recent experiences of the Red Army in China. But, granting all that, it was still unique. Politics became war by other means for the Vietnamese. Not that military skill was irrelevant, it was crucial if it served the long-term ends of wearing out the invaders. The theory of people's war, as the Chinese and Vietnamese call it, was so sophisticated that it even laid out the transition between the lowest levels of military resistance on through to eventual victory through conventional means.

Some have argued that people's war is necessarily communistic, but the last fifty years show it isn't. Not only have the Algerians used it successfully, but so have the Afghans. And, with bitter-sweet irony, the same type of war has been turned against some of its best communist practitioners in southern Africa and Southeast Asia. In Cambodia, the Vietnamese themselves could not crush the Cambodian rebels, well supported as they were by the U.S., China, and a significant proportion of the Khmer people.

This kind of war is certainly fought "for the hearts and minds" of the people, as everyone professes to know. But what is known, and what is done, are very different things, as the U.S. was to learn to its pain.

THE U.S. AND THE NAM

In response to the strategy of people's war, the U.S. offered hubris and technoscience. Henry Kissinger proclaimed, "A scientific revolution has, for all practical purposes, removed technical limits from the exercise of power in foreign policy." Kissinger went from this assumption of unrestrained power to develop his theories of limited war, which he later applied directly to Vietnam.[11] From this first principle of the triumph of scientific reason comes a natural corollary: the supremacy of rationality. David Halberstam noted this in his analysis of the "best and the brightest" who involved the U.S. in the Vietnam War.

> • If there was anything that bound the men . . . together, it was the belief that sheer intelligence and rationality could answer and solve anything. . . . Bundy was a man of applied intelligence, a man who would not land us in trouble by passion and emotion.[12]
>
> • He [McNamara], not only believed in rationality . . . he loved it. It was his only passion.[13]
>
> • McNamara himself admitted as much. For him, the life that wasn't ruled by rationality wasn't worth living.
>
> • "Who is man? Is he a rational animal? If he is, then the goals can ultimately be achieved; if he is not, then there is little point in making the effort."[14]

Fred Kaplan, who named McNamara and the other best and brightest the "wizards of Armageddon," noticed the same thing. "McNamara was coldly clinical, abrupt, almost brutally determined to keep emotional influences out of the inputs and cognitive processes that determined his judgments and decisions. It was only natural, then, that when Robert S. McNamara met the RAND Corporation, the effect was like love at first sight."[15] These new friends, worshipers of systemic analytical reason, agreed not always on how to fight the war, but always on how to judge it. From Harvard Yard to the beltway think tanks circling the Pentagon to the electronic shops and wilder think tanks of California it was agreed to fight the war logically, rationally, systematically, and with cold calculation.

On one level McNamara and his fellows knew that Vietnam was supposed to be fought as a political war. War is, after all, merely the extension of politics, isn't it? And war is, after all, messy, bloody, confusing, emotional, and unpredictable. But instead it became the war of the electronic battlefield, and the U.S. government not only lost the battle for the hearts and minds of the Vietnamese but the struggle for the hearts and minds of many Americans as well.

Illusions about the removal of "technical limits from the exercise of power" were based on a belief in a specific type or rationality, and especially in rationality's machines such as the computer. Kissinger and McNamara, both former Harvard bargaining theorists, believed war could be rationalized, that it could be managed. The military, for its part, believed completely in the superiority of firepower and logistics as coordinated with command, control, communication, and intelligence.[16]

Unsurprisingly, the actual war was run by "crisis management," which is systems analysis applied to a crisis. Everyone realizes there is a crisis. Somebody thinks through various possibilities, including the effects of effects (feedback), someone gives key factors certain numerical weights, someone assigns mathematical values (plus, minus, multiply, divide, or something more complex) to the relations between various factors, someone makes assumptions about the value of possible outcomes, and then a machine calculates the costs and benefits of different approaches. They call it a science.

Vietnam was the systems analysis war, the electronic war, the computer war, the technological war. From the point of view of the technophile analysts there was no reason they could have lost unless it was because the "peace movement" stabbed the military in the back. Others, including many who were there, saw it differently and it seems now that their views have prevailed.

The Vietnam War is a particularly good case of how unofficial knowledge can be used to change a society's conception of a complicated issue. Appeals to the "wisdom" of the grunts are made by many writers with quite different explanations as to why the war was lost, but the majority see it as a war that could not have been won.[17] In formal war discourse, only loyal officers, Pentagon bureaucrats, and official historians have an important point of view. All other accounts are marginalized, whether they are disloyal officers (like Hackworth), journalists (such as Bernard Fall), soldiers (as in the many memoirs), or Vietnamese (who also wrote their own books). For example, Gen. Vo Nguyen Giap, commander in chief of the People's Army, described U.S. strategy thus: "The United States has a strategy based on arithmetic. They question the computers, add and subtract, extract square roots, and then go into action. But arithmetical strategy doesn't work here. If it did, they'd already have exterminated us with their planes."[18] The sum of these many different voices, from General Giap to the Viet vets in the Senate or on the local corner to CBS to former President Bush to the *American Historical Review* to your reactions to this article, is our contemporary current discourse on Vietnam.

One book that has pulled many of these "marginalized" views together into one analysis is James Gibson's *The Perfect War: Tech-*

nowar in Vietnam. It examines the Vietnam War as seen by combat soldiers from the lower ranks, protesters to the war, dissident officials within government, and journalists, and it details how official power, patriotic ideology, flashy-destructive technology, and scientific rules of discourse were used to formulate and perpetuate U.S. policy. Gibson concludes that the official understanding of the Vietnam War can be called "the discourse of technowar" and that it was sharply regulated. "Technowar thus monopolizes 'organized scientific discourse' through multiple, but centralizing relationships among high-level position[s], technobureaucratic or production logic in the structure of its propositions, and the conventional educated prose style. The debate on Vietnam occurs within this unity."[19] He contrasts the official "unpoetic poetic" of the "technobureaucratic or production logic" (obvious by its propositions and style) with what he calls "the warrior's knowledge," which has many different viewpoints and insights and lacks a formal structure of concepts or any data in a regular sequence.

This warrior's knowledge often comes in the form of stories. The official discourse does not consider stories, poems, memoirs, interviews, and music valid forms of knowledge. They are disqualified because of their genre and their speaker. Nonfiction is valued over fiction and the memoirs of high-ranking officers are more important than any grunt's. And yet, in the long run it seems the grunt's view has won out.

Gibson's analysis is that the Vietnam War was lost because it was prosecuted as a rationally managed production system more interested in the appearance of scientificity (body counts, systems analysis) than real effectiveness. Managers such as McNamara insisted on numbers to explain the war but many of the numbers were lies. Gibson looks at a series of reports and other documents, such as the "point system" combat units used to judge their effectiveness, and decides, after a close reading of General Westmoreland's April 1967 report to President Johnson, that it

> presents Technowar as a production system that can be rationally managed and warfare as a kind of activity that can be scientifically determined by constructing computer models. Increase their resources and the war-managers claim to know what will happen. What constitutes their knowledge is an array of numbers—numbers of U.S. and allied

forces, numbers of VC and NVA forces, body counts, kill ratios—numbers that appear scientific.[20]

But this vision of rationality isn't a full picture of reality. Beneath official rationality the emotional can, and does, return in crazy and criminal acts. Consider these phrases by William Bundy, Robert McNamara, John McNaughton, and Richard Helms culled from the *Pentagon Papers* by Daniel Ellsberg about the rationale of the bombing of North Vietnam:

- The resumption of bombing after a pause would be even more painful to the population of North Vietnam than a fairly steady rate of bombing.
- "Water-drip" technique.
- It is important not to "kill the hostage" by destroying the North Vietnamese assets inside the "Hanoi donut."
- Fast/full squeeze . . . Progressive squeeze-and-talk . . .
- The "hot-cold" treatment . . . the objective of "persuading" Hanoi, which would dictate a program of painful surgical strikes.
- Our "salami-slice" bombing program.
- Ratchet.
- One more turn of the screw.[21]

Daniel Ellsberg (another Harvard bargaining theorist) admits that he heard such talk all the time from these men, and, while he often disagreed with the policies they advocated, he never saw what his wife did when she first read them. It is *"the language of torturers."*[22] Torture was the policy. "By early 1965, McNamara's Vietnam strategy was essentially a conventional-war version of the counterforce/no-cities theory—using force as an instrument of coercion, withholding a larger force that could kill the hostage of the enemy's cities if he didn't back down."[23] This strategy was based directly on Thomas Schelling's elaboration of game theory. In his book *Arms and Influence* Schelling applies his theory to limited war: "The power to hurt can be counted among the most impressive attributes of military force . . . War is always a bargaining process . . . the bargaining power . . . comes from capacity to hurt, (to cause) sheer pain and damage."[24] Or as Henry Kissinger put it, "In a limited war the problem is to apply graduated amounts of destruction for limited objectives and also to permit the necessary breathing spaces for political contacts."[25] By 1970 it is thus—"While troops are being brought home, the air war increases. It is a new form of war where machines do most of the killing and destruction. . . . mechanized war consists of aircraft, huge air bases, and aircraft carriers. The goal of the mechanized war is to replace U.S. personnel with machines."[26]

More than three million sorties (one plane on one attack) were flown by U.S. aircraft during the Vietnam War. Over 1,700 planes were lost, including drones. Over two hundred airmen were taken prisoner, and they became one of North Vietnam's strongest bargaining chips. The air force and the navy ran an ongoing contest to see who could fly the most sorties because much of their budget was determined in that manner. Often planes flew half full, or flew useless raids, just to keep the numbers up. Even though this massive application of air power proved a total failure, some military officers still feel more bombing could have won the war. Their faith in technology is all the stronger after its failure.[27] The various seductions of strategic bombing are more potent in the discourse than any balanced judgment of bombing technology's efficacy.[28]

Another example of the strange redirections the emotions of war took in Vietnam was the official approval given to killing by machines, while killing by people directly was often considered an atrocity. "It was wrong for infantrymen to destroy a village with white-phosphorus grenades, but right for a fighter pilot to drop napalm on it," noted one combat infantryman in a novelization of his Vietnam experience. He added that ethics "seemed to be a matter of distance and technology. You could never go wrong if you killed people at long range with sophisticated weapons."[29] This is a key discourse rule of mechanized warfare.

In *War Without End*, Michael Klare, gives a detailed account of this mechanized war and many of the institutions behind it. He examines the role of human-factors research, ergonomics, social-systems engineering, modeling, and simulations in the U.S. military's attempts to develop an automated electronic battlefield in Southeast Asia. Along with the scientific management, computerized communications, and data management, this battlefield also depended on sensors for metal, heat, and smells. Collected data was evaluated and sent to Udam, Thailand, where a computer system sorted it out and dispatched hunter-killer teams of helicopters. Anything living in the free-fire zones was a target.[30]

An effect of this vision of the clean "electronic" battlefield, were attempts to actually produce lifeless clarity with a massive herbicide attack on nature to improve visibility in the kill zones.[31] It seems that this illusion that war could be programmed was also behind the government's intermittently successful attempts to manage the mass media, to orchestrate the South Vietnamese military, and to manipulate the antiwar movement. But the best example of the application of information science to real-life contexts remains the prosecution of the war itself.

Klare points out that it was a gigantic infrastructure of researchers that planned the automation of the Vietnam War. Specifically he mentions Rand, the Special Operations Research Office, the Research Analysis Corporation, the Human Resources Research Office (HUMRRO), The Center for Research in Social Systems, the Institute for Defense Analysis (IDA), and the Stanford Research Institute, among others.[32] It was IDA, the Joint Chiefs' own think tank, that gave the biggest push to the electronic battlefield. An elite team of moonlighting university scientists, called the Jasons, proposed an "electronic" wall across the Ho Chi Minh trail. Although parts were built, it never even slowed the resupply of the North Vietnamese troops in the south.

Such thinking was too far removed from the political and military realities of the war in Vietnam. The U.S. elite expected the Vietnamese to live by U.S. models and up to U.S. simulations that were based on ungrounded political science assumptions and an exaggerated faith in system and technology. James Gibson concludes that in such a discourse system,

> Military strategy becomes a one-factor question about technical forces; success or failure is measured quantitatively. Machine-system meets machine-system and the largest, fastest, most technologically advanced system will win. Any other outcome becomes *unthinkable.* Such is the logic of *Technowar.* . . . Vietnam represents the perfect functioning of this closed, self-referential universe. Vietnam was *The Perfect War.*[33]

In this universe, autonomous weapons and sensors were to replace manpower on the battlefield. Prototype sensors were deployed right after the Korean War and first saw major use in Vietnam, as did the first working autonomous weapons. While both have been touted by some as great successes, it is important to note that the United States lost that war, and we lost most of the battles where they were deployed. Despite the sensors, the United States abandoned McNamara's wall, fought to a bloody draw at Khe Sanh, and finally suffered total tactical and strategic surprise during the Tet offensive.

The story of the smart bombs and remote-controlled drones is no better, although they performed over 2,500 sorties. So many drones were tried out over North Vietnam that U.S. pilots called it the Tonkin Gulf test range. During the planning for the Son Tay Rescue Mission, for example, all seven Buffalo Hunter recon drones sent failed to discover that the camp was empty, and six were shot down.

Smart bombs also had their share of failures. The Falcon, produced at a cost of $2 billion, was effective about 7 percent of the time instead of the 99 percent predicted by tests. Most pilots refused to carry it. The Maverick was also a failure, in part due to it being color blind.[34] Ironically, even the one big success of smart bombs, the use of a Hobo bomb to take out the Thanh Hoa bridge after a number of regular bomb runs failed, was a military failure since the use of a ford nearby meant the Vietnamese lost little supply ability.

As the war was running down, it became public that these weapons and sensors had been developed without any Congressional approval in what was one of the largest and most secret U.S. military research programs ever. In scale it was quite comparable to the Manhattan project and to the gigantic Black Budget research projects of the late eighties and early nineties.[35] Despite the manifest failures and the funding scandal, the research continued and led directly to present DOD plans for even further computerization because the same discourse system remained in place. In 1970 General Westmoreland predicted:

> On the battlefield of the future, enemy forces will be located, tracked, and targeted almost instantaneously through the use of data links, computer assisted intelligence evaluation, and automated fire control. . . . I am confident that the American people expect this country to take full advantage of this technology—to welcome and applaud the developments that will replace wherever possible the man with the machine.[36]

Or, left unsaid by Westmoreland, the option to make of the man a machine. One of the little-known aspects of Vietnam was the extensive use of stimulants and other drugs to help elite soldiers perform. By the end of the war, research on a wide variety of compounds for everything from controlling fear to improving night vision was being financed by the Pentagon. Such studies continue, as does even more research on automating warfare. Meanwhile, many outside observers have judged the U.S. performance in Vietnam quite harshly.[37]

In his history of *Command in War*, Martin Van Creveld concludes that the automated and electronic battlefield will be as confusing and chaotic as Vietnam was. On Vietnam he adds, "We have seen the future and it does not work."[38] Daniel Ellsberg is a little more brutal. "Whether as field tactic or foreign policy, our way of war now relies on the use of indiscriminate American artillery and airpower that generates innumerable My Lai's as a norm, not as a shocking exceptional case."[39] It is a conscious strategy.

They were both right, partially. Van Creveld was certainly right as far as low-intensity conflicts go; but the same high-tech strategy can work remarkably against the right enemy, as Saddam Hussein went out of his way to prove.[40] And Ellsberg is wrong when he calls the fire-power approach "indiscriminate." It was discriminate in Vietnam. It was meant to look good, (even if it killed many civilians) through numerous restrictions and zones and moratoriums, and it was certainly discriminate in Iraq-Kuwait in a very similar way.[41] Which brings us to the present.

CONCLUSION: THE HISTORICAL IS POLITICAL, THE HISTORICAL IS PERSONAL

The U.S. military has been haunted by Vietnam, and until the War to Restore the Emir of Kuwait, it didn't have many successes to help it forget. And, as great a victory as that was in military terms, it didn't end the Vietnam Syndrome. The euphoria that declared the Vietnam Syndrome over with the crushing of Saddam seemed hollow less than a hundred days after headlines screamed Bush's claim that "This War is Behind Us!" Bush is now gone and Saddam remains, showing that pure victories are still hard to achieve even in the desert. More sober analysts, including General Schwarzkopf himself, have always refused to equate the Iraqis with the Vietnamese, or the Vietnam War with shorter conflicts. To quote General Schwarzkopf: "I certainly don't give the Iraqis much credit. Ho Chi Minh and Gen Giap didn't live in luxury, didn't have seven different palaces, didn't drive white Mercedeses like Saddam Hussein. Hanoi had an entirely different class of leadership."[42] The marine combat veteran and former secretary of the navy, James Webb, also refuses to claim that the easy victory in Kuwait erases the lessons of Vietnam. He points out that we didn't lose in Vietnam because of our technology, but because of our opponent.

> We had one of the best-trained and best-equipped armies in American history in Vietnam. Our technology was just as good as it was in the Persian Gulf war. Not to denigrate what we accomplished against Hussein, but Hussein was no military strategist.
>
> If Ho Chi Minh had put 60 percent of his army in one spot where there were not any trees, we would have blown them away in 40 days too.[43]

That the Persian Gulf War erases the Vietnam Syndrome is just wishful, and dangerous, thinking. The Vietnamese won the first postmodern war because they had the proper strategy, motivation, and organization (including important allies) to match their enemies. The Soviets were driven from Afghanistan for similar reasons. Fundamentally, both Vietnam and Afghanistan ended the way they did because the people of the west and north aren't willing to support long bloody wars for the sake of empire, while many people of the east and south are willing to fight and die for the hope of something better than what they have now, or at least to drive foreign armies out of their countries.

The Vietnam syndrome isn't cured at home, either. There was a truly significant level of resistance to the Iraq War, despite the brilliant political mobilization orchestrated by the war movement. Antiwar forces didn't stop the war, but they came close. The war movement did triumph in the end, but it has a problem: it may not get an enemy like Saddam again for quite some time.

This is why, despite the dying children of Iraq, despite the massacres in Bosnia and Somalia and the Caucasus mountains, I can be optimistic. The protests to the Gulf War started with a level of support and sophistication that was only achieved during the old Movement days after years of organizing, and in the Gulf War protests there was a great deal less sectarian craziness and macho posturing. The many voices that the Vietnam War raised are still echoing in our culture and in the world as a whole.

Sure, President Clinton now promises to keep the U.S. military the strongest in the world, but he also plans to cut $50 billion from its budget since one of its prime rationales, the communist menace, is no more. As an anarchist I'm hardly going to put my faith in Clinton or even the ecologically aware Gore, but I am encouraged by the context in which they must operate. Yes, there are more wars than ever, but there is more peace activism than ever as well, from the United Nations to the grass roots. Vietnam showed the bankruptcy of anticommunist ideology and scientific warfare just as real bankruptcies have recently dramatically done away with illusions of Marxism's infallibility. We are left with a world without certainties, a world where the discourse is more open than it has ever been, even if the dangers we face, thanks to the incredible powers of technoscience, are the greatest ever as well. We are left with a world where bodies count even more than helicopter gunships, because, in the long run, human bodies are more articulate than any killing machine.

I expect that this administration will finally make peace with Vietnam, and the MIA families will make peace with their loss, and we can finally put the Vietnam War somewhere behind us, although never very far. Because as World War II marked the end of the modern era, Vietnam marks the beginning of the period we still live in, the postmodern age, and most of it has yet to be lived.

NOTES

1. Ben Kiernan, "The Vietnam War: Alternative Endings," *The American Historical Review* 97 (1992): 1118–37.

2. The term "postmodern war" was initially used, as far as I know, by Fredric Jameson when he labeled Vietnam the first postmodern war in his article "Postmodernism, or the Cultural Logic of Late Capitalism," *New Left Review* 146 (July-August 1984): 53–92. An extended discussion of postmodern war appears in my book, *Postmodern War: The New Politics of Conflict* (New York: Guillford, 1998).

3. See Seymour Melman, *The Permanent War Economy: American Capitalism in Decline* (New York: Simon and Schuster, 1974) [permanent war]; Stefan Possony and Jerry Pournelle, *The Strategy of Technology* (Cambridge, Mass.: University Press of Cambridge, 1970) [technology war]; Paul Edwards, "Artificial Intelligence and High Technology War: The Perspective of the Formal Machine," working paper no. 6, Silicon Valley Research Group, University of California at Santa Cruz (November 1986) [high technology war, technological war]; James Gibson, *The Perfect War: Technowar in Vietnam* (Boston: Atlantic Monthly Press, 1986) [technowar, perfect war]; Mary Kaldor, "The Imaginary War" in *Prospectus for a Habitable Planet*, ed. by Dan Smith and E. P. Thompson (New York: Penguin, 1987) [imaginary war]; Martin Van Creveld, *Technology and War* (New York: Free Press, 1989) [computer war];

Michael Klare, *War Without End: American Planning for the Next Vietnams* (New York: Knopf, 1972) [war without end]; Col. James Donovan, *Militarism U.S.A* (New York: Scribner, 1970) [Militarism USA]; Paul Virilio, *War and Cinema* (London: Verso, 1989) [light war]; James Derian, *Antidiplomacy: Spies Terror, Speed, and War* (Cambridge, Mass.: Blackwell 1992) [high modern war, cyberwar today]; Owen Davies, "Robotic Warriors Clash in Cyberwars," *Omni* January 1987): 76–88 [cyberwars as future wars]; Donna Haraway, personal communication (Winter 1991) [hypermodern war]; and Paul Virilio and Sylvere Lotringer, *Pure War* (New York: Semiotext(e), 1983) [pure war]. Although all of these labels have something to recommend them, none do justice to the complexity and sweeping nature of the recent changes in war. For example, Virilio's "pure war" does capture poetically the current deep penetration of war into culture, certainly in the West, especially into politics. But in a strong sense the nuclear climax of World War II was "pure war." What we have now is very "impure" war, called "imperfect" war in legalese, coming to the fore because pure total war has become, thanks to technoscience, suicidal. War is diffused throughout the culture, helping shift gender definitions, structuring the economy, selling products, electing presidents, and boosting ratings. But the actual battles are not decisive or heroic; they are confusing, distant, and squalid or one-sided.

4. For a more extensive discussion of postmodern theorists, see my "Excerpts From Philosophy and the Human Future: The Implications of Postmodern War," *Nomad* 3, no. 1 (1992): 31–39. While the work of Michel Foucault and Jean-François Lyotard has been helpful, in many ways I am more indebted to feminist postmodernists such as Donna Haraway, Leslie Adelson, Jane Flax, Linda Hutcheon, and Chris Weedon.

5. And I use "man" advisedly. Whether it is rational economic man, the rational actor of game theory, or the ideal rational man of cognitive science, this illusionary figure is always masculine.

6. A dynamic that is described in detail in my article "The Culture of War Cyborgs: Technoscience, Gender, and Postmodern War," in the special issue on *Technology and Feminism*, edited by Joan Rothschild, *Research in Philosophy & Technology* 13 (1993): 141–63.

7. For example, the U.S. military today is seriously researching antigravity, ESP, death rays, meditation, cold fusion, artificial intelligence, nanotechnology, and many other science fiction technologies.

8. David H. Hackworth and Julie Sherman, *About Face* (New York: Simon and Schuster, 1989).

9. Every student of the war should read Neil Sheehan's incredible *A Bright Shining Lie: John Paul Vann and America in Vietnam* (New York: Random House, 1988).

10. See Gerard Chaliand, *Revolution in the Third World*, trans. Diana Johnstone (New York: Penguin, 1978).

11. Gibson, 15, 21–23, quoting from Henry Kissinger, *American Foreign Policy* (New York, 1974), 57.

12. David Halberstam, *The Best and the Brightest* (New York: Fawcett Crest, 1972), 57.

13. Ibid., 288.

14. Robert Strange McNamara, May 1966. Qtd. Fred Kaplan, *The Wizards of Armageddon* (New York: Touchstone, 1983), 337.

15. Ibid., 51. Donna Haraway calls this weird matrix of feelings "the emotion of no emotion."

16. Andrew Krepinevich Jr., *The Army and Vietnam* (Baltimore: Johns Hopkins University Press, 1986), argues in great detail from original sources that the army's conversion to counterinsurgency doctrine was superficial and that Vietnam was fought as a conventional high technology war.

17. This is based on my own readings in the genre, including: Philip Caputo, *A Rumor of War* (New York: Ballantine, 1977); William Broyles Jr., *Brothers in Arms: A Journey from War to Peace* (New York: Avon, 1986); David Donovan, *Once a Warrior King: Memories of an Officer in Vietnam* (New York: Ballantine, 1985); Jonnie Clark, *Guns Up!* (New York: Ballantine, 1984); Robert Mason, *Chickenhawk* (New York: Penguin, 1984); John A. Parrish, M. D., *12, 20, & 5: A Doctor's Year in Vietnam* (New York: Bantam, 1972); Charles Henderson, *Marine Sniper: 93 Confirmed Kills* (New York: Berkeley Books, 1986); Michael Lee Lanning, *Vietnam, 1969–1970: A Company Commander's Journal* (New York: Ivy Books, 1986); Keith Walker, ed., *A Piece of My Heart: The Stories of Twenty-Six American Women Who Served in Vietnam* (New York: Ballantine, 1985); Peter Goldman and Tony Fuller, *Charlie Company: What Vietnam Did to Us* (New York: Ballantine, 1983); Mark Baker, ed., *NAM: The Vietnam War in the Words of the Men and Women Who Fought There* (New York: Morrow, 1981); Bernard Fall, *Street without Joy* (Harrisburg, Penn.: Stackpole, 1963), *Hell in a Very Small Place* (Philadelphia: Lippincott, 1967), and *Last Reflections on a War* (New York: Doubleday, 1967); Michael Herr, *Dispatches* (New York: Avon, 1978); C. D. B. Bryan, *Friendly Fire* (New York: Bantam, 1976); and Francis FitzGerald, *Fire in the Lake* (Boston: Little Brown, 1972).

18. Vo Nguyen Giap, *The Military Art of People's War: Selected Writings of Vo Nguyen Giap*, ed. Russell Stetler (New York: Monthly Review Press, 1970), 329.

19. Gibson, *The Perfect War*, 467.

20. Ibid., 115–16, 155–56.

21. Qtd. Daniel Ellsberg, *Papers on the War* (New York: Simon and Schuster, 1972), 304.

22. Ibid.; emphasis original. Herman Kahn called it the "attrition-pressure-ouch" theory. Ouch, of course, might mean thousands dead. Gregg Herken, *Counsels of War* (New York: Knopf, 1985), 210.

23. Kaplan, *Wizards*, 329.

24. Qtd. Ibid., 332.

25. Gibson, 22, quoting from Henry Kissinger, *Nuclear Weapons and Foreign Policy* (New York: 1957), 155.

26. Coca Crystal, "Airwar; Computerized Battlefield," first published in 1972 in the *Yippie Times*, reprinted in *The Secret History of the '70s* (New York: Youth Int. Party, 1982), 18–24.

27. For an eyewitness impression of the bombing of Hanoi, see Harrison

Salisbury, *Behind the Lines-Hanoi* (New York: Bantam, 1967), 188–98. He cites Hanson Baldwin of the *New York Times* for the number of U.S. planes lost. For a detailed account of the surface rivalry that warped the bombing campaign, and for an analysis of why opening up the restricted target areas in North Vietnam would not have changed the outcome of the war, see Loren Baritz, *Backfire: A History of How American Culture Led Us into Vietnam and Made Us Fight the Way We Did* (New York: Ballantine, 1985), 246–52. For the figure on U.S. sorties, he cites Thomas Thayer, "Air Power" in *The Lessons of Vietnam*, ed. W. Scott Thompson and Donaldson D. Frizzell (New York: Crane, Russak, 1977), 146–50. For a sample of the belief that more bombing would have won the war, see "Lessons Learned in the Air War over Vietnam" in *Proceedings — U.S. Naval Institute* (August 1987): 6. In this report on a forum of the same name held at the Naval Air Station in Pensacola, Florida, Admiral Moorer (ret.), who had been the chairman of the Joint Chiefs during the later part of the war, is quoted as saying that if the military had been given a free hand "we could have polished those clowns off in six months." Very funny, Admiral.

28. For an extraordinary discussion of the appeal of strategic bombing, see Michael Sherry's *The Rise of American Air Power: The Creation of Armageddon* (New Haven: Yale University Press, 1987).

29. Caputo, *Rumor*, 218.

30. Paul Dickson explains the centrality of computers in this type of war in *The Electronic Battlefield* (New York: Atheneum, 1976), 85:

> Due to the large number of sensors, the information from them relayed to the Center had to first be digested and sorted by computer before it could be passed along to target analysts who, in turn passed their assessments to the bases, which control the strike aircraft and order them to their targets. . . . Commonly, the pilot of the F-4 Phantom or whatever would not only not see his target but not even push the button that dropped the bombs—like so much else in Igloo White this was automated with the bombs released at the moment selected by the computer.

31. Klare, *War Without End*, 169–205.

32. Ibid., 80–90.

33. Gibson, *The Perfect War*, 23, 27; his emphasis.

34. On the number of drone sorties, see James Canan, *The Superwarriors: The Fantastic World of Pentagon Superweapons* (New York: Weybright and Taley, 1975), 310; for the Falcon's problems, see James Fallows, *National Defense* (New York: Vintage, 1981), 55; for the Maverick, see James Coates and Michael Kilan, *Heavy Losses* (New York: Penguin, 1984), 155; for the Buffalo Hunter drone failures see Richard Gabriel, *Military Incompetence: Why the American Military Doesn't Win* (Toronto: Collin, 1985), 58.

35. See Dickson, *Electronic Battlefield*, for an account of this scandal and some very important quotes from the debates between Senators Proxmire and Goldwater over the weapon systems themselves and their covert funding.

36. General William Westmoreland, Congressional testimony, 13 July 1970.

37. On drugs in Vietnam, see Elton Manizione, "The Search for The Bionic Commando," *The National Reporter* (Fall/Winter 1986): 36–38. For continuing research, see Richard Gabriel, *No More Heroes: Madness and Psychiatry in War* (New York: Hill and Wang, 1987). My *Postmodern War* looks in detail at the continuation of Vietnam policies in the U.S. planning for, and prosecution of, subsequent wars.

38. Martin Van Creveld, *Command in War* (Cambridge: Harvard University Press, 1985), quoted in Brian Bond, "Battlefield CI throughout History," *International Security* 11 (Spring 1987): 125–29.

39. Ellsberg, *Papers,* 236. From his essay "Bombing and Other Crimes," where he shows how the bombing and the policy for small unit combats were the same.

40. Although high-tech weapons are far from perfect, they are potent indeed in the right circumstances. For an analysis of their decidedly mixed role in the Iraq-U.S. war, see my article "Kuwait 1991: A Postmodern War," *Nomad* 3 (Spring 1933): 29–37.

41. Both wars had free-fire zones, especially for the B-52s. They had precision bombing attacks on numerous targets; some of which were horrible misses: they had various targets completely off limits; they aimed at command, control, communications, and industries in the rear areas and military units in the forward areas; and they were not really challenged in the air. Often targets were prioritized, even chosen, for purely political instead of military reasons. Good examples of this are the SCUDS and the sorties defending of Kurdish refugee camps.

42. David Lamb, "Reflections on 'Norman of Arabia,'" *San Jose Mercury News* (26 February 1991): A14.

43. Mike Capuzzo, "Once a hawk," *San Jose Mercury News* (3 April 1991): E12.

9

FROM VIETNAM TO THE GULF: POSTMODERN WARS?

Douglas Kellner

The Vietnam War has been frequently described as "postmodern," signifying its qualitative difference from previous "modern" wars. Fredric Jameson, for instance, has claimed that Michael Herr, in his Vietnam book *Dispatches*, evoked "the space of postmodern warfare." Moreover, Jameson believed that:

> The extraordinary linguistic innovations of this work may still be considered postmodern, in the eclectic way in which its language impersonally fuses a whole range of contemporary collective idiolects, most notably rock language and black language: but the fusion is dictated by problems of content. This first terrible postmodernist war cannot be told in any of the traditional paradigms of the war novel or movie—indeed, that breakdown of all previous narrative paradigms is, along with the breakdown of any shared language through which a veteran might convey such experience, among the principle subjects of the book and may be said to open up the place of a whole new reflexivity.[1]

Jameson is alluding here to the postmodern critique of representation and the skepticism that concepts, narratives, and theories do not represent "the real," but construct their own reality. It appears that the distance between language and reality grew in the Vietnam

War where the military discourse clearly did not correspond to the disturbing actuality of the war, but constituted mere lies and propaganda, articulating the arrogance of power. The military defined the war in their own terms, and thus official discourse functioned in its own linguistic sphere, radically at odds with the experience of the troops and the more inquiring members of the press. The troops in turn had trouble finding a language to describe their experience of the horrific experience of Vietnam, and reporters and writers like Herr had to struggle to put their own experience of the war in words, to capture its complexity and viciousness.

Jameson takes Herr's book on Vietnam as evidence of the impossibility of mapping the "postmodern" space of Vietnam and as itself part of the cultural logic of the postmodern. In dialogue with Jameson, I argue that the Vietnam War was a modern war and that Herr's *Dispatches* can be read as a modernist text. Through a close reading of *Dispatches,* I contend that Herr deploys recognizably modernist writing strategies, and, using Herr and some key theoretical texts on Vietnam, I argue for the modernity of the Vietnam War. At stake is developing a proper vocabulary for theorizing contemporary war and the differences and similarities between the wars in Vietnam and the Persian Gulf.

VIETNAM AS MODERN WAR

That fall, all that the Mission talked about was
control: arms control, information control,
resources control, psycho-political control,
population control, control of the almost
supernatural inflation, control of terrain through
the Strategy of the Periphery. But when the talk
had passed, the only thing left standing up that
looked true was your sense of how out of control
things really were.

Michael Herr

In many ways, the Vietnam War was a highly modern war that showed the pretensions and flaws of the project of modernity. J. William Gibson has demonstrated convincingly that Vietnam should be read in the context of the Cold War as an imperialist war designed to combat the spread of communism, claiming that it was motivated by the desire of the U.S. military and political establishment to discover new viable modes of warfare in the face of nuclear extinction and the doctrine of "mutually assured destruction" (MAD) that made nuclear war unthinkable. Accordingly, the U.S. military developed counterinsurgency strategies and tested these policies and new weapons systems in Vietnam in an attempt to impose capitalist versions of modernization on the developing world.

In Gibson's ironic title, Vietnam was "the perfect war" to establish U.S. hegemony over communism and to demonstrate the superiority of U.S. weapons and military systems because it was "unthinkable" that a peasant Third World army could defeat a high-tech military superpower. For Gibson, Vietnam is a modern "technowar" that utilizes the assembly-line system of production, scientific management, systems theory, and high-tech weapons systems to produce dead bodies and to defeat the Vietnamese "foreign Other." For Gibson the U.S. defeat in Vietnam discloses the limits of the reductionist model of technowar and its failed understanding of Vietnamese society and culture, thus revealing the limitations of the modern paradigm and its belief in technological solutions to all problems.

Technowar in Gibson's conceptualization is a result of the synthesis of politics, economics, and science and can be understood as a product of modernity and its mechanistic worldview. In a broader sense, the Vietnam War thus revealed some of the inherent flaws of modernity and the failures of its ways of seeing and contextualizing the world. Gibson cites the views of Henry Kissinger who held that U.S. foreign policy was predicated "on the assumption that *technology plus managerial skills* gave us the ability to reshape the international system and to bring domestic transformations in 'emerging countries.'"[2] Kissinger claims that there are virtually no limits to U.S. technical and political hegemony, just as for modern science there are no limits to its ability to control and dominate nature. Moreover, for Kissinger and the modern mind, power is measured solely in instrumental and technical terms. Kissinger also assumes that the U.S. and Western powers possess the knowledge necessary to control nature and "emerging countries," and that the system of global capitalism with its advanced war machines, science and technology, and managerial knowledge can control the natural and social worlds.

Kissinger indeed presumes that *only* the West knows reality and that the superiority of Western modernity is grounded in its "notion that the real world is external to the observer, that knowledge consists of recording and classifying data—the more accurately the better. Cultures which have escaped the early impact of Newtonian thinking have retained the essentially pre-Newtonian view that the real world is almost entirely internal to the observer" (qtd. Gibson, 16). Gibson rightly notes that Newtonian mechanics, however, is about nature and "says nothing about society, about human social relationships" (17). Thus, Kissinger is continuing a three-hundred-year-old tradition of modern thought that the social world can be controlled through the same techniques and forms of knowledge as the natural world, that the methods of control of the natural world can be applied to the social world.

Western modernity thus applies a mode of thinking about nature to human beings and assumes that humans are passive objects of domination, the stuff of social control. This is precisely what Adorno and Horkheimer conceptualized as "the dialectic of Enlightenment," when Enlightenment turns into its opposite, when instruments of liberation become means of domination, and a mode of objectifying thought that was intended to control and dominate nature also becomes a mode of objectifying and dominating human beings.[3] The world is projected as a closed system, subject to cybernetic control.[4] This model in turn conceptualizes thought as an instrument to dominate nature and arguably deforms and destroys nature, just as it objectifies and denigrates human beings.

For our purposes here, it suffices to suggest that the U.S. mode of technowar failed in Vietnam largely because it falsely believed that its superior technology would allow it to dominate the underdeveloped Vietnamese society. But, as Gibson argues, Vietnam was a guerilla war carried out as part of a national liberation movement that had the support of the majority of its citizens and was fought on a terrain familiar to the guerilla army and foreign to the invaders. Wars of national liberation are prototypically modern, producing modern nation-states and identities—beginning with the American revolution. Because of the intense nationalism generated by such struggles, it is difficult to defeat these movements. In addition, the Vietnam War was fought by the Vietnamese as a guerilla war, using the jungle, mountains, tunnels, and countryside in ways that resisted the overwhelming firepower of the modern U.S. war machine. Although postmodern theory has appropriated the metaphor of the guerilla for its political strategies, one could argue that the war of national liberation fought in Vietnam was a form of modern warfare and thus it is problematical to describe the war as "postmodern" *tout court.*[5]

Modern wars of national liberation attempt to develop a nation-state free from colonialist—or neocolonialist—domination. They are activated by intense nationalism, mobilize indigenous populations, and utilize a wide range of techniques of warfare. The Vietnamese war against U.S. intervention deployed anti-imperialist propaganda, communist and nationalist ideology, geopolitical pressures, and the more "modern" strategies and tactics of the North Vietnamese army, as well as the tactics of guerrilla warfare. The war was involved in modern power politics, in particular the struggles between world capitalism and communism, with the Vietnamese revolutionaries supported by China, the Soviet Union, and the socialist bloc, while the South Vietnamese government was propped up by the U.S. and its allies. Diplomatic and media struggles helped contribute to the eventual victory of the National Liberation Front, which waged an effective propaganda war as well as a military one. Thus, the Vietnam War was at once a peasant guerilla war that utilized highly modern means of communication, a prototypically modern national war of liberation, and an event in contemporary modern geopolitics that revealed the flaws of the modern paradigm and view of the world.

DISPATCHES AS MODERNIST TEXT

"Vietnam, man, Bomb 'em and feed 'em, bomb 'em and feed 'em."

Michael Herr

Herr's *Dispatches* represents the Vietnam War primarily as an out-of-control folly of the U.S. military and political establishment. Eschewing theoretical analysis, Herr presents his own experience and vision of Vietnam through use of both modernist and postmodernist literary techniques. Although many critics read Herr's text exclusively as an example of postmodernism, I suggest that it is best read as a modernist text. Jameson, for example, claims that *Dispatches* is "postmodernist" because of its fusion of different idiolects (i.e., grunts, official military slang, blacks, uneducated southerners, and

so on), its fragmentary collage of experiences and lack of a controlling narrative voice or vision, and its struggle to represent the seemingly unmappable experience and space of the Vietnam War.

Taking the latter issue first, I would argue that it is precisely
modernism that problematized representation in its polemic against
realism and traditional forms of writing. Modernists challenged traditional realist modes of representation through their use of highly
condensed symbols, allegory, the fracturing of narrative, invention of
new collage structures, and use of multiple points of view. Herr's *Dispatches* can be read from this perspective as a modernist search for
new modes of representation and types of writing needed to articulate
his experience of Vietnam and to tell the truth about the war. This led
Herr to break with dominant realist techniques and modes of writing—as well as the pseudo-objectivism of official journalism—and to
create a modernist collage structure that mixes symbols, allegories,
fables, anecdotes, straight reporting, and surrealist hallucinations to
represent Vietnam.

Obviously, texts, authors, and even schools of writing can be labeled "modern" or "postmodern" depending on one's theoretical constructs and what aspects of the object of analysis one chooses to target. While the fragmentary collage form of *Dispatches* seems to
assimilate it to modes of postmodern writing that break with conventional narrative forms, we see collage as having both modern and
postmodern variants. Within modernism, collage is usually the expression of a single artistic vision and it creates a complex text that
is formally innovative and that generates a wealth of interpretations,
as does, we would argue, the works of filmmakers Sergi Eisenstein,
Jean-Luc Godard, and Emile de Antonio, some of the art of Marcel
Duchamp and Robert Rauschenberg, or the rap music of Ice Cube
and Public Enemy. But on Jameson's own analysis (1991), a postmodernist collage would resist making statements and creating a
complex tapestry of meanings in favor of juxtaposing elements for
purely formal effects without hermeneutical depth—as in Jameson's
citing of Bob Perelman's "China" (28–30), his reading of the video
"AlienNATION" by the Chicago Art Institute (79 ff.), or some of the
collage paintings of David Salle that simply juxtapose images or fragments that do not coalesce into a greater whole or make significant
statements.[6]

On my reading, however, Herr's use of collage is a modernist one
in which the different idiolects are articulated as part of a modernist

narrative strategy, and his own narrative voice is privileged in an attempt to capture the truth of his experience of Vietnam and to communicate his experience to his readers.[7] Herr presents his text as a "witness act" to what is really happening in Vietnam, as his own personal expression of the experience, as his bearing witness to the madness of the war. Despite the lack of a conventional narrative structure and narrator, Herr is there on every page—controlling the narrative, articulating his vision, developing his own style, and above all telling his own story. Indeed, he is something of a romantic, placing himself—his sensations, his ego, his recollections—at the center of the narrative. Thus, it would be a mistake to read the text as evidence of a postmodern fragmentation of the subject, for however fragmented his experience, it is always that of Michael Herr, teller of his story, raconteur of his experience, the writer of *Dispatches*, and the survivor of Nam, that we are reading.

Furthermore, I suggest that the structure of *Dispatches* exhibits classical modernist literary and collage techniques, deploying symbolism and allegory as mapping strategies to capture the "truth" and "reality" of the war, whereas, on Jameson's own account, a postmodernist text would more radically, or ironically, problematize truth and reality, and fracture narratives to undermine the possibility of interpretation.[8] Although Herr avoids a conventional narrative and chronological account of the war, choosing instead to break the story into fragments, his text begins with a chapter titled "Breathing In" and closes with "Breathing Out," a modernist literary conceit that provides a certain rhythm and structure to the text. As Jakaitis argues, "the framing chapters emphasize the visceral quality of Herr's experience, implying that the war correspondent inhales a way of life or death that is not coincident with past experience and then must exhale that experience before he can return to the insulated civilization."[9] The title thus functions in typical modernist fashion as a polysemous signifier of "dispatches," both as messages and as means of exorcising painful memories and experiences. As a reader, one might get caught up in Herr's gripping dispatches and suck in one's breath, empathizing with the characters and the action. At the end, one might breathe a sigh of relief that the ordeal is over, that *Vietnam is over*, and that Herr and the reader at least have survived this horrifying experience.

In between the opening and closing vignettes, Herr utilizes a thoroughly modernist aesthetic strategy to map his experience of

Vietnam and to capture the truth of the ordeal. The opening section, "Breathing In," sets the stage and establishes the tone of Vietnam as a crazy, hallucinatory, high-tech war full of death and dying. Certain iconic images establish leitmotifs for the reading of the war: the *drugs* ("Going out at night the medics gave you pills, Dexedrine breath like dead snakes kept too long in a jar"); the *night patrols*, described by a grunt in war paint ("'Patrol went up the mountains. One man came back. He died before he could tell us what happened'"); the *helicopters* ("In the months after we got back the hundreds of helicopters I'd flown in began to draw together until they'd formed a collective meta-chopper, and in my mind it was the sexiest thing going"); the *bombing* and the contradictory U.S. relation to the Vietnamese ("'Vietnam, man. Bomb 'em and feed 'em, bomb 'em and feed 'em'"); the *jungle* ("'Aw, jungle's okay. If you know her you can live in her real good, if you don't she'll take you down in an hour. Under.'"); and, above all, the ubiquitous reality of *death* ("You could be in the most protected space in Vietnam and still know that your safety was provisional, that early death, blindness, loss of legs, arms or balls, major and lasting disfigurement—the whole rotten deal— could come in on the freakyfluky as easily as in the so-called expected ways, you heard so many of those stories it was a wonder anyone was left alive to die in firefights and mortar-rocket attacks").[10]

In these opening vignettes, Herr combines the sparse realism and clipped prose of a Hemingway with privileged signifiers that recur throughout the book, signifying the nightmarish and hellish reality of Vietnam.[11] A short section on the Tet Offensive ("Hell Sucks") follows, which sets up Tet as a key turning point, as a definite moment of genuine fear and chaos for the U.S. troops, as evidence that the war was really out of control, and that the United States and its allies could actually *lose* the war: the unthinkable Something Terrible that had never happened in U.S. military history, but which might actually happen this time. Herr writes:

> Almost as much as the grunts and the Vietnamese, Tet was pushing correspondents closer to the wall than they'd ever wanted to go. I realized later that however childish I might remain, actual youth had been pressed out of me in just the three days that it took me to cross the sixty miles between Can Tho and Saigon. In Saigon, I saw friends flipping out almost completely; a few left, some took to their beds for days with the exhaustion of deep depression. I went the other way, hyper and agitated,

until I was only doing three hours of sleep a night. A friend on the *Times* said he didn't mind his nightmares so much as the waking impulse to file on them. An old-timer who'd covered war since the Thirties heard us pissing and moaning about how *terrible* it was and he snorted, "Ha, we love you guys. You guys are beautiful. What the fuck did you think it was?" (72)

This passage highlights the centrality of the experience and the voice of the narrator, who passed from innocence to knowledge, from youth to an experience of the ways of the world, in the typical modernist configurations of the *Bildungsroman*, where the protagonist learns, grows, develops, and matures. Past illusions are destroyed and, eventually, the now-experienced war reporter puts Vietnam in context: war itself sucks. Such insight is precisely the sort of modernist epiphany that attempts to catch an experience or phenomenon in a pungent phrase or trope, that tries to draw out deeper meaning from surface experiences and events—although I argue that this epiphany requires theoretical supplementation to more adequately grasp the Vietnam experience. Thus, Herr's prose engages in precisely the sort of mapping of classical modernism, drawing on modernist strategies and the development of his own style and voice to tell the tale of his experience of Vietnam, to draw lessons from the episode, to communicate something true and important to his reader.

The next section of *Dispatches*, the longest and perhaps most gripping of the book, tells the story of the battle of Khe Sanh, in which the U.S. forces were under siege for weeks in a badly garrisoned up-country camp that could be overrun by the Vietnamese enemy at any time. Such was the chaos of the Vietnam War (and the openness to the press) that correspondents like Herr could actually live with the troops, take fire, and even fire back. After the camp at Khe Sanh is transformed into a genuinely defensible structure, the area recedes in importance as the North Vietnamese withdraw; the camp is then taken apart and the site is abandoned—after the beautiful surrounding hillsides have been pounded with U.S. firepower and napalm for weeks on end, and ecologically disfigured. The U.S. Air Force defoliation units "were called the Ranch Hands, and their motto was, 'Only we can prevent forests'" (Herr, 154). They succeeded to the shame of the nation and the disgrace of the U.S. military, which continued their ecocidal policies in the Gulf War.[12]

Herr's depiction of the siege of Khe Sanh is clearly an allegory concerning the insanity and futility of the Vietnam War, evoking how the U.S. took ground and fought to the death for totally unclear military or political objectives—and then moved on to the next pointless action. It is also an allegory about how the U.S. military hyped the war (presenting Khe Sanh as the "Western Anchor of Our Defense") and arrogantly claimed that it could not be taken (knowing perfectly well that it could at any moment). It also allegorizes the Alamo mentality that seized Lyndon Johnson, who, as Herr points out, was obsessed with Khe Sanh and determined that it would not "fall," as if his manhood and role as protector of U.S. mythology were at stake. Allegory is, of course, a literary mode, greatly favored by modernism, that takes seemingly unconnected or insignificant events and infuses them with greater meaning, evoking an order or meaning behind the seeming meaningless particulars. This is precisely the function of Herr's Khe Sanh episode, in which one highly publicized but militarily insignificant battle of the war is used to evoke the futility and wanton destructiveness of the whole intervention. Such use of modernist tropes and figures is typical of Herr's writing and at odds with the more fragmentary texts of postmodernism that resist allegory, deeper symbolic meanings, and unifying visions of the whole.

The Khe Sanh episode is followed by a set of fragments titled "Illumination Rounds" that attempt to depict certain truths of Vietnam. Utilizing modernist collage techniques, Herr tries to capture essential moments of Vietnam by using short vignettes that illuminate the broader contours of the war. The very title of the section recalls Walter Benjamin's concept of "illumination" and his argument that fragmentation, dialectical images, and collage are modernist strategies used to illuminate the complex conditions of modern life.

Following the personalizing impetus of modernism, which utilizes vivid characters as key figures of narration who articulate important truths or insight, Herr next delineates some "Colleagues" in a section that provides his perspectives on the role of the press. For Herr, Vietnam is about people, the grunts, their officers, and his press colleagues; thus his text operates not in a posthumanist register, but precisely within a modernist humanist frame. He tells stories about particularly memorable correspondents, focusing on his buddies Sean Flynn, the son of actor Errol Flynn, and Tim Page, a young British photographer renowned for his daring and eccentric personality. Flynn later disappeared in Cambodia, and Page was badly shot up, but returned with his humor intact and later published a book of photographs and memories—evoking a sense of the danger to all participants in the war, including the media.[13] Herr, however, eschews analytical analysis of the role of the media in Vietnam, preferring instead to use a constellation of privileged moments to illuminate their insertion into the Vietnam adventure.

Near the end of the section, he discusses his return to the "World" after nearly a year in Vietnam, but the concluding section mixes his postwar recollections with flashbacks to the war, a modernist device replicating his own experience (he couldn't let go of Vietnam upon his return), as well as that of the many Nam vets who could not forget or overcome their remembrances of the war in Southeast Asia. Thus, Herr codes his text as a narrative of experience, as exposure of deep truths about human life, as an account of a young man peering into the void, exploring the heart of darkness while recoiling and trying to get his life back together after exposure to the horrors of war—precisely the challenge of many who underwent the nightmare of Vietnam.

Herr's project is to undercut the conceptual universe of the Vietnam War managers, to disclose the deceptions and omissions of their discourse, and to show that conventional journalism which parrots the military version misses the truth of the war. By contrast, Herr is trying to map and tell the truth about Vietnam—his truth, to be sure, but a truth that illuminates and captures the Vietnam adventure as an odyssey of American experience. He especially attempts to capture the ordeal of the young who were wounded, or killed, during the decade-plus of the U.S.'s worst military debacle. Although there is no one central truth or overarching interpretation of Vietnam in Herr's narrative, he manages to tell an engaging and gripping story of his generation's (mis)adventures in Vietnam, an experience shaped by drugs, rock and roll, fear of dying, and the stench and anguish of death itself. Like many modernist texts, it is not possible to reduce *Dispatches* to a standard fictional narrative, for there is no beginning, middle, or end to the story.[14]

Crucially, Herr's text exhibits a lust and reverence for truth that is typically modern and is parodied or abandoned by many postmodernists. He notes how every grunt had a story "and in the war they were driven to tell it" (29). Herr claims that most of the troops *wanted* him desperately to tell the truth about what was happening in Vietnam, noting: "And always, they would ask you with an emotion whose intensity would shock you to please tell it, because they really did have the feeling that it wasn't being told for them, that they were going through all of this and that somehow no one back in the World knew about it" (206–07).[15] Thus, the troops and some of the reporters in the Vietnam War wanted to maintain a rigorous classical distinction between truth and lying. Unlike the Gulf War, there was no systematic implosion between truth and lies, between the hyper-reality of the official discourse and the reality of the war itself. That is, both the troops and the reporters in Vietnam knew that the official lies and hype were transparently ludicrous, that the body counts and optimistic reports were pure fabrications, that the official discourse was transparent propaganda.[16] In the war against Iraq, by contrast, the lies were equally extravagant, but the troops, media, and public seemed to accept at face value the mendacious discourse of the war managers—a theme that I explore later in the chapter.

During Vietnam, therefore, lying was not totally accepted by the troops as business as usual, as it was in the era of Reagan, Bush, and Clinton when lying became normal communicative practice. Herr tells of a wounded grunt in a hospital in Danang indignant with a Catholic chaplin who had lied to him about how bad his condition was, falsely telling him that his legs were okay when they were set for amputation. The next day, the now legless boy asked for the chaplin's cross, took it, looked him in the eye and said: "You lied to me, Father . . . You cocksucker. You lied to me" (175). Herr thus suggests that although one expected generals and military briefers to lie in Vietnam, the truth was still a sacred commodity to be preserved by honorable reporters and among the troops themselves. In the Gulf War, by contrast, truth and the vicious reality of the war disappeared completely in the hyperreal orbit of media representations.

REPRESENTING VIETNAM: NARRATIVE, COLLAGE, AND THEORY

And no moves left for me at all, but to write down
some few last words and make the dispersion,
Vietnam, Vietnam, Vietnam, we've all been there.
Michael Herr

Herr's *Dispatches* confronts the dilemma of representing the space of Vietnam and a war whose beginning, unfolding, trajectory, coordinates, and purpose were extremely difficult to understand and represent. On Jameson's account, the Vietnam War unfolded in an entirely new and unrepresentable postmodern space that transcended all the older habits of bodily perception, representing a "virtually unimaginable quantum leap in technological alienation" (45). Jameson takes a passage in Herr as emblematic of a postmodern literary strategy to articulate the impossibility of mapping postmodern space:

> He was a moving-target survivor subscriber, a true child of the war, because except for the rare times when you were pinned or stranded the system was geared to keep you mobile, if that was what you thought you wanted. As a technique for staying alive it seemed to make as much sense as anything, given naturally that you were there to begin with and wanted to see it close; it started out sound and straight but it formed a cone as it progressed, because the more you moved the more you saw, the more you saw the more besides death and mutilation you risked, and the more you risked of that the more you would have to let go of one day as a "survivor." Some of us moved around the war like crazy people until we couldn't see which way the run was taking us anymore, only the war all over its surface with occasional, unexpected penetration. As long as we could have choppers like taxis it took real exhaustion or depression near shock or a dozen pipes of opium to keep us even apparently quiet, we'd still be running around inside our skins like something was after us, ha ha, La Vida Loca. (Herr 8–9)[17]

Herr was trying to see as much of the war as he could see and tell, and as his acclaimed text demonstrates, he saw and told plenty. Indeed, the passage that Jameson himself cited indicates precisely that Herr was attempting to experience the war to the fullest in order to map its locales and significance. The passage suggests that he used the means of the helicopter to chart the specificity of motion in the terrain of Vietnam. Jameson claimed that Vietnam was a postmodern war because of the problem of mapping it, but the more Herr saw, the more he mapped, and in fact his book is a brilliant literary mapping of the war, catching key aspects of the experience, texture, flavor, stench, and horror of the war, above all the horror. Not by accident Conrad's modernist *Heart of Darkness* was the controlling metaphor of his enterprise, in which Western innocents are thrown into a foreign otherness that is overwhelming, exotic, incomprehensible, and destructive. This vision also informs Coppola's *Apocalypse*

Now (1979), for which Herr wrote the screenplay. In fact, Herr continued obsessively to map his Vietnam experience in his screenplay for Kubrick's *Full Metal Jacket* (1987).[18] This need to map and exorcise demons of modern experience is very much a part of the culture of modernism. Some writers have one story, one book, and one set of obsessions that constitutes their literary world and endowment. They have experienced something so terribly, so deeply, and so significantly that they really cannot think or write about anything else. Other topics pale besides It, the one story, and Herr's one story is his experience in Vietnam.

Thus, Herr can be read as a distinctively modernist writer and *Dispatches* seen as a characteristically modernist literary mapping that à la modernism, deploys metaphors, allegory, analogies, personal experiences, and good descriptive and evocative writing to map Vietnam and its site in the American psyche and contemporary history. A more properly postmodern text would distance itself from Herr's use of metaphor, symbol, and allegory, his obsessive attempt to capture the truth of Vietnam, and his repeated attempts to articulate his personal vision of the experience.

The widespread acclaim for Herr's text suggests that he quite successfully maps the experience and terrain of the Vietnam War. Jameson is perhaps too skeptical concerning the possibilities of mapping contemporary experience and too quick to proclaim the obsolescence of modernism in the current conjuncture. Perhaps Jameson also exaggerates "the lack of critical distance" in the experiencing of contemporary cultural texts (47ff), for it is not always the case that audiences are unable to see through media mystification and distortion, as a generation did in the case of Vietnam and eventually many did in the case of the Gulf War. "Critical distance," in a sense, is a standard and rather widespread feature of reflective consumption of cultural texts, a cognitive ability that has arguably developed during the Media Age, in which audiences become competent in reading media culture and codes, gaining competency in media literacy through experience and discussion—although it is not certain what political effects this sort of critical distance portends, a topic we will take up later in our studies.

Other writers have also depicted the Vietnam War as postmodern, such as Philip Kuberski who asks whether Vietnam was a "postmodernist war" because "its writing was foreign, heterogeneous, intrinsic." For Kuberski, the boundaries of the war "were hard to define," and because the war was "senseless," he raises the question of whether it might be seen as postmodern. Kuberski seems to answer in the affirmative, suggesting that: "the public war—reading and watching it as a teenager simply *made no sense to me* . . . we could not discover a pattern, a logic in the nomadic crises and encounters that organized reports every few months." He also argues more extravagantly that Vietnam is an allegory "of a postmodern, poststructuralist world divested of the coordinates that secure, confine, retain, within the barbed wire of latitudes, histories, and sentences, the prey of truth."[19]

But many modern wars "made no sense" to either the combatants or the citizens on the home front. There is a whole literature on the senselessness of World War I, of which *All Quiet on the Western Front* is only one example, and both the Korean and Vietnam War "made no sense" to many participants and sectors of the public.[20] In what sense does "senselessness" constitute the "postmodernity" of the Vietnam War? And rather than being devoid of coordinates, one could argue that Vietnam can be read as a guerilla war and as a war of national liberation against a neo-imperialist high-tech superpower, a terrain with its own spatiality and coordinates, more accessible, obviously, to the Vietnamese than to the Americans. Clearly, for the Vietnamese the war made sense as a war of national liberation against colonialist invaders and it was precisely this sense that enabled the Vietnamese to organize and defeat the U.S.-supported forces and apparatus of technowar.

In any case, the term "postmodern" is undertheorized in Kuberski's usage and the author does not convincingly argue for the postmodernity of the Vietnam War. In fact, there are several strong arguments for the modernity of the Vietnam War, some of which draw upon Herr's own book. As I have noted, the Vietnam War was a clash between neoimperialist forces and a national liberation movement over the control of a people and region. Whereas the neoimperialist forces sought to impose a certain economic and political order on a part of the world under the code word of modernization, Vietnamese society had quite different traditions, aspirations, and history. As Herr noted: "Vietnam was where the Trail of Tears was headed all along, the turnaround point where it would touch and come back to form a containing perimeter; might just as well lay it on the proto-Gringos who found the New England woods too raw and empty for their peace and filled them up with their own imported devils" (49).

Unfortunately, Herr doesn't pursue this insight, nor does he explore other key themes in depth, for his style combines the breakneck speed of the on-the-road beats with the now popular cyberpunks, both of whom are similar to Herr in style, vision, and theme.[21] Herr does not want to think too deeply about Vietnam, but to tell stories in order to try to capture his experience—which is both the strength and weakness of his text.

It is precisely historical research and theory that organizes such experiences into coherent order, that produces narratives and categories that help make sense of events, and that attempts to provide more comprehensive understanding and explanation. Whereas literature excels in capturing the texture, moods, and particularities of experience, theoretical concepts help illuminate the more general constitutive forces and defining features, while historical analysis helps provide contextual and narrative understanding of events by situating events in broader historical patterns and currents and by putting specific events and particulars into historical frameworks and narratives.

History and theory are thus necessary supplements to experience and those organizations and distillations of experience we call literature. Theory provides concepts that order historical research in a more cognitively satisfying manner, thus providing ways of seeing that help us organize and make sense of experience, that articulate a perspective that can be used to interpret events and phenomena, and that allow one a critical distance. Yet theory is not antithetical to narrative or fiction, and both can work together to illuminate experience, to provide historical vision, to make sense out of events like Vietnam. Thus, we do not see theory and narrative as agonistic, but as complementary modes of mapping. Theory has a narrative component, to be sure, but is not merely narrative, being also conceptual and analytical, using concepts to dissect, illuminate, and interpret social and historical (or psychological) realities. Conversely, literary narratives can provide material for theory and some can even be seen as prototheoretical, as in Pynchon's mapping of the warfare state and culture in *Gravity's Rainbow*.

Herr's narrative collage, however, lacks the historical contextualization found in theoretical texts on the Vietnam War, or documentary films such as Emile de Antonio's *In the Year of the Pig* (1969), which uses a modernist collage technique to present historical insight into Vietnam.[22] Combining historical documentary footage from a variety of archival sources with interview material, photographs, and contemporary documentary footage, de Antonio depicts French colonization of Vietnam, Vietnamese resistance under the leadership of Ho Chi Minh, and the American response after the defeat of the French in 1954. His panoramic documentary provides images and discourse that contextualize the Vietnamese experience in terms of its movement for national liberation against colonialization, providing a historical optic lacking in Herr's more literary collage.

On the other hand, it is precisely Herr's literary text and his use of metaphor, allegory, and narrative that provides a mélange of stories enabling access to the feel, experience, and texture of the Vietnam War. Gibson, too, points to the importance of what he calls "warrior's knowledge" selected from the experience of the participants to illuminate the events (461ff). But, in order to provide proper contextualization and understanding, literary insight should be supplemented by a multiperspectival optic which includes historical and theoretical analysis. From the perspective critical of social theory, the Vietnam War is primarily a modern war that attempted to augment U.S. global power by containing "communism" and by imposing a consumer economy on Vietnam under the code of modernization. Indeed, as Gibson shows, the form of "civilization" the U.S. brought to Vietnam was precisely that of modernity, in which the products and forms of life of the consumer society were exported to Southeast Asia.

Gibson describes in detail how commodification and commodities transformed the daily life of the people of Vietnam, and how the "pacification" camps, advent of urbanization, building of roads and modern systems of transportation and communication, and import of U.S. commodities were accompanied by rising inflation, crime, and the literal and figurative prostitution of Vietnamese society. "Modernization," then, was in practice a euphemism to describe the ecocide of the Vietnamese environment and the destruction of Vietnam's traditional culture and society. Modernization appears in Gibson's presentation as a set of processes that destroys traditional societies and brings into existence Western-style consumer societies and attendant industrial and technological revolution, secularization, social differentiation, urbanization, a centralized nation-state, consumer and media culture, and inclusion in the global economy of transnational capitalism.

The modernization process brought about by the Vietnam War was an attempt to violently impose capitalist modernity on Southeast Asia as part of the Cold War struggle between the U.S. and Soviet Union, representing two models of development and social organization. From this perspective and in retrospect, the Cold War was a sibling rivalry between two competing forms of modernization, capitalism and communism, that offered themselves as superior models of modernity. Thus, using historical and theoretical analysis to interpret phenomena like the Vietnam War contributes a necessary supplement to literary accounts such as Herr's book. Consequently, literary narrative, photo and print journalism, video and documentary, fictional cinematic representation, and historical and theoretical analysis provide supplementary aspects of a multiperspectivist account of Vietnam and thus together yield fuller understanding. Such a multiperspectivist optic must also include the perspectives of the Vietnamese that were lacking in most U.S. accounts and accessible to Western audiences primarily through documentary films made by the Vietnamese and distributed throughout the West.[23]

From the perspective of social theory and historical analysis, we can now see that the Vietnam War came at the high point of the Cold War and was a prototypical U.S. military intervention to contain communism. Vietnam can thus be interpreted as the continuation of the Korean War, an attempt to win it this time (actually to lose it much bigger), motivated by the domino theory, containment, and all the now obsolete discourse and fantasies of the Cold War. But it was largely a modern war that revealed the limitations of the modern paradigm of technocratic domination of nature and other people through the use of science, technology, and cybernetic control systems.

The war against Iraq, by contrast, came at the end of the Cold War, with the Vietnam generation military who suffered defeat in Vietnam (Norman Schwarzkopf, Colin Powell, and other generals and midlevel career military) wanting to win big this time, to overcome the Vietnam syndrome, to redeem the U.S. military, to recover their manhood and self-esteem—and perhaps protect the Pentagon budget from overzealous cuts.[24] The end of the Cold War revealed how useless and senseless the Vietnam War really had been (better to conquer Southeast Asia through Pepsi-Cola, Hollywood films, and popular music than helicopters and firepower). And so another war was necessary for the rebirth of American militarism, the Persian Gulf TV war, brought to you by the same folks who brought you

Vietnam, but this time they were going to win in a spectacular media extravaganza that would promote U.S. military power and weapons systems.

However, while Vietnam constituted an attempt to impose modernization on a traditional Asian society, the Persian Gulf TV war attempted to destroy the modernization that Iraq had achieved.[25] This time, the U.S. deployed all of the media, computer, high-tech weapons, and public relations strategies that have, since Vietnam, produced the most technologically overdeveloped society in the history of the world in order to overcome the so-called Vietnam syndrome, which inhibited U.S. use of its military power. And so let us now move from remembering the horrors that occurred in the jungles of Southeast Asia to recalling the events concerning the U.S. intervention in the deserts of the Persian Gulf during 1990–91.

CYBERWAR AND MEDIA SPECTACLE IN THE WAR AGAINST IRAQ

[The Gulf war] was the first space war. . . . [I]t
was the first war of the space age.
            General Merrill McPeak (March 1991)

The Vietnam War was thus not really a postmodern war, but a dirty old neo-imperialist modern war that attempted to stop a national liberation movement, to contain communism, to impose U.S. culture (i.e., "modernization") on the foreign other. The Vietnam War sought to test U.S. technology and military doctrine, trying to do what the military has always done—win battles and kill "enemies." The "Gulf War," by contrast, was arguably not a war at all, but a high-tech cyberspectacle in which the pitifully overmatched Iraqi troops were overwhelmed by the most massive and awesome military force ever assembled.[26] This required hyping up the Iraqi "enemy" as a genuine military power and threat and most of all demonizing its leader Saddam Hussein as both another evil Arab threatening the West and even another Hitler, in order for the mismatch to be overlooked and the U.S. forces not to appear as overbearing bullies. In perpetuating this image, the U.S. media dutifully transmitted every lie and piece of disinformation fed to them by the Bush Administration and the Pentagon.

In an important sense, the war against Iraq was a simulated war, a media spectacle, a TV war designed to hype the U.S. military, U.S. weapons systems, George Bush and his administration, and the United States as the number one superpower at the end of the Cold War, with the United States emerging as the policeman of the new world order.[27] It was postmodern in that, first, it was experienced by most of the world in real time and hyperreal media space as a political spectacle, as a carefully manufactured attempt to mobilize consent to U.S. policy, in which the distinction between truth and reality seemed to blur, and image and spectacle prevailed. Second, the war itself exhibited a new implosion between individuals and technology, previewing a new type of cyberwarriors and cyberwar. Thirdly, the war was a form of cyberwar, with information technology and new smart weapons systems prominently displayed (albeit excessively hyped). Thus, the Gulf War deployed both a new mode of high-tech warfare and a new experience of war as a hyperreal media event, as a postmodern political spectacle that demonstrated a new way to exploit "war" and new types of global political manipulation.

The Gulf War was the first war experienced in the cyberspace of live media and of videos of the military assault, and it provided a new level in the aestheticizing of war. In opposition to the analogic photographic images of the horrors of war in Vietnam, the electronic images of the Gulf War often created an audience delight in the play of signifiers, with TV audiences caught up in the spectacle of videos of precision bombing, the Scud and Patriot wars, air war over Baghdad, or tanks penetrating Kuwait in the ground war. These video images produced a euphoria of a high-tech spectacle parallel to the pleasures of computer and video games, or war movies, and the TV public, quickly addicted to the drama of the war, became enthralled with the spectacle and fascination of a new type of video. Images of the bombing of Baghdad, taken by night-cameras, produced an eerie, surreal vision of the war as an aesthetic phenomenon with digitized images of the green glow of missiles and artillery exploding in the night, almost like a cosmic Abstract Expressionist painting. Another type of image—of buildings, bridges, and military targets (but never civilians) being destroyed by laser-guided bombs—was photographed by cameras located on the bombs themselves; these conveyed the images to satellites where they were downloaded, recorded on videocassettes, and then shown to a worldwide audience via live satellite television. These images literally took the TV viewers into a new cyberspace, a realm of experience with which many viewers were familiar through video and computer games, the special effects of Hollywood movies, and cyberpunk fiction.

The Persian Gulf TV War also provided a simulation of live war, with direct satellite transmission of some of its events and images throughout the world. Representations of the war in Vietnam often took days to circulate from their production to their reception, and the images that circulated were filtered by media corporations and conventions. The Gulf spectacle, by contrast, was the first live, you-are-there TV war in which a global audience watched U.S. technology bombard a Third World country and demonstrate the superiority of its high-tech weapons systems and, incidentally, its media and communications systems (since it was CNN and U.S. media that primarily transmitted the images, discourse, and narrative of the war). It was the first sustained global TV war in which the entire world watched dramatic events unfold before its eyes in real time—McLuhan's global village becoming a reality in an era of computer and satellite communications in which live events could be transmitted instantaneously from one side of the globe to the other, allowing a media-mediated illusion of participation in "real" history.

It is therefore the dimension of live drama, of the illusion of seeing a real war in real time, that differentiates the Gulf from the Vietnam War—as well as the pleasure in the video images that conveyed the chimera of a clean high-tech war. The dominant images of Vietnam were dramatic and often bloody, while the characteristic images of the Gulf War were high-tech video images of aesthetic spectacle. In fact, although the Gulf War appeared to be live and unmediated, the production and circulation of its images were more managed and mediated than the images that came to define Vietnam. The events in Vietnam were open to a press allowed to travel around almost at will, and while the pictures, videotapes, and press reports often experienced delays, sometimes lengthy, due to the more primitive conditions of mass communications at the time, many of the images and reports that eventually circulated often stuck in the public mind and became icons of a brutal military misadventure. The Vietnam War also lingered on for years and it has been argued that press reports of the death, destruction, and stalemate may have cumulatively turned the audiences against the war.[28] The Gulf War, by contrast, was relatively brief and the U.S. government and military managed the flow of information and images from beginning to end through the "pool system" that controlled which of the press could describe and photograph the events and that censored every word and image produced in the conflict.[29]

Thus, on the whole, the "reality" of Iraqi suffering and ecocide were erased by high-tech simulacra that conveyed instead a vision of U.S. power and aestheticized war. Fascination with video and computer images also generated an aura of magic and power around the military that produced such spectacles, and it enhanced their credibility in a public eager to believe whatever it claimed. Not surprisingly, the media themselves were mesmerized by these simulacra, which they played and replayed repeatedly. CBS anchor Dan Rather spoke with awe when he presented "more remarkable video just released by the Defense Department," and CNN often opened each news segment with the videos of the bombing. The images of "clean" bombing seemed to give credence to military claims that they were avoiding civilian casualties and they endowed these high-tech wizards with power as well as credibility, providing an aura of veracity to whatever claims they made, claims that were seemingly grounded in technological omnipotence and evidence too compelling to doubt.

Such images exemplify what Jean Baudrillard calls "hyperreality," in which the images of the war substituted for the events of the war itself and appeared realer than real: the hyperreal, in which "the map precedes the territory."[30] Early on, military briefers began showing videotapes of the high-tech bombing, and the videos were replayed hour after hour, day after day, producing the notion of clean and precise bombing, coding the destruction as positive. The U.S. military's videocassette shows demonstrated that U.S. bombs always hit their targets, did not cause collateral damage, and only took out nasty military targets. This was intended to change the public perception of war itself, that the new technowar was clean, precise, and surgical, that the very nature of war had changed. War was thus something that one could enjoy, admire, and cheer about. War was fun, fascinating, and aesthetic, confirming the Italian futurist Marinetti's view that "war is beautiful." The videos created in its audiences a climate of joy in destruction, as when reporters clapped and laughed when General Horner said: "And this is my counterpart's headquarters in Baghdad," as a video showed a bomb blowing up the Iraqi air force headquarters. Just as video and computer games—or special-effects movies like *Star Wars*—produce a positive libidinal pleasure regarding destruction, so too the videos of high-tech bombing produced pleasure in the destruction of Iraq—at least among the audience that bought into the spectacle of high-tech destruction.[31]

The illusion was projected that only machines and not people are involved in the new high-tech warfare, which was supposedly bloodless and antiseptic. The targets of the released footage were always ugly buildings, usually serving military functions. The austere structures were seemingly always deserted, devoid of humans, so the bombing was coded as a positive surgical operation that methodically removed the instruments of the Iraqi war machine. Such medical discourse and the imagery of clean operations sanitized the war and represented the U.S. as a benevolent surgeon removing a malignant Iraqi disease. The discourse of a "clean war" and images of high-tech precision-bombing proved to be quite untrue, yet the constant replaying of tapes of laser-guided bombs taking out their targets produced spectacles of a clean and precise technowar, thus creating the impression that the military desired. Only after the war were figures released showing that 93 percent of the bombs dropped were not "smart" computer- and laser-guided bombs and that over 70 percent of the bombs missed their targets altogether.[32] It was also admitted that even the so-called smart bombs often produced a lot of dumb "collateral" destruction. In fact, it was claimed that the best explanation for the accuracy of some of the initial bombing raids, in contrast to the imprecision of the latter ones, is that the ability of the first bombs "to hit their targets would have been enhanced by homing devices at or near their targets, planted by U.S. agents in Iraq before the war started."[33]

These video images obscured how the bombs were being dropped on Baghdad, one of the largest cities in the Middle East, with a population of over four million inhabitants, and one of the centers of civilization, a city full of archaeological treasures that were in danger of being destroyed. The fact that the bombs were falling on Iraqi civilians and destroying their homes and social infrastructure was also obscured by the Nintendo-like video images of the pyrotechnics of modern warfare. The media, however, focused on the aestheticized images, or the military factors involved, without discussing the human and social dimension of the bombing. Whenever pictures from Iraq appeared to put in question the hyperreal model of a clean war with no collateral damage, the U.S. propaganda machine kicked in with disinformation, as when they claimed that an Iraqi infant-formula factory bombed by the U.S. was a chemical weapons facility, or when a civilian sleeping shelter bombed by the U.S. was a military command-and-control center. Indeed, one of the most striking aspects of the audience reception of the Persian Gulf TV War was the extent to which large numbers of people bought into the lies and propaganda.

Furthermore, not only were the supporters of the war living in a hyperreal space, but so were the opponents of the war. In both cases, "the map preceded the territory." In the case of the supporters of the war, the "maps" included the videocassettes of the bombing, the military briefings, the supportive media discourse, and the media spectacle of the war. Peter Arnett's disturbing reports and images from Baghdad were ignored by those who received their conception of the war from the Bush Administration and military, with well-orchestrated right-wing campaigns attacking Arnett and CNN. In the case of the opponents of the war, the map was Vietnam, and many who opposed the war simply saw it as another Vietnam, in which innocent young U.S. men and women would be the victims of the cynical war managers who used their soldiers as cannon fodder for geopolitical games.[34] Ron Kovic and other Vietnam vets worried about U.S. casualties and thousands of young Americans returning home in body bags or wheelchairs. Yet those who deployed the Vietnam analogy fell prey to the media disinformation whereby the Iraqi "enemy" was hyped as a powerful fighting force—armed with chemical and biological weapons, high-tech weapons systems, a battle-hardened army of over one million strong, and perhaps even nuclear weapons.[35]

Once the ground war began, this hype was shown to be empty rhetoric: many of the Iraqi troops stationed in the desert had deserted from Kuwait, the mostly conscript Iraqi army surrendered immediately, and those who did not were killed or buried in the sand by the U.S.-led juggernaut. U.S. soldiers involved in the ground war said that the assault on Kuwait was easier than their training exercises and the allied casualties rate (if one excluded "friendly fire" deaths) was said to be lower than a training exercise of that magnitude. Reporters were also amazed at the poor condition of Iraqi defenses and fortifications, and indeed even TV viewers should have been able to deduce the fraudulent nature of the hyping of the "Saddam line" from the pictures of Iraqi troops surrendering and the pathetic state of the Iraqi defenses in Kuwait.[36]

For the military as well as the TV audience, the war against Iraq was thus the first full-blown war of the infotainment age, the first really high-tech war, the first cyberwar in which nations and people were reduced to computerized data, the first war in which targets were literally reduced to abstract information, and in which technology provided much of the information, planning, and actual battlefield decisions. Cyberwar involves the use of technological information systems that attempt to cybernetically control and manage an electronic battlefield and the introduction of new technologies aiming at the increasing substitution of technology for human beings. Cyberwar opens up new spaces and terrains for warfare, including new realms of cyberspace, and constitutes new experiences and forms of warfare. It involves a high level of abstraction and reduction of humans, nature, and social environments to information, an attempt to systematically manage the theater of war with computer technology, and to replace human decision-making and action with new forms of military technology.

Of course, Vietnam previewed these developments. Yet the degree of computerization, reduction of people and land to information, and use of high-tech weapons systems were greater in the war against Iraq. Secondly, the implosion between humans and technology, and the emergence of cyberwarriors, as argued below, was much more highly developed in the war against Iraq. Moreover, the spectacle of the Gulf War was transmitted to the public and experienced differently from Vietnam through the medium of satellite technology and the sense that "you were there," thus making it the first really high-tech media and cyberwar in which cyberspace was a significant factor in both the execution of war and the transmission of its representations to a live worldwide audience.

In the Gulf cyberwar, Iraqi military forces and the entire country appeared to the war managers as data of information arranged in kill zones. Such mapping carried out a reduction of Iraqi reality to digital data in killing fields where "turkey shoots" systematically obliterated Iraqi targets—military, civilian, or indeterminate. In the war against Iraq it was the destruction of military equipment that was tabulated and not, as in the Vietnam War the number of dead soldiers (the infamous body counts). This contributed to a model of a high-tech war that was merely destroying machines and not people.

Information technologies, simulation modeling, and execution of an overall plan were thus much more highly developed and operative in the war against Iraq than in Vietnam. It was extremely difficult to map the forces and movements of an enemy that hid under cover of jungle or even tunnels, as in Vietnam. "Information" was deployed in the war against Iraq, however, as a mapping of terrain, of Iraqi forces, and of their movement. These mediated high-tech images effected a dehumanization and reification of the Iraqi people and their culture.[37] People and their homes were abstracted in the digitized information and then destroyed in the bombing raids—which deployed old-fashioned B-52s and horrendous antipersonnel bombs, as well as a few of the newer laser-guided bombs. Furthermore, information also served as a mode of organizing consent to the war, marked by fetishism of "facts" and their collapse into propaganda, disinformation, and outright lying. The Persian Gulf TV War media discourse was characterized by a daily piling on of insignificant facts via TV and the press to overwhelm the spectator with trivia, to marshal military facts and jargon so as to produce a consensus that the war was necessary, just, and successful. The tremendous proliferation of "facts" and military commentary overwhelmed the political context and the real issues and buried the events of the war and their consequences in the technocratic, twenty-four-hours-a-day military discourse, which disseminated details about weapons systems and military events in largely statistical terms. The progress of the war was also presented in terms of military statistics concerning how many Iraqi tanks, planes, or artillery were destroyed. There was an overload of facts and information about the "Operation Desert Storm," memorialized after the slaughter in a series of books that were basically Gulf War trivia and propaganda books.[38]

This military discourse and the books, videos, and other artifacts that later commodified the war against Iraq were highly misleading, indeed in some cases totally fraudulent, for the story of the war was the successful media campaign that covered over the more distressing aspects of the high-tech murder of the Iraqi people and the ecocidal destruction of the environment so as to mobilize consent to the war as an exalted U.S. victory. The U.S. media campaign, with its propaganda, disinformation, and manipulation, was really what was striking about the war against Iraq. Although the military hyped up its activities as heroic, strategic, and tactically brilliant, it was no great military feat to slaughter the hapless Iraqis. The military event was secondary in comparison to the ways in which the media manufactured consent to the U.S. war policy and covered over the actual effects of the war despite the existence of high-tech communications technologies.

One could argue that the seeming lack of concern for veracity by the TV audience demonstrated a decline in an interest in truth from the time of the Vietnam War when there had been a widespread desire to discover what was really going on, as evidenced by Herr's book and its reception, and the extent and impact of the antiwar movement. The past decades seem to exhibit a steady erosion in the discourse and interest in truth in U.S. politics, disclosing an erosion in the norms of modern epistemology and politics. In the Vietnam and Watergate eras, a certain premium was put on truth and the uncovering and punishment of lies and government wrongdoing. In the Reagan-Bush-Clinton era, however, a widespread tendency has been evident to ignore the facts of events like the Grenada and Libyan bombing, the Iran-Contra affair, the Panama invasion and Gulf War, and the Clinton scandals. Distinctions between truth and lies, reality and simulation, propaganda and public discourse have been judged in terms of their effects on public opinion rather than truth content.

Moreover, political events themselves seem to have less and less force and staying power as the media moves on to the ever new spectacle and scandal. Hence, the ephemeral nature of the Gulf War's effects could be taken as symptomatic of the fickleness of the audience in a media age that quickly passes from one event to another, without deep immersion or lasting effects. Indeed, by 1992, the war against Iraq was almost an already forgotten war, just a hyperreal blip on the media screen that was not able to mobilize support for George Bush's reelection. The fate of a media war seems to be that a hyped-up political spectacle has no more lasting effects than a popular TV miniseries or sports event. Here today, gone tomorrow. Unless a war, for instance, articulates real threats, problems, or conflicts that vitally effect the public, the media event will be forgotten—as was the failed U.S. military intervention in Lebanon, the Grenada invasion, the Libyan bombing, the Panama invasion, or Desert Storm. While parades and victory celebrations continued to get media attention during the summer of 1991, by the fall the supposedly great Gulf War victory was almost forgotten, supplanted in interest by the spectacle of the 1992 Presidential campaign and then relegated to the realm of historical amnesia.

While the Bush reelection team planned to exploit the war against Iraq to the maximum, its polls and focus group surveys indicated that people really didn't care about the war,[39] and were beginning to raise serious questions about Reagan-Bush prewar policy, the lies of the war, and/or the unsatisfying aftermath, which allowed Saddam Hussein to slaughter his Kurdish, Shiite, and other oppositional forces in Iraq and to remain in power, still an irritant to the Western powers. Bush's media war established Saddam Hussein as "another Hitler," as the evil demon in a Manichaean scenario, and a successful resolution according to the frames of media culture required that the evil be removed. But Saddam remained to taunt Bush and deny him of symbolic victory; and to the present day Saddam has continued to provoke subsequent U.S. administrations. Thus, the war against Iraq did not bring stability to the Middle East, did not establish U.S. hegemony in the region or geopolitically around the globe, did not prevent necessary military budget cuts, did not guarantee the reelection of George Bush, and, crucially, did not get rid of Saddam Hussein. Therefore, it could not be counted as a genuine U.S. military triumph. Rather, it was a "triumph of the image," as one of the anthologies on the Gulf War and media put it, and certainly not a lasting political victory.[40]

CONCLUDING REFLECTIONS

The Gulf War was represented by the Pentagon and the media as the anti-Vietnam: efficient, high tech, short, and successful. In a sense, the Korean, Vietnam, and Persian Gulf TV Wars all manifested near-apocalyptic confrontations between the U.S. and its allies of the moment and a small third world country.[41] In all three cases, the smaller country was subject to extreme devastation, although the Korean War is usually seen as a stalemate, the Vietnam War as a defeat, and the Iraq War as a triumph for the U.S. In a sense, all of these wars are linked, with Vietnam appearing as another Korea, another attempt to contain communism that would vindicate the honor and efficacy of the U.S. military but actually delegitimized it in the first U.S. defeat. The war against Iraq is the first major post-Cold War military confrontation, yet it, too, was formulated as an attempt to avoid "another Vietnam" and to overcome "the Vietnam syndrome." There is also a certain historical symmetry in these juxtapositions: Korea began the proliferation of the military-industrial complex and national security state with the maintenance of, in Bruce Cumings' words, a permanent "huge and expensive peacetime armed force at home and abroad in the interests of global hegemony."[42] Vietnam occurred in what we can now see as the middle of the Cold War, and the U.S. intervention, as Gibson suggested, was motivated by the drive to stem communist aggression and to test new U.S. counterinsurgency techniques and conceptions of limited war. The war against Iraq comes at the end of this era, occurring precisely when the Cold War became obsolescent and with it the entire apparatus of the National Security State and its bloated Military-Industrial Complex.

Technowar provides a bridge from modern to postmodern war as it substitutes technology for human skills and action. The assembly-line model of warfare eventually creates a high-tech model of war where humans and technology implode and advanced technology makes possible new forms of warfare. The forms of postmodern war that we have discussed represent a progressive displacement of humans by technology, and the creation of new spaces and sites of warfare. The ultimate in postmodern war, which could make life on earth itself "post," would be nuclear war, the war that so far has not happened, the war that would perhaps end all human wars and life itself. Critics of high-tech war worry that as technology replaces human beings, by taking humans out of control and decision-making loops, the possibility of accidental nuclear war increases. Indeed, de Landa worries about nuclear accidents and technology out of control in fully automated cyberwar and calls for the development of weapons systems in which humans maintain control and interact creatively with technology, rather than being its object and servomechanism.[43] Rochlin also cites the danger of accidents that emerge from automated high-tech battlefields and high-tech wars in which humans are forced to react ever more quickly to high-speed, high-tech systems and presents case studies of accidents that have happened in high-tech environments over the past decade, thus warning that humans must maintain control over their technology.[44]

Earlier, philosopher of war Paul Virilio criticized the accelerating speed of modern technology and indicated that it was creating technology out of control, which in the case of military technology could lead to the end of the human race.[45] Recent wars and the potential for nuclear holocaust thus reveal militarism and war as absolutely unacceptable ways of resolving conflict; they reveal contemporary warfare as genocidal and ecocidal. As George Gerbner points out: "Wars in the twentieth century have killed 99 million people (before the Gulf War), twelve times as many as in the nineteenth century and twenty-two times as many as in the eighteenth century. Other hostilities, not counting internal state terrorism, are resulting in an estimated one thousand or more deaths per year."[46] The human sensorium can simply not withstand the lethal effects of modern warfare technology, recalling a warning by Walter Benjamin: "[T]raffic speeds, like the capacity to duplicate both the written and the spoken word, have outstripped human needs. The energies that technologies develop beyond the threshold of those needs are destructive. They serve primarily to foster the technology of warfare, and of the means used to prepare public opinion for war."[47]

Technowar is not only lethal to the human body, but to the natural environment. Indeed, the Gulf War had an incredibly destructive effect on the environment, creating ecological holocaust in the Gulf and, through the effects of the Kuwaiti oil fires, producing dramatic changes in world weather patterns, even threatening to create nuclear winter conditions that would block out sunlight through vast areas of the world.[48] The U.S.-led allied military relentlessly bombed Iraqi nuclear, chemical, and biological weapons facilities, releasing perilous elements into the environment. Reports abounded of hazardous materials loose in Iraq, and allied troops as well as Iraqis were exposed to dangerous materials, resulting in widespread Gulf War-syndrome diseases—similar to the experience of Vietnam vets exposed to Agent Orange who suffered mysterious diseases after returning from combat duty. In addition, the U.S. bombing of Iraqi oil installations caused fires, oil spills in the Gulf, and pools of oil in the desert—ironically destroying vast resources of the very commodity that the war was supposedly being fought over. The Iraqis, too, created oil spills, using oil as a weapon, and started oil fires with the result that by the end of the war in March 1991, Kuwait was in flames, producing the worst industrial-military pollution that the world had seen.

The U.S. propaganda machine blamed the Iraqis for most of the environmental holocaust, accusing them of "environmental terrorism," but in fact there is significant evidence that U.S. bombing was responsible for much of the oil spills, at least some of the fires, and the dangerous pollution caused by the bombing of Iraqi nuclear and weapons facilities.[49] In fact, technowar itself is ecocide; contemporary weapons of mass destruction are in and of themselves deadly to ecological habitats. Consequently, the technology of mass destruction is simply too lethal and destructive of human bodies, civilization, and the natural environment to be permitted as a mode of conflict resolution.

NOTES

1. Fredric Jameson, *Postmodernism, or, the Cultural Logic of Late Capitalism* (Durham, N.C.: Duke University Press, 1991), 45. Further references will be cited parenthetically in the text. Many individuals have followed Jameson in interpreting the Vietnam War as "postmodern," as the studies in this book attest. Likewise, many books, articles, and dissertations read Herr's *Dispatches* as a postmodernist text. So far the concept of "postmodern war" has not been adequately developed, though see Chris Hables Gray's *Postmodern War* (New York: Guilford Press, 1998) for serious attempts at conceptualization with much interesting material, and also Steven Best and Douglas Kellner, *The Postmodern Adventure* (forthcoming).

2. James Gibson, *The Perfect War: The War We Couldn't Lose and How We Did* (New York: Vintage, 1986), 15. Further references will be cited parenthetically in the text.

3. See T. W. Adorno and Max Horkheimer, *Dialectic of Enlightenment*, trans. John Cumming (New York: Continuum, 1972).

4. See Paul Edwards, *The Closed World: Computers and the Politics of Discourse in Cold War America* (Cambridge: MIT Press, 1996).

5. A genealogy of guerilla war would reveal that the struggles of indigenous peoples against the Spanish and other European colonizations produced forms now identified as guerilla war, and the imperialist powers produced treatises on how to defeat guerilla warfare. Gilles Deleuze and Felix Guattari in *The Anti-Oedipus* (1977) and *A Thousand Plateaus* (1987) adopt the figure of the guerilla nomad as their model for new postmodern identities, replacing the modern model of the rational and unified subject. Michael Bibby has suggested in correspondence that the discourses and morphologies of the postmodern arise out of "the specific historical conditions and cultural practices generated by the U.S. intervention in Vietnam. The postmodern celebration of the mobile nomad, for example, stems from French Situationist readings of Third World guerilla practices, not the other way around. The fragmentation of global economy that Jameson describes seems an effect of the first world investment in containing wars of liberation, the breakdown of a centralized military-industrial economy which was precipitated for the U.S. by the failures of the Vietnam War—and thus, I would argue that these 'postmodern' conditions can be described as such only in a post-Vietnam historical moment." Moreover, I would suggest that bomb culture and the Cold War also contributed to the matrix that engendered the postmodern adventure and that indeed helped generate Vietnam. Finally, I would also add to Bibby's account that the debates and events of the 1960s, in part a reaction against Vietnam, also contributed to producing the discourses of the postmodern and that the 1960s concept of revolution was transposed into the postmodern conception of a historical rupture or break. See Best and Kellner, *The Postmodern Turn* (New York: Guilford, 1997). The question is, however, to what extent the discourses of the postmodern best describe the complex of events, structures, and processes that constitute the trajectory from the end of World War II to our present moment.

6. On the postmodern turn in the arts, and differences between modernism and postmodernism, see Best and Kellner, *The Postmodern Turn*, chapter 4.

7. Jameson describes the articulation of personal style and vision as a key feature of modernism, encompassing a cultural style and logic, and he sees the disintegration of the subject and decline of personal and artistic style as characteristics of the postmodern era. *Postmodernism*, 14ff. In our reading, however, Herr, like Pynchon, has a very distinctive voice, style, and vision, and very modernist aims (i.e., demystification, telling the truth, creating a complex aesthetic structure that elicits interpretation, and so on), and thus we would qualify him as a modernist artist, who, however, deploys some postmodern literary techniques.

8. Fragmentation did not first appear in postmodernist cultural artifacts. Recall Lukàcs's attack on "The Ideology of Modernism" in *Realism in Our Time* (New York: Harper and Row, 1964) in which he complained that "decadent" modernist writers reveled in the description of the "disintegration of personality," as well as "the disintegration of the outer world" (25). Moreover, Herr's use of collage fragmentation and other modernist techniques can be read as an attempt to map the experience of the Vietnam war and to convey its truth, as we argue below. Thus, in this reading, Herr does not share the postmodern rejection of concepts of truth and reality and instead deploys a modernist epistemology and narrative strategy.

9. John M. Jakaitis, "Two Versions of an Unfinished War," *Cultural Critique* 3 (1986): 195.

10. Michael Herr, *Dispatches* (New York: Vintage, 1977), 4, 6, 9, 10, 14.

11. Brady Harrison in the present collection suggests that Herr constructs postmodern simulacra of the experiences of Vietnam, producing cinematic screens to capture the movielike aura of the war in Vietnam, and that therefore his text is a postmodern simulacra that attempts to capture the hyperreality of the war. This is certainly a provocative reading, but I would argue that the medium of Herr's *Dispatches* is literature, that he uses words to construct his images, and that this is exactly what the great modernist writers—many of whom drew on cinematic techniques—have done to capture complex experiences.

12. See the discussion later in this chapter.

13. See Tim Page, *Page After Page* (New York: Atheneum, 1989). In 1993, a TV movie, *Frankie's Place*, was broadcast on the Arts and Entertainment network, which featured the adventures of Flynn and Page.

14. Herr points out that no one agrees as to the Vietnam War's beginning, and as U.S. politics over the past decades war makes clear, the war has not yet ended for the American psyche, despite the best efforts of the U.S. political and military establishment to overcome "the Vietnam syndrome" in the Gulf War.

15. Herr also tells how some U.S. military officials resented the reporters (200ff.), but the overwhelming thrust of his story concerns the desire of especially the younger troops to tell the truth about the war, to engage in a "witness act" that would confirm their experience—precisely Herr's own mission.

16. To be sure, the generals, politicians, and media lied regularly in both the Vietnam and Gulf Wars, but it is not clear that propaganda and lying constitute a war's postmodernity, as propaganda and lies are part of almost all wars. See the demonstration by Philip Knightly, *The First Casualty* (New York: Harcourt, Brace, Jovanovich, 1975).

17. Jameson continues to quote Herr on the experience of moving about in helicopters (without using the paragraph break in Herr's text), commenting in conclusion: "In this new machine, which does not, like the older modernist machinery of the locomotive or the airplane represent motion, but which can only be represented *in motion*, something of the mystery of the new postmodernist space is concentrated" (45). The force of this distinction is not clear and the text cited indicates, contrary to Jameson, that Herr used the helicopter to travel about to try to map the space of Vietnam, to capture the experience of the war, part of which constituted motion in helicopters, an experience not necessarily qualitatively different from the use of helicopters in Korea and World War II—though they were admittedly used more extensively in Vietnam and became an icon of the war, both in its sight and sound, an image utilized in the beginning of Emile de Antonio's documentary *Vietnam: Year of the Pig* (1969) and in Coppola's *Apocalypse Now* (1979).

18. Herr was also associate producer of Kubrick's film; incidents and dialogue of the film come right out of *Dispatches*, and so Herr's telling and retelling of his one story constitute up to this point his life's work, although he has published a novel *Walter Winchell* and coauthored *The Big Room*.

19. Philip Kuberski, "Genres of Vietnam," *Cultural Critique* 3 (1986): 181, 187.

20. On the senselessness of World War I, see the collection of photographs and texts by Ernst Friedrich, *War Against War* (Seattle, Wash.: The Real Comet Press, 1987), and the introduction by Kellner. On Korea, see Bruce Cumings, *War and Television* (London: Verso, 1992).

21. Herr does mention the impact of war movies on the fantasies of those involved in Vietnam and suggests the salience of the Western mythology as well, but he does not pursue the linkage between the genocide in Vietnam to the earlier genocide against Native Americans. But once again in Vietnam, it was the cowboys against the Indians (an analogy that Herr mentions and that is fleshed out in *Apocalypse Now*) and once again millions of native peoples were slaughtered because they refused to submit to domination by the "Great White Race" and its underlings. Once again the "Fantasies of the Master Race" consisted of subjugating native peoples, bringing civilization to the wilderness, and taming (and, if necessary, eliminating) the "savage." See Ward Churchill, *Fantasies of the Master Race: Literature, Cinema and the Colonization of American Indians*, ed. M. Annette Jaimes (Monroe, Maine: Common Courage Press, 1992). The racist and imperialist Western fantasy persisted in the Gulf War. Ramsey Clark recounts how U.S. military briefer, Marine General Richard "Butch" Neal said on February 18 that the U.S. wanted to be sure of speedy victory once it committed ground troops to "Indian country." Clark comments: "In two words, he revealed that the U.S. military honors its racist history and intended another slaughter of 'sav-

ages.'" *The Fire This Time: U.S. War Crimes in the Gulf* (New York: Thunder's Mouth Press, 1992), 208.

22. On de Antonio, see the introduction to his work by Douglas Kellner in *Painters Painting* [CD-ROM] (Voyager, 1996), and the forthcoming collection of his writings edited by Kellner and Dan Streible.

23. Some Western filmmakers and documentarians also attempted to present the perspectives of the Vietnamese as in the French film *Loin de Vietnam* (1967) and various other documentaries. The Vietnamese themselves also produced agitprop documentaries and later fictionalized narratives of the war, articulating their perspectives. One must realize that every perspective is subject to limitations and manifests the biases and interests of the producers—precisely why one needs multiperspectivist seeing in order to understand complex phenomena.

24. The memoirs published by Generals Schwarzkopf (1993) and Powell (1995) reveal the traumatic experience of Vietnam for their generation of the military and how they viewed the Gulf War as an attempt to compensate for the loss of Vietnam. For critiques of their memoirs, see Kellner, rev. of *It Doesn't Take A Hero*, by Norman Schwarzkopf, *Z Magazine* (April 1993): 66–69; and the critiques of Powell's activity in Vietnam by Robert Parry in *The Consortium* (15, 22 July 1996).

25. Many Iraqis and other Arabs are convinced that the Gulf War was fought to destroy the power of Iraq, which had modernized and created a strong military force and modern secular society that threatened Western interests and those conservative regimes like Saudi Arabia and Kuwait that maintained traditionalist Islamic social values despite economic modernization. On this reading, the war was an attempt to destroy Iraq's modernity through the high-tech military powers of the West. For Arab perspectives on the war, see Mohammed Heikal, *Illusions of Triumph: An Arab View of the Gulf War* (New York: Harper/Collins, 1992).

26. And thus we prefer to speak of the "U.S. war against Iraq," or "the Persian Gulf TV War." This account draws on Douglas Kellner, *The Persian Gulf TV War* (Boulder, Colo.: Westview Press, 1992), which describe the events of 1990–91 as a high-tech media spectacle orchestrated for television and experienced as a new kind of live, direct, immediate (but highly mediated) media event, providing a new mode of governing and mobilizing consent to government and military policies.

27. Of course, a complex event like the war against Iraq was overdetermined by economic motivations (control of oil and petrodollars) mixing with geopolitical concerns (U.S. hegemony in the Middle East, destruction of Iraqi power) and more specifically domestic economic and political interests (i.e., Bush's reelection, preservation of the Pentagon budget, promotion of U.S. weapons systems, and so on); see the analysis in Kellner, *The Persian Gulf TV War*. Although there is a complex political history behind the war, much of it still unknown, we will simply analyze it here as a media event and political spectacle in the postmodern adventure, as well as a stage in the evolution of postmodern war.

28. The effects of the media coverage of Vietnam are highly contested.

The right wing and significant portions of the U.S. military claim that the media lost the war through its negative and critical coverage. Scholars such as Chomsky, Gibson, Hallin, Herman, and others claim that in fact the U.S. media coverage was overwhelmingly supportive. While the latter analysis is basically correct, given the length of the war, the mere fact of its extended coverage, whether positive or negative, may have contributed to turning the public against the war. In addition, many of the defining images of Vietnam coded the war as horrific, as a brutal, bloody, and senseless military intervention, thus eventually helping to position the majority of the public against the war. By contrast, the war in the Gulf was relatively brief and tightly controlled, as a media spectacle orchestrated by the U.S. government and transmitted by compliant media corporations eager for high ratings and profits.

29. See Kellner, *The Persian Gulf TV War.*

30. Jean Baudrillard, *Simulations,* trans. Paul Foss, Paul Patton, and Philip Beitchman (New York: Semiotext(e), 1983), 2.

31. Indeed, kids playing video and computer games that celebrate mayhem and destruction are being integrated into a cyberwar machine through the generation of their digital skills and tendencies to see violence as fun and as aesthetic spectacle.

32. On 16 March 1991, Air Force General Merrill McPeak, in charge of the bombing campaign, admitted that only 7 percent of the bombs were the laser-guided, high-tech variety, while 93 percent were the old dumb bombs. The same day, the *Washington Post* published an article by Bernard Gellman in which a high Pentagon official admitted that the U.S. bombs missed their targets over 70 percent of the time. Much information was also released after the war, indicating that the patriot missile was a dismal failure, causing more damage than it prevented, and U.S. government documents also revealed that the accuracy rate of the Cruise missile was much lower than previously claimed, that Apache helicopters failed to perform over 50 percent of the time, and that the "friendly fire" ratio of U.S. troops killed by their own weapons was the highest in history. See Kellner, *The Persian Gulf TV War.*

33. From *Anti-War Briefing Week Four,* cited in the *Covert Action Information Bulletin* 37 (Summer 1991): 11; and James Adams, in *Dispatches from the Gulf War,* ed. Brian MacArthur (London: Bloomsbury, 1991), 250ff. The aesthetic spectacle of the Scuds versus Patriots covered the fact that the Patriot was largely fraudulent, failing to intercept most of the Scuds and compounding the damage. See Kellner, *The Persian Gulf TV War,* chapter 4. Yet the spectacle of Patriots seemingly knocking out Scuds provided powerful advertisements for U.S. technology. And thrilling duels appeared to demonstrate U.S. technological omnipotence.

34. Amusingly, macho movie star Sylvester Stallone, Rambo himself, also saw the coming war as another Vietnam when he warned that a war with Iraq could produce thousands of American casualties. The article was published in a tabloid weekly, *Star* 4 December 1990: 5, with the headline, "You Don't Have to Jeopardize One Man," and an opening paragraph that read: "Rambo yellow? A pacifist wimp? Could be. Sylvester Stallone is urging President Bush: Bring back our troops from the Persian Gulf." Thus, both

Stallone and some antiwar activists saw the events in the Gulf through the lenses of Vietnam and failed to see that the war against Iraq was really a carefully orchestrated high-tech massacre.

35. Iraqi-American Nabil Al-Hadithy tells of discussions with U.S. peace activists before the war in which he insisted that the war would be a military rout and slaughter of the Iraqi people, whereas the peace activists insisted that it would be another Vietnam, with thousands of U.S. soldiers brought back in "body bags" and wheelchairs. Many in the peace movement were thus living in the image of Vietnam, failing to see the significant differences. See Al-Hadithy, "The Education of American Consciousness," in *War After War*, ed. Nancy J. Peters (San Francisco: City Lights Books, 1992), 60–61. Alvin and Heidi Toffler in their book on "third wave" war also argue that congressional critics of the Gulf War often interpreted the events through the frames of previous wars and an older model of warfare. *War and Antiwar: Survival at the Dawn of the Twenty-first Century* (Boston: Little, Brown, 1993), 74ff. The Tofflers' distinction between second- and third-wave wars, however, leaves out all the concrete historical factors that produced the wars in Vietnam and the Gulf, just those factors that we are concerned with articulating.

36. TV-simulation models showed powerful Iraqi defenses with sand berms, ditches of oil around them to be set on fire, dangerous artillery, minefields and barbed wire protecting Iraqi positions, and the threat of chemical weapons. The actual images of the Iraqi defenses, transmitted during the "ground war," however, showed forlorn bunkers in the sand with hardly any defenses at all. In addition, the Iraqi "soldiers" on the front line of defenses were largely conscripts with little training or discipline. Thus, the U.S. was able to produce a hyperreal model of powerful Iraqis that was dutifully transmitted by the media.

37. Other modes of abstraction and dehumanization than the digital-informational, however, were also operative. As the "turkey shoot" and other animal metaphors suggest, the U.S. forces also saw Iraqis as animals to be hunted and killed. One of the disturbing things about the war was the glee and euphoria of U.S. forces returning from destroying Iraqi tanks or targets, as if it were great fun to engage in high-tech slaughter. The libidinal pleasure in playing video and computer games, war simulations, and viewing movies was thus transferred to the activity of destroying Iraqi "targets."

38. CNN, of course, produced a book on the Gulf War (celebrating its trivia), as well as several videocassettes, while Time-Warner put out a CD-ROM version of the war. For an analysis of CNN and CBS videos of the war, see Michelle Kendrick, "Kicking the Vietnam Syndrome: CNN"s and CBS's Video Narratives of the Persian Gulf War," in *Seeing Through the Media: The Persian Gulf War*, ed. Susan Jeffords and Lauren Rabinovitz (New Brunswick, N.J.: Rutgers University Press, 1994), 59–76. Gulf war trivia dominates the "instant" books of James Blackwell, *Thunder in the Desert* (New York: Bantam, 1991) and James F. Dunnigan and Austin Bay, *From Shield to Storm: High-Tech Weapons, Military Strategy, and Coalition Warfare in the Persian Gulf* (New York: Morrow, 1992), while CNN's military commentator, Retired

General Perry Smith, provided a brief for the TV networks' use of military commentators in his *How CNN Fought the War* (New York: Birch Lane Press, 1991). Some Gulf War books provide legitimation of specific services with Norman Friedman, *Desert Victory* (Annapolis, Md.: Naval Institute Press, 1991), celebrating the navy's role, while other books celebrate the army and air force. Such books should be read as part of the ideological apparatus of the war itself.

39. Stories circulated about a glossy high-tech video of the war that the Bush campaign was going to play up at the Republican convention and use in the 1992 Presidential election, but it was dropped when it received a poor response by audiences. Bush himself appealed to his great triumph in the Gulf War with some audiences, but the issue never really became a key issue of the election, with people apparently concerned more with the economy and their own future than the past military triumphs of a man who had wanted to inaugurate a "New World Order," but had ended up a failed president with no domestic program and no reasons for people to reelect him.

40. See Hadmid Mowlana, George Gerbner, and Herbert I. Schiller, eds., *Triumph of the Image* (Boulder, Col.: Westview Press, 1992).

41. Cumings writes that these wars "had an objective quality in which the greatest power on earth pulverized a small Third World country that dared to challenge it, and therefore, ideological pleading to the contrary, all had an incommensurability of the enemy that allows no human being, on reflection to exult in American victory. If David took different forms, from the unknown Kim Il Sung to the avuncular Ho Chi Minh to the central-casting villainy of Saddam Hussein, Goliath was ever present." *War and Television,* 17.

42. Ibid., 17.

43. See Manuel de Landa, *War in the Age of Intelligent Machines* (New York: Zone Books, 1991).

44. See Gene I. Rochlin, *Trapped in the Net: The Unanticipated Consequences of Computerization* (Princeton, N.J.: Princeton University Press, 1997).

45. See Paul Virilio and Sylvere Lotringer, *Pure War* (New York: Semiotext(e),1983); and Virilio, *Speed and Politics*, trans. Mark Polizzotti (New York: Semiotext(e), 1986). Also see Kellner, "Virilio, War, and Technology," *Theory, Culture & Society,* forthcoming.

46. Gerbner, "Persian Gulf War: The Movie," in *Triumph of the Image,* 264.

47. Cited in David Levi Strauss, "(Re)Thinking Resistance," *War After War,* 37; for further dramatic documentation of the increased lethality of contemporary warfare, see Keegan, 199x.

48. See Kellner, *The Persian Gulf TV War,* and Hawley, *Against the Fires of Hell.*

49. See Kellner, *The Persian Gulf TV War,* 94ff, on the propaganda war, over who caused environmental destruction. As to who was actually responsible for the ecocide, Clark points to sources that blame U.S. bombing for much of the oil spills, and a later Canadian report attributes much of the

ecological damage in the Gulf to U.S. and allied military action; T. M. Hawley, *Against the Fires of Hell*, documents ecological damage from the Gulf War, blaming both Iraqi and allied action, and argues that war is simply not an option for settling disputes in the present era; and Betty Jean Craige sums up the long-term environmental effects of the Gulf War and argues that ecological and global interdependency make such events unacceptable. See *American Patriotism in a Global Society* (Albany: State University of New York Press, 1996).

Contributors

PHILIP D. BEIDLER is Professor of English at the University of Alabama. His books include *American Literature and the Experience of Vietnam; Re-Writing America: Vietnam Authors in Their Generation;* and *Scriptures for a Generation: What We Were Reading in the 60s.* He is also author of articles on American writing from the colonial and classic periods to the present. His most recent book is *The Good War's Greatest Hits: World War II and American Remembering.*

MICHAEL BIBBY is Assistant Professor of English at Shippensburg University and author of *Hearts and Minds: Bodies, Poetry, and Resistance in the Vietnam Era.* He has published articles on antiwar poetry, Black Liberation poetry, and GI Resistance poetry and is currently working on a book-length study of African American poetry and the racial uncanny from 1945–55.

MICHAEL CLARK is Professor of English and Comparative Literature at the University of California, Irvine. In addition to books on Michel Foucault and Jacques Lacan and articles on literary theory and early American literature, he has published "Remembering Vietnam," in *The Vietnam War and American Culture,* edited by John Carlos Rowe and Rick Berg, and "Vietnam: Representations of Self and War," in *Wide Angle* (1985). With John Rowe, he has also conducted two community reading and discussion groups on the Vietnam War in a state-wide project sponsored by the NEH and the California Council of the Humanities.

CYNTHIA FUCHS is Associate Professor of English and Codirector of Film Studies at George Mason University. With Chris Holmlund, she coedited *Between the Sheets, In the Streets: Queer, Lesbian, Gay Documentary*. She is a regular film reviewer for the *Philadelphia City Paper, Nitrate*, and *Addicted to Noise* and the author of many articles on film and popular culture.

ERIC GADZINSKI is Assistant Professor of English at Lake Superior State University, Sault Sainte Marie, Michigan. He is currently at work on a book that features Vietnam-era soldier-poetry in defining a poetics of trauma and its relation to contemporary poetics. His articles have appeared in the journal *To*.

CHRIS HABLES GRAY is the author of *Cyborg Citizen* and *Postmodern War* and the editor of *The Cyborg Handbook*. He has been an Oregon State Center for the Humanities Fellow, a NASA Fellow in Aerospace History; and an Eisenhower Fellow to the Czech Republic. Currently he is an Associate Professor at the University of Great Falls in Montana. He is currently researching the role of information technology in peace making for his next book, *Real Peace*.

BRADY HARRISON is an Assistant Professor of English at the University of Montana. He has written on the literatures of the Vietnam War and American imperialism, and his articles have appeared in *American Studies, Southwestern American Literature*, and *The Journal of Men's Studies*. He is currently at work on *Manifest Defeat: The Imperial Self in American Literature*.

DOUGLAS KELLNER is Professor of Philosophy at the University of Texas at Austin. He is author of many books and articles on social theory, politics, history, and culture, including *Critical Theory, Marxism, and Modernity; Jean Baudrillard: From Marxism to Postmodernism and Beyond; Television and the Crisis of Democracy; Postmodern Theory: Critical Interrogations* and *The Postmodern Turn*, both coauthored with Steven Best; *The Persian Gulf TV War*; and *Media Culture*.

TONY WILLIAMS is Professor of Cinema Studies at Southern Illinois University at Carbondale. His articles have appeared in *Inventing Vietnam: The War in Film and Television*, edited by Michael Anderegg; *America in Vietnam/Vietnam in America*; and *From Hanoi to Hollywood: The Vietnam War in American Film*, edited by Linda Dittmar and Gene Michaud. He also coauthored *Italian Western: Opera of Violence* and *Jack London: The Movies*.

INDEX